Naturalistic Hermeneutics

Naturalistic Hermeneutics proposes the position of the unity of the scientific method and defends it against the claim to autonomy of the human sciences. Mantzavinos shows how materials that are "meaningful," more specifically human actions and texts, can be adequately dealt with by the hypothetico-deductive method, the standard method used in the natural sciences. The hermeneutic method is not an alternative method aimed at the understanding and the interpretation of human actions and texts, but it is the same as the hypothetico-deductive method applied to meaningful materials. The central thesis advocated by Mantzavinos is, thus, that there is no fundamental methodological difference between natural sciences, social sciences, and humanities.

Advanced students and professionals across philosophy, social and political theory, and the humanities will find this a compelling and controversial book.

Professor C. Mantzavinos holds the Chair in Economics and Philosophy at the Witten/Herdecke University, Germany.

Naturalistic Hermeneutics

C. MANTZAVINOS
Witten/Herdecke University

Translated from German by Darrell Arnold
in collaboration with the author

CAMBRIDGE
UNIVERSITY PRESS

CAMBRIDGE UNIVERSITY PRESS
Cambridge, New York, Melbourne, Madrid, Cape Town, Singapore, São Paulo

Cambridge University Press
40 West 20th Street, New York, NY 10011-4211, USA

www.cambridge.org
Information on this title: www.cambridge.org/9780521848121

First published 2005

Printed in the United States of America

A catalog record for this publication is available from the British Library.

Library of Congress Cataloging in Publication Data

Mantzavinos, Chrysostomos.
Naturalistic hermeneutics / C. Mantzavinos; translated from German
by Darrell Arnold in collaboration with the author.
p. cm.
Includes bibliographical references (p.) and indexes.
ISBN 0-521-84812-1
1. Hermeneutics. 2. Naturalism. I. Title.
BD241.M28513 2005
121'.686–dc22   2004062840

ISBN-13 978-0-521-84812-1 hardback
ISBN-10 0-521-84812-1 hardback

For Anthoula

A reader who does not have time to read the entire book might well start by reading Chapter 4 to the end of the book since Part II (the constructive one) is largely independent of Part I (the critical one).

Contents

Preface

It is common to view human actions as meaningful and to view texts and other by-products of human action as meaningful material. It has also become common to view as problematic or impossible the apprehension of meaning with the method of the natural sciences. This book shows that it is possible to hold the view that human actions are meaningful, and at the same time the view that human actions and all meaningful material can be dealt with scientifically using the method prevalent in the natural sciences. I defend, in other words, the thesis that there is no fundamental methodological difference between the natural sciences, on the one hand, and the social sciences and humanities, on the other.

In order to accomplish my aim, I present two kinds of arguments, critical and constructive. In Part I of the book, I present a set of primarily critical arguments against the accentuation of the problematic of meaning, both in its strong and in its weak version. The strong version alleges that the totality of the facts in the world are endowed with meaning. This radical thesis normally involves the text metaphor, which is transferred to the world as a whole, and it is correspondingly maintained that the text model is universal. In the weak version, the possibility of grasping causal connections is commonly admitted for the realm of nature, but not for societal reality, a realm in which only meaning can be apprehended. In principle, then, this is a variant of the old dualism of man and nature. In both versions, placing the accent on the meaningful components of the facts that constitute the world has two significant implications: Understanding is viewed as the sufficient way to access these meaningful components, and hermeneutics is viewed as the discipline specifically suited to deal with this way of accessing reality. The set of primarily critical arguments presented in Part I intend to show that it is not fruitful to dramatize the problematic of meaning.

More specifically, I critically discuss three hermeneutic conceptions in which the problematic of meaning arises – both in its strong and in its weak versions – and is treated differently from the natural sciences, that is, is treated as impervious to the standard scientific method. For this, I have chosen the approaches of Dilthey, Heidegger, and Gadamer, not only because they present the most influential hermeneutic views in the German-speaking world, but also because they are sources of inspiration for the hermeneutical wave that is flooding the French- and English-speaking worlds. I proceed here by choosing and discussing in detail a particular problem that arises in connection with the hermeneutic conception of each respective author and that is of great systematic relevance. In Chapter 1 I deal with the problem of the autonomy of the human sciences and argue that they are not methodologically autonomous. In Chapter 2 I deal with the hermeneutic circle, because it is the main point of reference in the standard arguments of those who plead for the special status of the social sciences and the humanities. In Chapter 3 I discuss the hermeneutic claim to universality and show why hermeneutics is not universal.

In Part II, I proceed to offer a set of constructive arguments proposing a way to deal with the problematic of meaning based on methodological naturalism. In accord with this position, the occurrences in the societal world can be viewed as natural events in continuity with other natural events. Consequently, in dealing with such occurrences, there is no need for a different method from that used in the natural sciences. In all areas in which increasing our knowledge about the real world can be presupposed as an aim, hypotheses can be formulated, consequences can be drawn by deduction, and these can be tested against empirical data. This operation, known as the 'hypothetico-deductive method,' is a methodological procedure that is in principle applicable to every subject matter, whether it is meaningful or not. Since the analytic philosophy of science has been too stepmotherly in its treatment of the concrete problems that come up when dealing with meaningful material, I attempt to work out the concrete application of the hypothetico-deductive method for this case. It is shown here that, with the help of the hypothetico-deductive method, the apprehension of the meaning of actions as well as the apprehension of the meaning of texts can take place without any difficulty, whereas employing the method of understanding propagated by antinaturalism to solve these problems proves to be of no avail.

Since the notion of the hypothetico-deductive method is central to the whole enterprise, I want to be more specific about its exact character right at the outset. There are two essential characteristics of this method. The first consists in the fact that scientific work is generally viewed as being related to hypotheses. The propositions put forward in scientific work are not viewed as absolutely certain propositions, but as fallible hypotheses. The second characteristic consists in the fact that the hypotheses are tested by means of the deduction of consequences from them and by checking how well these consequences fit in with our experience and with our other well-supported beliefs. The empirical data with the help of which the hypotheses are tested manifest great variety. In the humanities and the social sciences the empirical data to a large degree consist of meaningful material, a fact that can in some cases complicate the process of testing the hypotheses but does not in principle render it impossible.

As will be shown in more detail, the proposal of the hypothetico-deductive method does not deny that different research styles and diverse research techniques dominate the various disciplines, nor does it deny the different structure of the object areas. As will be worked out, for example, in Chapter 1, the idea of the unity of the method is to be confused neither with the demand for a universal language nor with the demand for a unified science; instead it is a minimalistic requirement to set up hypotheses whenever one attempts to acquire knowledge and to test them critically using empirical evidence.

The protagonists of the hypothetico-deductive method, Popper and Hempel, originally viewed it as a method that is directed toward deductive causal explanations in the sciences. This seems to me to be the decisive weakness of their analysis. These original proponents of the hypothetico-deductive method always portrayed scientific activity as explanatory activity, which rightly led many representatives of scientific disciplines such as history, law, and so on to protest. There is no reason to presume that alleging the existence of individual facts is of less scientific interest, however. I regard it as the main thrust of my argument to extend the range of application of the hypothetico-deductive method to what I call the 'reconstructions of the nexuses of meaning.' What is meant by that and how exactly it is supposed to happen are, in a way, the central enterprise of this book.

Acknowledgments

My first intuitions regarding the subject matter of this book go back to 1997, when I was at the University of Freiburg, and in the long gestation of it I have profited from interactions with many people whom I wish to thank.

The person whom I would like to thank most is Herbert Keuth for supporting my philosophical work for many years and in many different ways. I had many useful discussions with Hans Albert when writing this book that have been decisive not only for the ideas presented in it, but also for my broader intellectual life; I would like to thank him for them, and also for his many helpful comments on drafts of this book. Tassos Bougas, my fatherly friend, has offered his intellectual support very generously once again, and I would like to thank him for that, in particular because I know that he disagrees with my main argument in the book. I had the great luck to have Stefan Magen sitting in the office next to mine while I was at the Max Planck Institute in Bonn; this brilliant colleague of mine was the first to read my drafts, comment on and evaluate them – always with patience and good will, for which I am grateful. I owe particular thanks to Axel Bühler for all I have learned from him and for his valuable comments on draft chapters of the book.

I learned a lot from talking to Paul Sniderman during our walks in the streets of Bonn and Berlin, and I am really thankful for that. In addition, I would like to thank him for actively supporting my project.

I owe particular debts to Christoph Engel, not only for his penetrating comments on the various drafts of the book, but also for unreservedly supporting the project, thought he thoroughly disagreed with its core ideas. Petros Gemtos, my teacher in Athens, once again helped me clarify my thoughts on a series of issues that are dealt with in the book; I am grateful for this as well as for his general support throughout many years.

I am also particularly grateful to Michael Heidelberger, Anton Friedrich Koch, and Peter Schroeder-Heister for supporting my work.

I want particularly to thank Raine Daston for a useful interaction when we were both visiting Harvard that helped me decisively to give my thoughts their final shape. Gerd Gigerenzer has provided valuable written comments on Chapter 5 for which I want to thank him.

For profitable discussions I want to thank Martin Beckenkamp, Raymond Boudon, Merlin Donald, Peter Hall, Russell Hardin, Friedrich-Wilhelm von Hermann, Stathis Kalyvas, Terry Moe, Richard Moran, Tim Scanlon, Oliver Scholz, Alisson Simmons, Francis Steen, and Mark Turner.

I had the opportunity to present the main arguments of this book in seminars at George Mason University, Yale, and Bonn (Lohmar), and I would like to thank the participants for their helpful comments. In addition, I would like to thank the institutions that have hosted me during the different stages of completion of this book: the Department of Law and Economics at the University of Bayreuth, the Department of Political Science at Stanford University, and the Department of Philosophy at Harvard University. Though I had been working on the book when I was at those institutions, I did nearly all the writing at the Max Planck Institute for Research on Collective Goods in Bonn. I would like to express my deep appreciation to the academic and nonacademic staff of this special institution for providing a wonderful place for me to write this book.

I am indebted to my editors at Cambridge University Press, Lew Bateman and Stephanie Achard, for supporting the project. I would also like to thank Louise Calabro and Helen Greenberg for the production editing and copyediting of the book.

Though the book is now being published in the English language, I originally wrote it in German. I had the great luck to have the gifted philosopher Darrell Arnold as the translator of the (still unpublished) original German manuscript. We spent countless hours together working on the translation, and I am particularly indebted to him for mastering this task, which was especially difficult due to the peculiar character of the text.

Lastly, I want to thank my family in Greece for all their love and support during the work on this book and my wife, Georgia, for her care and love during all those years we have been together.

Bonn, September 2004

Naturalistic Hermeneutics

PART I

HERMENEUTIC DEAD ENDS

1

The Claim to Autonomy of the Human Sciences

A Critique of Wilhelm Dilthey's Hermeneutic Conception

1.1 WILHELM DILTHEY'S HERMENEUTIC CONCEPTION[1]

Contemporary discussions about philosophical hermeneutics are largely inspired by the conception of Wilhelm Dilthey, who is viewed as the founder of philosophical hermeneutics. Although more recent research[2] has convincingly shown that general hermeneutics was systematically developed much earlier, as *hermeneutica universalis* – above all in the work of Georg Friedrich Meier (1718–7)[3] – Dilthey's work remains the source of information and, in part, of legitimation for contemporary hermeneutic reflections.[4]

---

[1] *Note:* When possible, I have used standard translations of the texts of Dilthey, Heidegger, and Gadamer. Other translations from German into English are by Darrell Arnold (D. A.) unless otherwise noted. For direct quotations, when possible I have given the page references to both the German and English editions. The German page number is given first, followed by the English one. The normal textual references throughout this work are to the German editions of the texts.

[2] See especially the articles in Bühler (1994).

[3] Compare Meier (1757/1996), who developed a general theory of signs and a general art of interpretation. Meier spoke of the principle of hermeneutic equity as the most general principle of all interpretive rules. Compare, for example, Meier (1757/1996, §39): "The hermeneutic equity (aequitas hermeneutica) is the tendency of the interpreter to hold that meaning for hermeneutically true that best comports with the flawlessness of the originator of the sign, until the opposite is shown" (trans. D. A.).

[4] And indeed, to a greater extent than the work of Schleiermacher, above all, because Dilthey's hermeneutics was connected with the claim to the foundation of the human sciences and was embedded in a general philosophical conception, namely, in his

Dilthey's goal was to work out the philosophical foundations of the human sciences, and to do so historically and systematically. His plan was to write six books, which would be divided into two volumes. This remained a torso, because Dilthey published only the first volume, entitled *Introduction to the Human Sciences* (1883).[5] This volume contains above all a historical account, which was to set the stage for the epistemological foundation planned for the other volume.[6] Nevertheless, the first two books of the introduction also contain systematic thoughts; besides, already in Dilthey's lifetime, his systematic work, *The Formation of the Historical World in the Human Sciences* (1910), was published, which according to the publisher, Groethuysen, was to be integrated into the second volume of the planned introduction to the human sciences (GS VII, IX). These two books, which were published by Dilthey himself, as well as his famous article "The Rise of Hermeneutics" (1900)[7] and a few other smaller works, will serve as the foundation for my discussion of his hermeneutic conception.

Dilthey attempted to show that the human sciences comprise an independent whole alongside the natural sciences. Human sciences are understood as "all the disciplines that have socio-historical reality as their subject matter" (GS I, 4/SW I, 56). Dilthey diagnosed a dualism between the 'realm of nature' and the 'realm of history' and postulated the incommensurability of the mental order with the order of nature on the basis of the facts of the unity of consciousness

philosophy of life. For more on the historical influence of his work, see Anz's fitting characterization (1982, 59): "Without Dilthey's presentation of the history of hermeneutics and without his reinterpretive elaboration, Schleiermacher's hermeneutics would have hardly achieved the character of a paradigm; without his unending epistemological efforts to make 'understanding' the basis of all 'sciences of the acting man' and of the 'socio-historical reality', Heidegger's project of 'existential hermeneutics' would hardly have been possible; without his foundation of the human sciences, critical of metaphysics and speculative idealism as it was, Gadamer certainly would not have attempted to develop philosophical hermeneutics as the 'prima philosophia'" (trans. D. A.).

5 As Bernhard Groethuysen, his colleague and the editor of many of his works, notes in the preface to the first volume of the collective works of Dilthey: "That was a source of anguish for him his entire life, and all his work was, in the final analysis, aimed at making it possible for a second volume to follow the first volume of the *Introduction*" (GS I, V/trans. D. A.).

6 This follows Dilthey's own remarks in the preface to the first volume of the *Introduction* (GS I, XV/SW I, 47).

7 See Dilthey (GS V, 317–38/SW IV, 233–58).

and the spontaneity of will, which can only be found in the mental order. Correspondingly, it is impossible to extract mental facts from the mechanical order of nature. For Dilthey, the 'content' of the human sciences is "the socio-historical reality insofar as that reality has been preserved in human consciousness as historical information and has been made accessible to scientific study as information about society extending beyond its current state" (GS I, 24/SW I, 76).

If the irreducible 'mental facts' of the socio-historical reality are defined as the epistemological object of the human sciences, then the question of the possibility of analyzing them arises. What does access to mental facts look like? Dilthey suggests proceeding in two steps. In the first step, psychology should deliver an analysis of life units, that is, the psychophysical individuals, which are the elements of which society and history are made. On the basis of this analysis, the 'enduring formations,' which are the objects of social research, are then to be examined. Dilthey views both the 'cultural systems' and the different types of the 'external organization of society' as among the enduring formations. "The facts which constitute the cultural systems can be studied only by means of the facts recognized by psychological analysis. The concepts and propositions which form the basis of our knowledge of these systems are dependent on the concepts and propositions developed by psychology" (GS I, 46/SW I, 96). Something similar applies to second-order facts, which constitute the external organization of society, such as the family, the state, the church, associations, and so forth.

It should be emphasized that in his discussion of this two-step procedure for analyzing the 'lasting forms' of socio-historical reality, Dilthey appears to approach very closely a consistent methodological individualism. Methodological individualism is well known as the meta-theoretical postulate[8] according to which all social phenomena must

---

[8] The first, so far as I know, to give this idea the name 'methodological individualism' was Joseph Schumpeter in his Habilitation thesis *Das Wesen und der Hauptinhalt der theoretischen Nationalökonomie* (1908), and he used this as a clear contrast to political individualism: "We must clearly distinguish between political and methodological individualism. They haven't the least in common. The former begins with general principles, such as the view that freedom contributes more to the development of people and to the general good than anything else, and builds a series of practical propositions on the basis of this; the latter does nothing of the sort, it makes no claims and has no special presuppositions. It only means that in describing certain processes, one starts with the action of individuals" (1908, 90 f./trans. D. A.).

be explained through the situations, dispositions, and presuppositions of individuals[9] – or, expressed differently, that the social reality is to be explained by the interplay between individual actions under different conditions.[10] As we shall see later, Dilthey challenges, in principle, the possibility of explaining social phenomena and proposes another way of dealing with social formations, the soundness of which is still to be examined. Nevertheless, Dilthey repeatedly argues that in an analysis of the social formations or of the external organization of society, one should never lose track of the individual. He notes, for example: "The family is the womb of all human order, of all group-life. [...] Nevertheless, this unity – the world's most concentrated form of volitional unity binding individuals – is only relative. The individuals that are joined together in it are not completely absorbed in it; the individual is ultimately for and by himself" (GS I, 74/SW I, 123). This methodological individualism, however, is not to be confused with an ontological individualism – that is, with the thesis that in social reality only individuals exist – and Dilthey does not appear to hold this view. Thus he maintains: "[T]he sciences of the cultural systems and of the external organization of society are related to anthropology primarily through physical and psychophysical phenomena which I have designated as second-order facts. The analysis of these phenomena, which are produced by the interactions of individuals in society and are *in no way fully reducible to anthropological facts*, determines to a significant extent the theoretical rigor of the particular human sciences which they underlie" (GS I, 11/SW I, 163; emphasis added).

---

[9] For example, Watkins (1953, 729): "[The principle of methodological individualism] states that social processes and events should be explained by being deduced from (a) principles governing the behaviour of participating individuals and (b) descriptions of their situations."

[10] For example, Albert (1998, 18). A discussion of methodological individualism from a philosophical perspective, unfortunately, bundled with a confused analysis of the 'zero method,' can be read in Popper's classical *The Poverty of Historicism* (1957/1991, 136ff.). A discussion of methodological individualism from a sociological perspective is presented in Vanberg (1975), above all in chapter 8, and in Bohnen (1975, 2000). For a discussion of the role of methodological individualism in economics see Arrow (1994), Suchanek (1994, 125f.), Kirchgässner (1991, 23f.), and, above all, Blaug (1992, 42ff.). Methodological individualism was discussed in political science in connection with rational choice theory in the 1990s. See Green and Shapiro (1994, 15f.) and selections in Friedman (1996), but also Riker (1990) and Elster (1986).

The psychological foundation of the human sciences, joined with methodological individualism, could lead the reader to expect Dilthey's conception to be a program that operates with nomological hypotheses. However, Dilthey intends to do something else. On the one hand, he does indeed mark himself off from the philosophy of history by emphasizing that the particular human sciences are capable of producing "real theories" because they are based on the *analytic method* and they are related to reality, that is, they have an *empirical orientation*. On the other hand, he doubts that laws are possible in the human sciences. To defend this, he introduces a distinction between explanative and descriptive psychology. If a social scientific program that wants to operate with nomological hypotheses is based on an explanatory, natural scientific psychology, then the alternative proposed by Dilthey – of descriptive psychology as the fundamental science – can never lead to nomological knowledge in the human sciences.[11] But even if the goal is not to produce nomological hypotheses, the descriptive psychology will inextricably lead to a dead end.

This special type of psychology is not concerned with regularities in the order of psychic processes, but with regularities in the sense of a psychic structure. It is concerned with the pattern according to which psychic facts are regularly connected with one another by an inner, experienceable relation, and the regularity consists in the relation of parts to a whole (GS VII, 15/SW III, 35f.). Dilthey's descriptive psychology is concerned with inner experience (Anz 1982, 67), which attempts to grasp psychic facts together with their structure. This apprehension of mental states "arises from the lived experience (*Erlebnis*) and remains linked to it. In the *lived experience (Erlebnis)*, the processes of the *entire mind* work together. It is endowed with a nexus, while the senses only present a manifold of particular data. The individual operation is brought to lived experience (*Erlebnis*) by the totality of inner

---

[11] In his words: "Psychology can be a foundational human science only if it stays within the limits of a descriptive discipline that establishes facts and uniformities among facts. It must clearly distinguish itself from explanative psychology, which strives to derive the whole human, cultural world by means of certain assumptions. Only on the basis of this descriptive procedure can such an explanative psychology attain precise and unprejudiced material that makes possible the verification of its psychological hypotheses. But above all, only in this way can the particular human science obtain a foundation which is itself secure; at present even the best psychological accounts build one hypothesis upon another" (GS I, 32 f./SW I, 84).

life, and the nexus through which it is related with the entire inner life belongs to immediate experience" (GS V, 172/trans. D. A.).

Now, it is possible to raise numerous objections to this type of psychology, which employs the concept of lived experience (*Erlebnis*) as an inclusive term for all mental states. Above all, the common objection is that this must be more precisely specified.[12] Besides, the fundamental question remains unanswered concerning "how we can have knowledge of the states of other people's minds" (Scholz 2001, 76). A descriptive psychology that concentrates on the first-person perspective cannot offer access to the experiences of other persons, regardless of what is meant by experience.[13] Besides, as soon as a regularity of any kind can be identified – in this case the "regularity consisting in the relation of parts to a whole" – it is always possible to grasp it with a nomological hypothesis. A hypothesis is nomological by virtue of the form of the sentence in which it is formulated, not its content, so a regularity of the kind Dilthey is analyzing could easily be nomologically apprehended.

Perhaps because of the immanent difficulties of this conception, there is less and less discussion of the psychological foundation of the human sciences in his later works. In fact, it is fully plausible to maintain that Dilthey changed his view. Lived experience (*Erlebnis*) remains the foundational category, but the human sciences are no longer concerned with the methodological knowledge of psychic processes, "but with re-experiencing, with understanding them. In this sense *hermeneutics* would then be the real foundation of the human sciences" (Groethuysen, GS VII, VII/trans. D. A.). If the young Dilthey is characterized by the search for an Archimedean point for knowledge,

---

[12] Dilthey is a very honest thinker, and he does not attempt to evade difficult questions. Thus, in this context he asks (GS VII 28/SW III, 49): "What happens now if I pay attention to this lived experience and ask myself what it contains? Here is a second important problem for the foundation of the human sciences." In the pages that follow the quotation, however, one unfortunately does not find much that is concrete, except for a discussion of the "partial transcendence" of the objects from the lived experience (*Erlebnis*).

[13] See Kalleri (1993, 70) as well: "Even if one, for example, presumes that self-understanding can be proven from a psychological basis, it is still not clear how understanding of something alien is possible, especially in its individuality, because understanding as re-experiencing, is also a process of one's own inner perception" (trans. D. A).

which he believes he has found in the certainty of the lived experience, the mature Dilthey attempts to give a hermeneutical underpinning to the human sciences, which would definitively establish their autonomy.

1.2 ON THE ROLE OF UNDERSTANDING

In his well-known article "The Rise of Hermeneutics" (1900), where Dilthey deals with "the problem of the *scientific* knowledge of individuals and indeed the main forms of human existence in general," he asks: "Is such knowledge possible, and what means are at our disposal to attain it?" (GS V, 317/SW IV, 235). Thus the question arises about the objectivity and the general validity of knowledge of the states of other minds. Distancing himself from his earlier opinions, Dilthey ascertains that inner experience is not enough to secure an objective view of other persons (GS V, 318/SW IV, 235). He thus proposes a specific process for achieving such knowledge, namely, understanding. "[T]he existence of other people is given us at first only from the outside, in facts available to sense, that is, in gestures, sounds, and actions. Only through a process of re-creation of that which is available to the senses do we complete this inner experience. Everything – material, structure, the most individual traits of such a completion – must be carried over from our own sense of life. Thus the problem is: How can one quite individually structured consciousness bring an alien individuality of a completely different type to objective knowledge through such re-creation? What kind of process is this, in appearance so different from the other modes of conceptual knowledge? *Understanding* is what we call this process by which an inside is conferred on a complex of external sensory signs" (GS V, 318/IV, 236).

It must immediately be emphasized that Dilthey characterizes understanding, ambivalently, as a 'process.' To a certain extent, this ambivalence is constitutive of the entire discussion on understanding, and, indeed, in Dilthey and many modern proponents of hermeneutics. On the one hand, with understanding a *type of knowledge* is meant, which is oriented toward certain signs and symbols. Understanding thus appears to be a subcategory or a subclass of knowing. On the other hand, understanding appears to be a *method*, and in fact the method proper for the human sciences, which among other things is supposed to legitimize the claim to the autonomy of those sciences.

Now, it would be desirable for clarity in the discussion if this process –
the understanding – were interpreted either as a type of knowledge
or as a method. Unfortunately, Dilthey does not do this, although it
must be immediately pointed out that his discussion of this process is
less confusing and less mystical than that of Gadamer and Heidegger.
Nonetheless, it remains ambivalent.

So, on the one hand, understanding is brought into connection with
lived experience (*Erlebnis*) and expression: "Thus thought receives a
definite function in relation to life. In its tranquil flow, life constantly
produces all sorts of realities. Many of its remnants are deposited on
the banks of our little ego" (GS VII, 6f./SW III, 27). Lived experiences
are thus formed and brought to expression. "The givens [...] are always manifestations of life. They appear in the world of the senses, but
express something spiritual, which they make it possible for us to cog-
nize" (GS VII, 205/SW III, 226). These manifestations of life, which
draw from the source of life, encompass everything mental: texts as
well as individual human actions and all sorts of 'objectifications of
life.' The process of understanding consists in mentally grasping these
texts, these human actions, and these objectifications of life, that is,
in knowing. Understanding appears to be nothing more than a specific *type of knowledge*, namely, the perception of specific objects, which
is available in principle to every person, not only to the social scientist. Thus, in the discussion of the elementary forms of understanding, Dilthey sketches out an operation that can be characterized as
a fully normal, if not banal, sociopsychological communicative process. "Understanding comes about, first of all, through the interests
of practical life where persons rely on interchange and communication. They must make themselves understandable to each other. One
person must know what the other wants. This is how the elementary
forms of understanding originate" (GS VII, 207/SW III, 228).

On the other hand, Dilthey repeatedly speaks of understanding
as 'transposition' (*hineinversetzen*), 're-creating' (*nachbilden*), and 're-
experiencing' (*nacherleben*) (GS VII, 213ff./SW III, 234ff.) and interprets it as "the fundamental procedure for all further operations of
the human sciences" (GS V, 333/SW IV, 252). The impression thus
arises that understanding ought to be a *method*, and, in fact, the specific
method for the human sciences. What does this method look like in
concreto, and what is its logical status? "The fundamental relationship

on which the process of elementary understanding depends is that of an expression to what is expressed in it. *Elementary understanding is not an inference from an effect to a cause.* Nor must we conceive it more cautiously as a procedure that goes back from a given effect to some part of the nexus of life that made the effect possible" (GS VII, 207f./SW III, 228f.). It is thus clear that understanding is proposed as an alternative to explanation. Unfortunately, one searches in vain for a concrete specification of the logical status of this method. Besides a few poetic phrases, such as "Understanding is a rediscovery of the I in the Thou" (GS VII, 191/SW III, 213), it is only stated that understanding is not supposed to be a logical operation: "There is something irrational in all understanding, just as life itself is irrational; it cannot be represented in a logical formula" (GS VII, 218/SW III, 239). The question arises then: What kind of method is it supposed to be exactly?

One point seems clear: Understanding is neither a *mental* process nor a *logical* operation, that is, neither a *type of knowledge* nor a *logical method* for acquiring knowledge. But what, then, does it deal with? "Here too we are not dealing with logical construction or psychological analysis but with analysis of interest for a theory of knowledge" (GS VII, 205/SW III, 226). Here the ambivalence culminates. This "analysis of interest for a theory of knowledge," as we can conclude, is a nonlogical method, which, while being generally valid, does not lead to nomological knowledge about mental facts, although such mental facts may be grasped. It is the hermeneutic method à la Dilthey, which proposes that scholars in the human sciences tap the manifestations of mind by means of re-experiencing and transposition.

1.3 THE PROBLEM OF THE AUTONOMY OF THE HUMAN SCIENCES

The ambivalence of the method of understanding would have been a lesser evil had Dilthey not connected a claim to the autonomy of the human sciences with it. Dilthey's systematic claim was thus to plead for the autonomy of the human sciences on the basis of this hermeneutic method.[14] This claim has been carried forward since Dilthey's time

---

[14] In this sense, he remains indebted to Droysen's historicism, which, as is well known, proceeds from a radical dichotomy between nature and history and views understanding as "the most perfect knowledge possible for humans" (Droysen, 1943, 26).

without interruption and is still often made in philosophical discussions today. I will present the two main arguments for this position before I critically evaluate them in Section 1.4. These are, of course, general arguments. I will, however, above all point to the corresponding texts in Dilthey's work, because the arguments are archetypically represented there.

I. The Argument of the Internal Perspective

The first argument for the autonomy of the human sciences states that there is a basic difference between our interpretation of the natural and the social reality. The attitude of the natural scientist toward nature is fundamentally different from that of the social scientist toward society. The natural scientist assumes an external perspective toward nature; the social scientist, an internal perspective toward society. In connection with this thesis, a further thesis is often proposed – namely, that the two perspectives cannot be reduced to one another. The method of the natural sciences consists in explaining the regularities in nature with the help of law-like statements. The method of the social sciences consists in comprehending social reality on the basis of understanding. Understanding is thus the means available to the researcher to apprehend the meaning of texts, actions, and social phenomena.

The archetypal statement of this position is to be found in Dilthey's words:[15] "This leads us to the source of the difference in our relations to society and to nature. Social states are *intelligible to us from within*; we can, up to a certain point, reproduce them in ourselves on the basis of the perception of our own states; our representations of the historical world are enlivened by love and hatred, by passionate job, by the entire gamut of our emotions. Nature, however, is dead for us. Only the power of our imagination can give it an aura of inner life. [...] *Nature is alien to us. It is a mere exterior for us without any inner life. Society is our world*" (GS I, 36/SW I, 88; emphasis added).

II. The Method–Object Argument

Very closely connected to the argument of the internal perspective, though still independent of it, is another thesis, which I call the

---

[15] See, for example, Jung (1996, 55).

'method–object argument.' This thesis states that the scientific method has to be suited to its object. If the object of the scientific analysis demonstrates certain characteristics ontologically, then a scientific method has to be used that is suitable for dealing with these characteristics. This argument thus postulates the primacy of the object of inquiry over the method of inquiry. In the natural and social sciences, this means concretely that the difference in the structure of the natural and social ontology forces the researcher to employ respectively different methods to research different objects. Correspondingly, the human sciences are supposed to be autonomous of the natural sciences.

In Dilthey this argument is expressed most clearly in the following quotation: "This understanding does not just designate a distinctive methodological approach that we assume over against such objects. The difference between the human and natural sciences is not just about the stance of the subject toward the object; it is not merely about a kind of attitude, a method. Rather, the procedure of understanding is grounded in the realization that the external reality that constitutes its objects is totally different from the objects of the natural sciences. Spirit has objectified itself in the former, purposes have been embodied in them, values have been actualized in them, and understanding grasps this spiritual content that has been formed in them" (GS VII, 118/SW III, 141).[16]

1.4 WHY THE HUMAN SCIENCES ARE NOT METHODOLOGICALLY AUTONOMOUS

The two main arguments for the autonomy in the human sciences, which I have discussed in the previous section, originate in archetypical form in Dilthey, but they are also present in postmodern dressing in the contemporary discussion, and indeed with diverse emphasis and to various degrees. I would like to contrast the claim to methodical autonomy with the thesis for the unity of method. This meta-theoretical thesis states that all sciences employ the same method insofar as they aim to increase our knowledge of the real world. This method consists in the formulation of hypotheses, the deduction of consequences from

---

[16] See also the discussion in Rodi (1995, 197).

them, and the testing of them with the help of empirical data. This process, which was first analyzed as the hypothetico-deductive method by Popper and Hempel and has been amply discussed and more clearly specified in modern philosophy of science, is a methodical procedure, which can in principle be applied to all facts, whether natural-scientific or social-scientific. Science is always concerned with the formulation of hypotheses (in the case of the theoretical sciences more specifically with theoretical explanations), and the normative idea of methodological unity has, among other things, the heuristic-constructive function of steering the creative potential of scientists to discover and test such hypotheses.

Now, this idea denies neither the different *research styles* and *research techniques* that dominate the various disciplines nor the *different structure of the object areas*. The daily work in molecular biology, political science, and philology employs, of course, different research styles. With the help of technologically highly developed instruments, molecular biology, for example, studies the structure of human DNA. With the help of qestionnaires in interviews, political scientists study the structure of public opinion. With the help of manuscripts that have been preserved in archives, philologists study the structure of the Aristotelian opus. All of these scientists work, in accord with the research style of their discipline, with the help of their specialized research techniques and attempt to grasp the specific structure of their research object. This diversity in research styles, research techniques, and object areas is fully compatible with the idea of the methodological unity of the sciences. The setting up of theories, namely, of systems of propositions, which are conceived as hypotheses, and the critical testing of these theories using experiments or other observations, constitutes a methodical procedure, bearing on cognitive problem solving in accord with critical rationality (Albert 1978, 37).

Besides, the idea of the unity of method in all empirical sciences is by no means identical with the demand to unify the sentences of the individual sciences in a universal language, for example, in the language of physics.[17] By no means is it to be confused with the requirement for

---

[17] As is well known, this influential program was propagated by Carnap in the 1930s. See, for example, Carnap (1932); and for a critical discussion of this thesis, see Bodammer (1987, 145–9) and Gemtos (2004, 159ff.).

a unified science, that is, for establishing a unified system of propositions, on the basis of which we can explain all phenomena as long as a
common conceptual apparatus is used and a series of reductions are
made.[18] The idea of the unity of method is rather a *minimalistic requirement* for all empirical sciences to search for theoretical explanations
on the basis of regularities or to formulate hypotheses about singular
events and to critically test them.[19] Against this background, I would
like to take up the two main arguments in favor of the autonomy of
the human sciences.

I. On the Argument of the Internal Perspective

The thesis that the social and natural sciences assume different pos-
tures toward their research objects is certainly undeniable if interpreted to mean that natural and mental facts can be accessed differently. It is certainly true that we have privileged access to mental
facts and that we can have immediate knowledge of our own 'mental
condition' or mental operations.[20] But it is certainly not true that nature is alien to us. We are also part of nature, and, beyond that, we

---

[18] As is equally well known, this demand was developed within the framework of logical
positivism. As Albert (1993, 53/trans. D. A.), however, has appropriately noted, it
is concerned "with an epistemological Utopia, reminiscent of Leibniz's idea of a
mathesis universalis. It originates in a static view of knowledge, determined by an
ideal, final condition of sciences, which ignores the development of the sciences and
the controversies prevailing in them, which over-accentuates the logical structure of
knowledge and which bans the heuristic problematic from the philosophy of science."

[19] As Albert has emphasized in this context, this idea is, in principle, metaphysical, and
it normally appears in connection with further metaphysical presuppositions (1978,
39/trans. D. A.): "The epistemological program of the theoretical empirical sciences
is thus also inspired by certain metaphysical presuppositions, which for their part have
effect on the methodological conceptions connected with it. Among these is not only
the presupposition of a reality independent of human subjects, but, beyond that, the
presupposition that this reality is in principle able to be known; the presupposition
of the existence of laws, the possibility of constructing explanations on the basis of
those laws and, finally, the presupposition connected to all of these hypotheses – the
possibility of a more or less accurate depiction of real facts which is entailed in the
classical idea of truth."

[20] How exactly this access is to be conceptualized is an important but different problem
from the one at stake here. In any case, the dominant perceptual model of introspection seems to encounter a number of serious difficulties, and the "inner eye"
metaphor tends to be seriously misleading, as Richard Moran convincingly shows
in his excellent essay on self-interpretation (2001, 12ff.). Yet a distinct problem is
whether this access is *immediate*, and if so, in what sense. It seems that knowledge
about one's self is immediate if it is not inferred from observational evidence. See

are less familiar with a series of social phenomena than with natural phenomena: Put quite plainly, we are better acquainted with gravity than with monetary systems.

It is important to note that in any case the privileged access only relates to the *generation* of hypotheses, not to the *validity* of them. The fact that our self-consciousness can be interpreted, that we are organisms availing of a 'feeling of what happens' (Damasio 1999), may make it possible for the social scientist to successfully project his or her own mental operations onto the actions of other actors and in this way to develop a good theory of the social world. This, however, need not be the case. There is hardly reason to presume that the specific possibility of reflecting on one's own mental operations, characteristic of humans, simultaneously offers a method for generating true hypotheses about the function of our own and other people's mental operations. To the contrary, there is surely reason to presume that the property of being able to reflect on our own mental operations – in the past usually called 'intuitionism' and now appearing in the philosophical discussion under the auspices of self-consciousness – is fallible in principle: fallible both in grasping one's own mental states and in projecting the individual opinions, feelings, and the like onto other persons. A series of neurological pathologies, above all anosognosia, may most clearly demonstrate the fallibility of this property precisely because they are extreme cases of mistakenly interpreting one's own mental life.[21]

Moran (2001, 10): "The claim that introspective awareness is not inferred from observational evidence is what is usually intended by the claim that it is 'immediate'. As a claim about the mode of awareness, this just means that such judgments are not inferred from anything epistemically more basic. Beyond that, immediacy does not entail anything about the epistemic authority of the judgments."

[21] See the description of this illness of the famous neurologist Antonio Damasio (1999, 209f.): "The word *anosognosia* derives from the Greek *nosos*, 'disease', and *gnosis*, 'knowledge', and denotes the inability to recognize a state of disease in one's own organism. [...] Neurology has no dearth of bizzare conditions, but anosognosia is one of the strangest. The classical example of anosognosia is that of a victim of stroke, entirely paralysed in the left side of the body, unable to move hand and arm, leg and foot, face half immobile, unable to stand or walk, who remains oblivious to the entire problem, and who reports that nothing is possibly the matter. When asked how they feel, patients with anosognosia answer with a sincere, 'I am fine.'" See also the presentation of a case by another well-known neurologist, Elkhonon Goldberg (2001, 136): "Whatever the explanation, I find one patient, a successful international entrepreneur who suffered a massive right-hemispheric stroke, unforgettable. His performance on language tasks was perfectly intact, indicating the sparing of the

Besides, when dealing with the issue of the dualism between internal and external perspectives, one should take serious note of the newest developments in brain research. With the help of functional magnetic resonance imaging and various other brain imaging techniques, it is now possible to map precisely those neurological processes in the brain that correspond to certain expressions and other observable behavior of the subjects under study. This, of course, means neither that the privileged access to one's own mental operations has been eliminated nor that the internal perspective can automatically be reduced to the external one. However, all these developments in modern brain research[22] indicate that natural scientific methods can, in principle, be applied to human behavior. The degree to which such methods will help in the explanation of materials that are 'meaningful' remains an open question. In Chapters 5 and 6, I will point to some explanations of that sort and attempt to show how one can approach the question of the meaning of actions and texts from the perspective of empirical science. In any case, there is no reason to deny that meaningful objects, the traditional domain of the human sciences, cannot be just as well explained as objects that are not meaningful, the traditional domain of the natural sciences.[23]

In any case, the argument of the internal perspective is not able to legitimize the claim to the methodological autonomy of the human

left hemisphere. His performance on visuospatial tasks, requiring drawing or manipulation of visual forms devoid of meaning, was devastated, indicating severe damage to the right hemisphere. He was spatially disoriented to such a degree that he was unable to learn the layout of my modestly sized office and kept getting lost between the examination room, the reception area, and the bathroom. Yet he insisted that he has fully recovered, that nothing was the matter with him, and that he had to immediately fly to Cairo to finalize a business deal. There was no chance that he would have gotten anywhere near Cairo. He would have become hopelessly and completely lost the moment he got out of the taxicab at Kennedy International Airport. His wife and daughter understood this very well and, to their credit, arranged for his involuntary hospital admission despite his furious protestations."

[22] See Sections 5.5 and 5.6.

[23] The question of the system of description used is less relevant in this. As long as we are concerned with explaining mental functions or semantic structures, it is possible to formulate the phenomena to be explained using concepts that traditionally originate in the human sciences. In formulating the theoretical hypotheses, which specify the processes or the mechanisms that explain the corresponding phenomena, it is possible to use the concepts of the natural sciences. The problem of the incompatibility between the first-person perspective and the third-person perspective is thus not of a *linguistic nature*, at least not primarily. I will come back to that point in Section 5.4.

sciences, because it refers to the *context of discovery*, not the *context of justification*. Even if the privileged access to mental facts is able to function as an acceptable source of hypotheses in individual cases, that will by no means render the requirement to test these hypotheses obsolete. And testing hypotheses against the facts with the help of methodical procedures is precisely what constitutes the kernel of the unity of method for which I argue here.[24]

II. On the Method–Object Argument

The thesis that the scientific method must be adjusted to the object of research cannot be meant to express merely that different objects are accessible only through different *research techniques*. This thesis would be trivial, because no one can seriously maintain, for example, that the movement of planets can be studied with the same research techniques as the consumer behavior of Americans. On the other hand, this thesis can be put forward as a methodological consideration, according to which the transfer of the methods of the natural sciences to the social sciences and humanities leads to bracketing certain phenomena insofar as they cannot be grasped with these methods.[25] The argument thus states that that part of reality traditionally treated in the social sciences and humanities (in Diltheyean terminology, the 'historical–social scientific reality') cannot be apprehended with the methods of natural science, whereby this latter

---

[24] See also Popper's classical remark (1957/1991, 135): "For we can say [...] that it is irrelevant from the point of view of science whether we have obtained our theories by jumping to unwarranted conclusions or merely by stumbling over them (that is by 'intuition'), or else by some inductive procedure. The question, 'How did you first *find* your theory?' relates, as it were, to an entirely private matter, as opposed to the question, 'How did you *test* your theory?' which alone is scientifically relevant."

[25] See, for example, Rodi's comment (1995, 197/trans. D. A.) regarding Dilthey's proposals: "In reality these are not concerned with the expression of a fuzzy affinity of world views, but with a sober methodological consideration. It aims at the relationship between the object and the research method: the method must suit the object, not vice-versa. Dilthey's criticism of a one-sided intellectualistic epistemology is based on this inappropriate relationship between method and object. Thus for Dilthey, 'mutilation' means, that by transferring methods from the natural sciences to the human sciences, certain areas of life are methodologically bracketed insofar as they defy being comprehended and processed with these methods."

term is typically meant to signify the methodical procedure of testing hypotheses.

Now, the question arises concerning what is meant by 'apprehending' this socio-historical world. A defender of the claim to autonomy, Frithjof Rodi, seems to use it to mean, for example, "the underlining of meaningful states of affairs, opinions and works" (1995, 207).[26] Whether the activity of "making apparent the significance" of a phenomenon (206), for example, of a work of art, should be characterized as scientific, because it is motivated by an "epidigmatic epistemological interest" supposedly characteristic of a specific human science is a question that I do not want to address here. It remains puzzling, in any case, how such an activity can be oriented on any standards or regulative ideas. The mere ἐπίδειξις, that is, the mere pointing out of matters of fact and the demonstration of the significance of something is an activity that every layman can engage in, and it cannot, in my opinion, be characterized as a *method*, let alone a scientific one.

The method–object argument may appear more effective if one uses it to emphasize the primacy of the object studied over the method of inquiry. Formulated as a methodological rule, this thesis states that it is advisable to gain clarity about the characteristics of the object of inquiry before establishing how the object is to be studied: "First gain certainty about the ontology of what you want to study, then draft the method for studying it!"

This maxim appears to be closely connected to the doctrine that Popper referred to as 'essentialism' (1957/1991, 26ff.). In accord with this doctrine scientific research is concerned with grasping the essence of things and with analyzing them. One starts with the question "What is a social fact?" or "What is an institution?" and then attempts to develop statements to answer this "What is x?"–question. One thus attempts to penetrate to the essence of things, to grasp their essence cognitively, and to treat them scientifically. The method–object argument is a further development of the essentialist thesis based on a

---

[26] Earlier, Georg Misch had already proposed a similar theory (1933/1994). He took on the heroic task of developing a logic that granted a legitimate place to the 'evocative expression.' On the basis of this evocative expression, "the expression of the living essence of things in their self-determination (*Selbstmacht*) and significance" would supposedly be possible (1994, 512/trans. D. A.).

methodological twist. It states that it is reasonable, from the perspective of scientific methodology, to answer the "What is x?"–question before making a decision on the appropriate method. In the cases of interest here, this means specifically that, for the human sciences, one poses and answers the question "What is x?", that is, "What is our object of inquiry?" and decides afterward on the proper method. Philosophical hermeneutics answers this question with "x are mental facts," and it then proposes that understanding is the appropriate method.

This type of thinking inevitably leads to dead ends, above all, because the direction in which it channels the researcher's cognitive capacities is unproductive. If one deals with the question "What is x?", then it is possible, in the end, to come to a more or less precise description of what the characteristics of x are, but it is never possible to show how x is connected with other facts in this world. In this, it does not matter whether x is a natural or a mental fact. Even if x is a natural object, dealing with the question "What is x?" will only lead to a procedure that could only enable an exact depiction of the features of this fact, independently of whether one calls this procedure 'understanding' or not.

The alternative is to start with a problem and to formulate propositions aimed at solving that problem. In accord with this approach, the scientific work begins with a problem, which can originate in any object area, and it consists in formulating problem solutions and subjecting them to critical testing. The problem to be solved is formulated with the help of natural or artificial linguistic tools, which above all help to simplify communication in the scientific community about the problem being dealt with. The goal of this type of activity is to deepen our knowledge of how to solve problems that arise in both the natural and the social world. The methodological requirement to do this by working out hypothetical solutions to problems and critically testing them is productive insofar as it may succeed in directing the researchers' cognitive abilities toward paths that will finally allow us to change our natural and our social environment.

So, instead of beginning with a detailed specification of the relevant ontology and then reflecting on the appropriate method for accessing this ontology, it is possible to begin with a problem that we find interesting, and then to put forth hypotheses susceptible to criticism about how to solve that problem. Obviously, it is nonetheless possible to opt for the first alternative as, for example, Heidegger does. The dead end that this type of thinking leads to will be the subject of the next chapter.

2

The Hermeneutic Circle and the Paralysis of Thought

A Critique of Martin Heidegger's Hermeneutic Conception

2.1 MARTIN HEIDEGGER'S HERMENEUTIC CONCEPTION

At the center of Martin Heidegger's thought lies the question of being. His main work, *Being and Time*, published in 1927, begins with a
quotation from the platonic Sophist, in which one of the first formulations of the question of being is posed: "δῆλον γὰρ ὡς ὑμεῖς μὲν ταῦτα
(τί ποτε βούλεσθε σημαίνειν ὁπόταν ὂν φθέγγησθε) πάλαι γιγνώσκετε,
ἡμεῖς δὲ πρὸ τοῦ μὲν ᾠόμεθα, νῦν δ' ἠπορήκαμεν ...": (Plato, Sophist
244a). In an English version of Heidegger's translation: "For man-
ifestly you have long been aware of what you mean when you use
the expression 'being.' We, however, who used to think we understood it, have now become perplexed."[1] And nearly thirty years later,
in his 1956 article "What Is Philosophy?", Heidegger still thinks that
the question of being is the main question of philosophy. This time
he cites a classical topos from Aristotle: "καὶ δὴ καὶ τὸ πάλαι τε καὶ νῦν
καὶ ἀεὶ ζητούμενον καὶ ἀεὶ ἀπορούμενον, τί τὸ ὄν;" (Met. 21, 1028b). In
the English version of Heidegger's translation: "And thus, as was in
the past, is now too and will be ever more, that towards which (philosophy) is moving and towards which it again and again does not

---

[1] *In German:* "Denn offenbar seid ihr doch schon lange mit dem vertraut, was ihr
eigentlich meint, wenn ihr den Ausdruck "seiend" gebraucht, wir jedoch glaubten
es einst zwar zu verstehen, jetzt aber sind wir in Verlegenheit gekommen."

find access: the question – what is being? (ti to on)" (Heidegger 1958, 53).[2]

Already in §2 of *Being and Time*, Heidegger more precisely specifies the question of being as the question of the meaning of being, and one would fairly expect an analysis of the concept that would be able to develop or clarify the meaning of the term 'being.'[3] Heidegger first establishes that in our everyday language we possess a vague average understanding of Being (5/25), but he does not offer an analysis to contribute to the clarification of the concept. Instead, he chooses another starting point.

Initially, he correctly maintains that many things are meant by the term 'being' (*seiend*), and then he asks which being best reflects Being in general. In his words: "But there are many things which we designate as 'being' [*seiend*], and we do so in various senses. Everything we talk about, everything we have in view, everything towards which we comport ourselves in any way, is being; what we are is being, and so is how we are. Being lies in the fact that something is, and in its Being as it is; in Reality; in presence-at-hand; in subsistence; in validity; in Dasein; in the 'there is'. In *which* entities is the meaning of Being to be discerned? From which entities is the disclosure of Being to take its departure? Is the starting-point optional, or does some particular entity have priority when we come to work out the question of Being? Which entity shall we take for our example, and in what sense does it have priority?"

---

[2] *In German*: "Und so ist denn einstmals schon und auch jetzt und immerfort dasjenige, wohin (die Philosophie) sich auf den Weg begibt und wohin sie immer wieder den Zugang nicht findet (das Gefragte dieses): Was ist das Seiende? (τὶ τὸ ὄν)."

[3] According to Ernst Tugendhat in an excellent article, which poignantly expresses the results of his thirty years of work on Heidegger, "The question of the meaning of x has a clear meaning if an expression is meant by 'x'" (1992, 109). And he continues: "And thus Heidegger's question of being would not be a problem either, were it meant to question the meaning of 'Being'; and that is also the only thing that comes of the Plato quote introduced on page 1 (Heidegger translates correctly: 'what you mean when you use the expression 'being'). But Heidegger proceeds immediately to drop the quotation marks and says: 'Thus it is valid to question the meaning of Being anew', and every expert knows that Heidegger is not speaking about the word Being. But then what is he talking about? We are confronted in this first paragraph of the work with one of the typical Heideggerean shifts in which, in a harmless, first formulation, it is suggested that one understands something, which in the second formulation is no longer meant that way, and we are not told what then is being talked about" (ibid).

(6f./26). A few lines later Heidegger reveals his proposal: "This entity which each of us is himself and which includes inquiring as one of the possibilities of its Being, we shall denote by the term '*Dasein*'. If we are to formulate our question explicitly and transparently, we must first give a proper explication of an entity (Dasein), with regard to its Being" (7/27). Put more simply, Heidegger here opts to use the being of man (using the terminology of Dasein as his starting point) in order to attain a sufficient answer to the question of the meaning of Being.

It would now be legitimate to expect arguments concerning why the answer to the meaning of Being should be expected in reference to the Dasein rather than in reference to any other being[4] and concerning why this answer should even be reflected in an exemplary being in the first place. Instead of this, however, Heidegger admits quite openly and honestly that the option he has chosen amounts to a logical circle. Just after the end of the previously quoted text, he continues: "Is there not, however, a manifest circularity in such an undertaking? If we must first define an entity *in its Being*, and if we want to formulate the question of Being only on this basis, what is this but going in a circle? In working out our question, have we not 'presupposed' something which only the answer can bring? Formal objections such as the argument about 'circular reasoning', which can easily be cited at any time in the study of first principles, are always sterile when one is considering concrete ways of investigating. When it comes to understanding the matter at hand, they carry no weight and keep us from penetrating the field of study" (7/27).

What is openly and unambiguously stated here is the author's admission that in answering his basic question, which is also supposed to be the main question of philosophy, he is moving in a logical circle.[5] Every reader who views the respect for logical rules as a minimal

---

[4] (Tugendhat 1992, 116) remarkts that, in general, "'Seiend' in German" is, "in contrast to the Greek term, a strange artificial concept that seems old-Frankish." This, however, cannot serve as a valid criticism, since every author is free to use any expression to simplify the exposition of his thoughts.

[5] In other texts from his work – for example, in his Freiburger inaugural lecture – Heidegger states expressis verbis that his philosophical conception does not respect the rules of logic: "If the power of the intellect in the field of inquiry into the nothing and into Being is thus shuttered, then the destiny of the reign of 'logic' in philosophy is thereby decided. The idea of 'logic' itself disintegrates in the turbulence of a more original questioning" (Heidegger 1943, 1998, 40/ 1993, 105).

requirement for philosophy ought to stop reading *Being and Time*, on page 7, for it is clear by this point at the latest that the author does not wish to respect the rules of logic. Yet it is possible to be tempted to continue reading the main work and other works of Heidegger in order to find out whether the thinking of this philosopher constitutes a serious alternative to thinking that follows the elementary rules of logic.

What is offered, and what I cannot pursue in detail here, is a series of conceptual determinations, which are presented in an aura of apodictic importance and validity as a fundamental ontology. The entire description follows with the help of logical contradictions and tautologies, and Heidegger's goal is to achieve the "essential" or "original" views. In what follows, I offer a short summary of Heideggar's main thesis in *Being and Time*, which is relatively systematic by Heidegger's standards. In doing this, I will proceed in accord with the classical hermeneutic principle of charity in its weakest form (the strong form, of attributing as few obviously contradictory beliefs as possible, is unfortunately not applicable to Heidegger): I will thus presume *that the author is aiming to speak sensibly about something.*[6]

The question of the meaning of Being possesses both an 'ontological' and an 'ontic' priority (§3 and §4 of *Being and Time*). As we have seen, Heidegger postulates that an answer to the question of Being ought to set forth from the Dasein. The main thesis is that in the 'I am,' the so-called 'existence,' a different meaning is included than in the 'it is,' which he also characterizes as 'presence-at-hand' (*Vorhandenheit*).[7] Thus it appears that to answer the question of

---

[6] In his classical article "Überwindung der Metaphysik durch logische Analyse der Sprache" (1931), Carnap attempted to show, on the basis of an example from Heidegger's work (in accord with the criteria of meaning of the Vienna circle), that Heidegger's sentences are pseudo-sentences, since they do respect the grammatical rules of syntax but not those of logical syntax, and they are thus meaning*less*. Tugendhat (1992, 9off.) pursues a similar strategy, which on the basis of the recent advances in logic and in the analytic philosophy of language also attempts to show that the Heideggerean question of being is meaningless. I would like to go beyond the criticisms of Carnap and Tugendhat and presume the most generous interpretative rule: Since the rules of logic are not to be viewed as sacrosanct, not even to mention the meaning criterion of logical positivism, *I would like to presume that Heidegger did attempt to say something sensible,* and then I would like to analyze how frutiful his endeavor was.

[7] Cf. Tugendhat (1992, 126): "In SuZ, and even before it, Heidegger came across a second fragment of 'is' that is at least as interesting, with the question of the being

Being, what is known as an 'existential analytic of Dasein' is necessary. This analysis or 'analytic' of man or of Dasein does not make use of the results of the empirical sciences, such as, for example, anthropology, psychology, and biology, which also take human beings as their research object (§10). It is thus 'existential'. What does that mean? It means that man or 'existence' is analyzed with the help of what are known as 'existentials' instead of with the help of categories: Humans are thus not to be viewed as one species of a thing that exists parallel to other things; instead, they enjoy a special status, which it is imperative to analyze in reference to the idea of existence. This special status is expressed conceptually, among other things, such that the being of the existing person is defined as 'in each case mine' (*je meines*). This 'in each case mineness' (*Jemeinigkeit*) thus ought to exclude any 'objectifying' of man and underline the thesis that man is not an exemplar of a species.

The 'existential analytic of Dasein' raises a very high, indeed a colossal, claim: It is to supply a fundamental ontology from which all other ontologies can spring. In other words, this is not about the regional ontologies analyzed by Husserl, upon which the various empirical sciences are founded.[8] So, it is not only about working out the essential structures of the concerned regions upon which the corresponding sciences can then be erected. Beyond that, it is about supplying a fundamental ontology that constitutes the foundation of all regional ontologies. Unfortunately, the logical status of this fundamental ontology, that is, the 'existential analytic of Dasein', is not explained. Nor is it explained how an interested reader is able to attain the same essential knowledge.

Be that as it may, this fundamental ontology offers a series of results, which I sketch out here: the basic constitution of Dasein, that

of Dasein. I suppose that here lies one of Heidegger's earliest intuitions. First, he was convinced very early on that a fundamentally different meaning lies in 'I am' – he called it 'existence' – than in 'it is', which he characterized as presence-at-hand [*Vorhandenheit*]; and second, he was (already at the same time) convinced that it must be possible on the basis of 'I am' to understand anew the meaning of Being as a whole."

[8] See, e.g., Husserl (Ideen I, 1913/1980, 19/Ideas I, 57): "Every concrete empirical objectivity, together with its material essence, finds its proper place within a *highest* material genus, a '*region*' of empirical objects. To the pure regional essence belongs then *a regional eidetic science*, or, as we can also say, a *regional ontology*. [. . .] We can express this also in this way: *Every factual science* (empirical science) *has essential theoretical bases in eidetic ontologies*."

is, of man, is being-in-the-world. Put more simply: Humans find themselves in an environment. This environment is spatial: "Space is rather 'in' the world in so far as space has been disclosed by that Being-in-the-world which is constitutive for Dasein" (111/147). Part of this spatial environment is social in that other people (existences) are to be found there. Heidegger formulates this, saying that Dasein implies being-with (*Mitsein*). "The world of Dasein is a *with-world* [*Mitwelt*]. Being-in is *Being-with* Others. Their Being-in-themselves within-the-world is *Dasein-with* [*Mit-dasein*]" (118/155). This "argument," that humans find themselves in an environment, is allegedly even good enough to come to grips with the issue of the existence of the external world. Being-in-the-world is part of the basic constitution of existent things. According to Heidegger, the difference from the typical philosophical analysis consists in the fact that the "Dasein, as Being-in-the-world[,] has the tendency to bury the 'external world' in nullity 'epistemologically' before going on to prove it" (206/250). Heidegger offers a simpler solution to the problem: "Along with 'Dasein as Being-in-the-world, entities within-the-world have in each case already been disclosed. This existential-ontological assertion seems to accord with the thesis of *realism* that the external world is really present-at-hand" (207/251). The fundamental ontology thus hereby comes to grips with the issue of realism with a dogmatic determination: The external world is real, because the basic constitution of Dasein is being-in-the-world. In other words, the issue of realism is solved by the fact that man lives in an environment.[9]

The first section of *Being and Time* concludes with the summarizing observation that Dasein, earmarked by being-in-the-world, is to be understood as care that already expresses the entirety of Dasein.[10] In Heidegger's own words: "What have we gained by our preparatory analysis of Dasein, and what are we seeking? In Being-in-the-world,

---

[9] Heidegger ignores not only the issue of realism but also the problem of truth, which I cannot get into here. See, however, Tugendhat's important article, in which he reaches the conclusion: "But the interpretation of Heidegger's analysis of the concept of truth in the SuZ already makes it possible to establish the thesis that Heidegger evades the problem of truth by making the concept of truth to one of his foundational concepts, and by the way he does this. The fact that he calls 'disclosedness' itself truth leads him not to relate it to truth, but to essentially disconnect it from truth" (Tugendhat 1984, 286).

[10] See Schulz's interpretation (1953/1954, 72ff.), which is connected to the idea of the entirety of Dasein.

whose essential structures centre in disclosedness, we have found the basic state of the entity we have taken as our theme. The totality of Being-in-the-world as a structural whole has revealed itself as care. In care the Being of Dasein is included. When we came to analyse this Being, we took as our clue existence, which, in anticipation, we had designated as the essence of Dasein" (231/275). The fruits of this complex 'existential analytic of Dasein,' which constitutes half of the main work, are then banal descriptions of man, nothing more and nothing less. Man is characterized as a 'Dasein' that is 'in-the-world,' where other men also are. Man is characterized as an 'existence,' and it is established that he is 'thrown' into the world and that it is possible for him to act – "[given that] the Being of the being 'man' is *Being-possible*" (143/183). In addition, man is to be understood as a whole and as care.

In the second part of the work, these banal descriptions of man are then brought into connection with time. Here the analysis of death is assigned great significance, and death reveals itself to be "that *possibility which is one's ownmost, which is non-relational, and which is not to be outstripped [unüberholbare]*" (250/294). Page-long descriptions clarify that death is not to be outstripped as the 'ownmost possibility,' and that viewed both subjectively and objectively – that is, intersubjectively – it is uncertain when man will die. The entire analysis is offered in the 'jargon of authenticity' [*Jargon der Eigentlichkeit*] (Adorno, 1964),[11] which makes it considerably more difficult to understand the descriptions. The main thesis of the second section of *Being and Time* is that temporality is the meaning of the being of Dasein. "*Temporality reveals itself as the meaning of authentic care*" (326/374). What does that mean? If one seeks not to problematize the analysis of the past or of 'certainty' so much and checks out the more systematic Heideggerian analysis of the future, then "[b]y the term 'futural' we do not here

---

[11] This is jargon insofar as authenticity and inauthenticity are not defined as two contrary concepts by Heidegger, but are closely connected: "But inauthenticity is based on the possibility of authenticity. Inauthenticity characterizes a kind of Being into which Dasein can divert itself and has for the most part always diverted itself; but Dasein does not necessarily and constantly have to divert itself into this kind of Being" (259/303). The dictionary of Feick/Zeigler (1991) is a very useful introduction to this jargon. It contains the most important definitions of the concepts that Heidegger uses in his works.

have in view a 'now' which has *not yet* become 'actual' and which some-time *will be* for the first time. We have in view the coming [*Kunft*] in which Dasein, in its ownmost potentiality-for-Being, comes towards itself" (325/373). Man, Dasein, is related to the future in his ac-tions, in his thoughts, and in his entire life. But isn't that the same as maintaining that man is 'Being-possible'? (143/183). This is noth-ing other than a reformulation of the existential 'Being-possible,' and the main thesis is that man is oriented toward the future. This thesis is trivial.

In accord with the weakest form of the principle of charity, it would be possible to attempt to rebut this charge of triviality. In the final analysis, the author does offer an analysis of temporality as primordial time. This 'primordiality thesis' states that the future is more primor-dial than the vulgar future. Vulgar time is natural time, and thus that which is normally understood as time, the series of moments that stand in a relationship of earlier and later. Yet, in fact, it is false to main-tain that the future is more primordial than the vulgar future. For as Tugendhat (2001, 20) appropriately noted, "if we could not presume that there is a time after the present one, in which I will either live or die, there would be nothing that I could approach in the manner Heidegger describes as the coming-towards-oneself. Thus one sees that, in reality, the coming-towards-oneself in this allegedly original sense presupposes the time Heidegger tends to name vulgar, that is, the following of events" (trans. D. A.). With this, Heidegger's primor-diality thesis is refuted. "Heidegger's analysis of the temporality of Dasein is reduced to the harmless thesis that man is a being that not only – like every natural being – proceeds through a series of moments of time, but that he is also related in every moment of his waking life to the impending time" (ibid). And that is trivial.

The main work, *Being and Time*, concludes with the following questions: "Is there a way which leads from primordial *time* to the mean-ing of *Being*? Does time itself manifest itself as the horizon of *Being*?" (437/488). After 437 pages, the opening question, the question of Being, has still not been answered. The reason is, as I have attempted to show in my outline, that the 'existential analytic of Dasein' was a course that led to trivialities.

It would be possible to retort that this charge of triviality may ap-ply to the published parts of *Being and Time*, but that that work was

published as a torso.[12] Perhaps the charge does not apply to
Heidegger's later work. In the later Heideggerean production there is
a well-known inversion of the argumentation, known as the 'turn.' In
this later work the author still does not follow the rules of logic, but I
shall refrain from this here. In this phase of his development, the author remains preoccupied with the question of Being, but a reversal of
the argumentative structure is apparent. In *Being and Time*, the starting
point for answering the question of Being is man, Dasein. The main
argument was that with the help of an 'existential analytic of Dasein'
it would be possible to open up the Being of the being Dasein, so that,
in the next step, something could be said about Being (in general). In
the *Letter on Humanism* (1947) the opposite is maintained. Existence
is no longer the starting point; Being itself is the 'wherefrom.'[13] "Man
is rather 'thrown' from Being itself into the truth of Being, so that ek-
sisting in this fashion he might guard the truth of Being, in order that
beings might appear in the light of Being as the beings they are. Man
does not decide whether and how beings appear, whether and how
God and the gods or history and nature come forward into the clearing of Being, come to presence and depart. The advent of beings lies

---

[12] As is well known, Heidegger did not publish the third section of the first part of *Being
and Time* in his lifetime, not to mention the second part. Tugendhat presumes (1992,
132) "that when Heidegger began the investigations that led to *Being and Time*, and
when he wrote the second section, he had a vague faith that it would somehow work
out, although a single clear look would have shown that this was impossible. It makes
no sense to transfer a structure prepared for the analysis of consciousness or Dasein
to something else – even if it be Being. And thus the reason that Heidegger did not
write the third section of *Being and Time* proves to be entirely banal. Those on the
outside can easily see that Heidegger's vision was not only difficult to carry out, but
absurd, and in one way or another Heidegger must have had some clear hint of this."
  Figal (1999), who is generally positive about Heidegger's work, treats in some
length a seminar that Heidegger held in the summer semester of 1927 entitled
"The Fundamental Problems of Phenomenology," which Heidegger himself characterized as a "new elaboration of the third section of part I of *Being and Time*" and
which appeared postum (as volume 24 of the collected works, GA 24). He reaches
the following conclusion (93): "The introduction of the horizontal scheme of the
presence tranforms the structure of time in its threefold structure, and without this,
philosophy can no longer be explained from the structure of the everyday Dasein.
With that, the program of a fundamental ontology failed."

[13] There the author also gives the reason why the third section of *Being and Time* was
not published. It was not because of the appointment to Marburg, as Figal (1999, 49)
maintains; rather, "the questionable section was not written because thinking failed
in this 'turn', and so, it did not get through with the help of language of metaphysics"
(20).

in the destiny of Being. But for man it is ever a question of finding what is fitting in his essence that corresponds to such destiny; for in accord with this destiny man as ek-sisting has to guard the truth of Being. Man is the shepherd of Being" (Heidegger, 1947, 2000b, 22f./Heidegger, 1993, 234).

What we have before us is an argument directly opposing that in *Being and Time.* All a person can do is to find 'what is fitting in his essence' that corresponds to the destiny of Being. In other words, people should be prepared for 'Being'; 'Being' comes to man and clears him up; that is, something not exactly specified approaches man, and he must be prepared for or be anticipating it. The question naturally arises of what that 'Being' ultimately is. In the *Letter on Humanism*, only a couple of lines after the previously quoted text, there is an answer: "Yet Being – what is Being? It is It itself. The thinking that is to come must learn to experience that and to say it" (ibid.). It is clear that this is a trivial tautology. 'Being' is itself.

What is known as 'the turn' thus does not pertain to a clear explication of the concept 'Being'; it pertains to the fact that the argument is oriented from 'Being' to Dasein rather than the other way round. But this turn (or this turnaround) in the argumentation is not further specified. One merely finds out in various passages, for example, that "only so long as the clearing of Being propriates does Being convey itself to man"[14] (*Humanism*, 28/1993, 240) or that the arrival or the "absence of the truth of Being is at stake" (Introduction to *What Is*

---

[14] It is characteristic that this illustration in the *Letter on Humanism* is formulated precisely as an answer to the question of the degree to which this new argumentative structure is compatible with that in *Being and Time.* The complete quote is (Humanism, 28/1993, 240): "But does not *Being and Time* say on p. 212, where the 'there is / it gives' comes to language, 'Only so long as Dasein is, is there [*gibt es*] Being'? To be sure. It means that only so long as the clearing of Being propriates does Being convey itself to man. But the fact that the *Da*, the clearing as the truth of Being itself, propriates is the dispensation of Being itself. This is the destiny of the clearing." As Karl Löwith convincingly shows in his analysis of Heidegger's turn, "the existentials from *Being and Time* are in fact not abandoned, but they are re-defined, re-thought, and turned around to mean something different than what they originally did" (1984, 140/ trans. D. A.) Although the argumentative structure is clearly different, indeed standing in direct opposition to the earlier one, Heidegger uses the same concepts and maintains that he has always meant the same thing. But if this were the case, why would he then speak of a 'turn' at all? This is yet another logical contradiction, which we will ignore within the interpretative framework laid down in the volume.

Metaphysics? 10, trans. D. A.). Thus it is possible to take the message of the later Heidegger to be that people need to be ready for something. And that is both vague and trivial. The reproach for triviality thus also applies to his later work.

In sum, it is possible to say that Heidegger's philosophy is trivial and, in addition, often logically untenable. If that is true, the question of the intention of his philosophy seems less interesting. In the end, it plays less of a role whether the evocatively expressed garlands (Topitsch)[15] of an "apostate Christian ideologue" (Stegmüller)[16] is a "godless ideology" (Löwith),[17] a "teaching about salvation without a God" (Albert),[18] or whether it occurs as God's invocation after all (Bougas).[19] Those who make respect for the rules of logic a minimal requirement for philosophy will reject this philosophy. And those who are less concerned with logic will be confronted with a trivial philosophy that is not able to contribute to the solution of a single philosophical or any other sort of problem.[20]

2.2 ON THE ROLE OF UNDERSTANDING

We noted in the preceding section that Heidegger does not say anything about the logical status of his statements. In some of his texts, however, he explicitly speaks about the method he uses and about the

---

[15] See the chapter on Heidegger in Topitsch (1990), especially 110ff.

[16] See Stegmüller (1989, 156).

[17] See Löwith (1984, 124ff.).

[18] See Albert (1994, 2).

[19] See Bougas (1991, 114). In this excellent article, Bougas convincingly shows that in the final analysis Heidegger in fact sought and propagated recourse to God: "This 'other thinking' does not have an *affirmative*, but only a *questioning* and *aporetic* character: It does not offer an answer, it lingers with the questionable and the problematic. It makes due the 'preparing for readiness', it becomes awaiting expectation and longing for 'revelation', with which it clearly takes on religious tones: Heidegger speaks in this context about the 'piety of thinking'. With these presuppositions it is no wonder that Heidegger's late philosophy ends in the *call to God*, whose arrival is desired: 'Only a god can save us' he professes in a Spiegel interview, a resigned confession, which appears to consummate Heidegger's philosophy of being [...] Thus Heidegger's 'godless ideology' – the expression stems from Karl Löwith – ends with the *relinquishment of reason*, which so to say kneels before a hidden, unknown godliness."

[20] In the words of Karl Jaspers, it is "a teaching that does not teach anything except for how one can eloquently express this nothing: the great art of saying that he has nothing to say" (1978, 172).

role of understanding. As early as in his lectures in the War Emergency Semester 1919 on "The Idea of Philosophy and Problem of World-view," he discusses the "Phenomenology as a Pre-theoretical Primordial Science" (the second part of the lecture). The influence of his teacher, Husserl, is still very clear, and the analysis of the structure of lived experience (*Erlebnis*) (§§13–15) is carried out fully in accord with the Husserlean *"principle of all principles: that every originary presentive intuition is a legitimizing source of cognition, that everything originarily* (so to speak, in its 'personal' actuality) *offered to us in 'intuition' is to be accepted simply as what is presented as being, but also only within the limits in which it is presented there*" (Husserl, Ideen I, 43 f./ Ideas I, 44).[21] In his dispute with Natorp, he defends the Husserlean phenomenology, notably in its true reflexive form,[22] and the hermeneutic intuition is discussed only briefly and unsystematically on the last page of the lecture course (Heidegger GA 56/57, 117/Heidegger 2000a, 98).

In the summer semester of 1923 he then held a lecture course, "Ontology – The Hermeneutics of Facticity," in which Husserl's reflexive phenomenology was for the first time transformed into a hermeneutic phenomenology. The title, which at first sounds strange, is more fully described at the beginning of the lecture. "'*Facticity*' is

---

[21] So Heidegger argues fully in Husserl's sense about the experience (*Erlebnis*) that a question causes: "The question is lived, is experienced [*erlebt*]. I experience. I experience something vitally. When we simply give ourselves over to this experience, we know nothing of a process passing before us [Vor-gang], or of an occurrence. Neither anything physical nor anything psychic is given. But one could immediately object: the experience is a process in me, in my soul, therefore obviously something psychic. Let us look at it carefully. This objection is not to the point, because it already *reifies the experience rather than taking it as such, as it gives itself*" (Heidegger GA 56/57, 65 f/ Heidegger 2000a, 55; emphasis added). He also takes over other expressions of Husserl, such as the discussion of the "indetermined determinability" (Heidegger GA 56/57,14/Heidegger 2000a, 12). The original quotation from the Ideas I (129/156) is: "It should also be mentioned that what is given at any particular time is usually surrounded by a halo of undetermined determinability [...]." In the German original (Ideen I, 129): "Zu erwähnen ist ferner, *dass das jeweilig Gegebene zumeist umringt ist von einem Hof von unbestimmter Bestimmbarkeit* [...]")

[22] Husserl's work, as is well known, went through different stages of development, and Husserl's phenomenology accentuated different things at each of them. Nevertheless, the fact that the phenomenological method moves in acts of reflection (e.g., Ideen I, 1913/1980, 144/Ideas I, 174) is the core thesis of Husserl's philosophy, which accordingly should certainly be characterized as reflexive phenomenology. For a defense of this thesis – especially in the Anglo-Saxon world – against the interpretation that Husserl is primarily a theoretician of meaning, see Hintikka (1995, 82ff.).

the designation we will use for the character of the being of 'our' 'own
Dasein'. More precisely, this expression means: *in each case* 'this' Dasein
in its being-there *for a while at the particular time* (the phenomenon
of the 'awhileness' of temporal particularity, cf. 'whiling,' tarrying
for a while, not running away, being-*there*-at-home-in . . . , being-*there*-
involved-in . . . , the being-there of Dasein) insofar as it is, in the character of its being, *'there' in the manner of be-ing*. Being-there *in the manner
of be-ing* means: not, and never, to be there primarily as an object of
intuition and definition on the basis of intuition, as an object of which
we merely take cognizance and have knowledge. Rather, Dasein is *there*
for itself in the 'how' of its ownmost being" (GA 63, 7/4). That is a
cumbersome definition of the concept of 'man'. 'Hermeneutics' is also
defined, once as "the announcement and making known of the being
of a being in its being in relation to . . . [me]" (10/7) and then more
simply: "In the title given to the following investigation, 'hermeneutics'
is *not* being used in its modern meaning, and in no sense does it have
the meaning of such a broadly conceived doctrine *about* interpretation. In connection with its original meaning, this term means rather:
a definite unity in the actualizing of ἑρμηνεύειν, that is, of the *interpreting
of facticity* in which facticity is being encountered, seen, grasped, and
expressed in concepts" (14/11).

Hermeneutics is thus the construal or interpretation of facticity, that
is, of man. But because it is man that interprets himself, 'hermeneutics' is to be understood "as the self-interpretation of facticity" (in accord with §3 of the lecture). In other words, hermeneutics is nothing
more than the way man interprets himself.[23] Thus, in principle, *Being
and Time* repeats what the students learned in summer semester lectures of 1923: "The phenomenology of Dasein is a *hermeneutic* in the

---

[23] Heidegger (1999) maintains on page 12: "The relationship here between hermeneutics and facticity is *not a relationship between the grasping of an object and the object grasped,*
in relation to which the former would simply have to measure itself. Rather, interpreting is itself a possible and distinctive how of the character of being of facticity"
(emphasis added). Just afterward, on the same page, however, he maintains: *"The
theme of this hermeneutical investigation is the Dasein* which is in each case *our own* and
indeed as hermeneutically interrogated with respect to and on the basis of the character of its being and with a view to developing in it a radical wakefulness for itself"
(emphasis added). As long as it is possible to presume that the 'theme' of a study
also constitutes its 'subject matter', this is yet another contradiction.

primordial signification of this word, where it designates this business of interpreting. [...] [I]t contains the roots of what can be called 'hermeneutic' only in a derivative sense: the methodology of those human sciences [...]" (37f./62). This is clearly a transformation of Husserl's phenomenological program. The imperative of Husserl's philosophy "to return to the things themselves" condenses the central message of his reflexive phenomenology, which is to describe the contents of consciousness. His view was in fact that, with the aid of phenomenological ἐποχή, one could attain 'pure consciousness,' which for its part was not affected by the process of the phenomenological bracketing or reduction.[24] He was thus concerned with describing this phenomenological residue – that is, the lived experience (*Erlebnis*) as it is given – from a first-person perspective.

There is much in this program that can be objected to; for one, no intersubjectively testable method is proposed. The entire procedure, however, remains comprehensible, at least in principle. In Heidegger's hands, the Husserlean program is silently distorted and pushed in the counterproductive direction of a hermeneutic of facticity. The description of the lived experience (*Erlebnis*) in the reflexive phenomenology of Husserl is transformed into an interpretation of Dasein, that is, of man. As was shown in Section 2.1, the basic constitution of Dasein is characterized as its 'being-in-the-world,' and for the world of Dasein, the environment (*Mitwelt*) is viewed as constitutive. This depiction stands in direct contradiction to the main idea of Husserl's reflexive phenomenology: The point of Husserl's phenomenology is that, with the aid of ἐποχή, the world of natural perception will be switched off. The whole phenomenological region and pure consciousness will first be made accessible if the phenomenological ἐποχή is performed as a fully conscious act. Heidegger's elaboration of Dasein as 'being-in-the-world' is consequently a clear distortion of Husserl's reflexive phenomenology. In addition, the hermeneutic of facticity, in the form of the existential analytic of Dasein, provides the trivial knowledge that we presented in Section 2.1. Thus, it is fair to maintain that *Heideggers's hermeneutics is a distortion and, at the same time, a trivialization of Husserl's reflexive phenomenology.*

---

[24] I cannot go into details here. See Husserl (Ideas, §§32–4).

Within the framework of this hermeneutic phenomenology, understanding is accorded an independent place. Understanding is not interpreted, as it usually is, as a cognitive relationship to other persons or as intentionality. Rather, in the ontology lecture course of 1923, it is pointed out (15/12): "This understanding which arises in interpretation cannot at all be compared to what is elsewhere called understanding in the sense of a knowing comportment toward the life of another. It is not comportment toward... (intentionality) in any sense, but rather a *how of Dasein* itself." Understanding is thus not a concrete mental operation but, as is said in *Being and Time*, "*the existential Being of Dasein's own potentiality-for-Being*" (144/184). In other words, understanding can be interpreted as one of the ways (or the way) that people are, their way of being, a mode (or the mode) of human existence in general. In principle, this is nothing more than a further defining characteristic of the concept of 'man', which, in accord with Heideggerean jargon, is presented as 'existential' in order to dramatize the problem at hand. Certainly this further 'existential', the understanding, would be a less important component of the Heideggerean philosophy if it had not been discussed in connection with the circle of understanding, which I turn to next.

2.3 THE PROBLEM OF THE HERMENEUTIC CIRCLE

In accord with the course followed in this first part of the book, I would like to choose and discuss in more detail a very precise problem that arises in connection with Heidegger's work and is of great general significance. It concerns the problem of the hermeneutic circle. This is of fundamental importance because the hermeneutic circle serves as a standard argument for all those who raise a claim for the autonomy of the human sciences or propagate an alternative methodology for the human sciences.[25] In this and the following section, my concern will thus be to check the soundness of this argument. I will proceed by

[25] In Stegmüller's words (1986b, 28/1988, 103): "[T]he circle of understanding seems to be the rational core which remains after we eliminate all irrational factors from the thesis of the distinction or special position of the humanities vis-à-vis the natural sciences."

listing and briefly sketching out three variations of the problem. In the following section, I will critically discuss these variations and appeal to alternative solutions.

I. Is the Hermeneutic Circle an Ontological Problem?

An important part of Heidegger's philosophy is the treatment of the problem of the hermeneutic circle, which arises in connection with his analysis of understanding. There the hermeneutic circle is presented as an ontological problem, and the question arises of what is meant by that and whether in fact the hermeneutic circle is this kind of problem. Heidegger, first of all, correctly emphasizes that things become 'understandable' only if we experience them *as* something. He notes that only interpretation with "the structure of something as something" (149/189) can take place. "Whenever something is interpreted as something, the interpretation will be founded essentially upon fore-having, fore-sight, and fore-conception" (150/191). This is what is known as the idea of the 'fore-structure' of understanding, which is presupposed in every act of understanding. "Any interpretation which is to contribute understanding must already have understood what is to be interpreted. [...] But if interpretation must in any case already operate in that which is understood, and if it must draw its nurture from this, how is it to bring any scientific results to maturity without moving in a circle, especially if, moreover, the understanding which is presupposed still operates within our common information about man and the world? Yet according to the most elementary rules of logic, this *circle* is a *circulus vitiosus*" (152/194).

The problem of the hermeneutic circle need not be solved by showing respect for the rules of logic and attempting to avoid the circle. "What is decisive is not to get out of the circle but to come into it in the right way" (153/195). And that is the case precisely because the hermeneutic circle is not a *logical* circle, but is meant to present an ontological problem: "This circle of understanding is not an orbit in which any random kind of knowledge may move; it is the expression of the existential *fore-structure* of Dasein itself. It is not to be reduced to the level of a vicious circle, or even of a circle which is merely tolerated" (ibid.).

II. Is the Hermeneutic Circle a Logical Problem?

In the contemporary discussion, the previously quoted views of Heidegger are very often called upon as a source of legitimation.[26] The philologist Friedrich Ast (1778–1841), however, was probably the first to draw attention to the circularity of interpretation (Ast 1808, 178ff.). He pointed to "[t]he foundational law of all understanding and knowledge," which is "to find the spirit of the whole through the individuals, and through the whole to grasp the individual"[27] (178). This circle of understanding is thematized by Hans-Georg Gadamer, the main representative of philosophical hermeneutics (whose views we will deal with in the next chapter), in the following manner: "The anticipation of meaning in which the whole is projected, is brought to explicit comprehension in that the parts, determined by the whole, determine this whole as well. This is familiar to us from learning foreign languages. We learn that we can only try to understand the parts of a sentence in their linguistic meaning when we have parsed or construed the sentence. But the process of parsing is itself guided by an expectation of meaning arising from the preceding context. [...] Thus the movement of understanding always runs from whole to part, and back to whole. The task is to expand in concentric circles the unity of the understood meaning" (GW 2, 57/1988, 68). Does this "circular relationship" (ibid.) present a logical problem?

III. Is the Hermeneutic Circle an Empirical Problem?

The hermeneutic circle is typically viewed as either an ontological or a logical problem and is analyzed correspondingly. However, the question arises of whether the phenomenon that the hermeneuticists think of and characterize as the circle of understanding does not present an empirical problem after all. By that, I mean that the movement of understanding from the whole to the part and back to the whole is a

---

[26] See, for example, Gadamer's article "On the Circle of Understanding," where he notes: "Heidegger's hermeneutical reflection has its point not so much in proving the existence of a circle as in showing its ontologically positive meaning" (GW 2, 59/1988, 71).

[27] Schleiermacher (1999, 329) characterizes as a hermeneutic principle the fact "that the same way that the whole is, of course, understood in reference to the individuals, so too, the individual can only be understood in reference to the whole."

mental operation that plays out in the brain of every interpreter and could be analyzed with the tools of empirical science. In this case, the circle of understanding has nothing to do with ontology or with logic, but rather with the representation of knowledge in the mind of the interpreter, which would present the following empirical problem: How does the cognitive system of the interpreter perceive, classify, and understand written signs? Is this mental operation automatized, and what sort of cognitive mechanism is activated so that the meaning of part of a written expression is only available to the interpreter in dependance of the whole and vice versa?

2.4 WHY THE HERMENEUTIC CIRCLE DOES NOT PARALYZE THOUGHT

If the hermeneutic circle were either an ontological or a logical problem, then this might indeed have very serious consequences. Should the hermeneutic circle be found to be a real ontological problem, this would mean the end of the subject–object distinction constitutive of modernity. For Heidegger's discussion of the hermeneutic circle refers to the structure of the being-in-the-world.[28] In accord with his interpretation, understanding is not an attitude that man assumes toward certain objects, but his very being-in-the-world itself.[29] In other words, if Heidegger's analysis of the circle of understanding were correct, then one might be inclined to accept his ontological consequences as well and to admit that the subject–object distinction is perhaps to be rejected in favor of an 'existential analytic of Dasein.' On the other hand, if the hermeneutic circle were a logical problem, then this would mean that the foundations of the human sciences were insecure and their scientific character was endangered. In either case, thinking would be paralyzed: In the first case, we would only be capable of producing trivialities; and in the second case, the human sciences would be logically lamed. In what follows, I would like to show that the hermeneutic circle is neither a genuine ontological problem nor a logical problem and that, consequently, philosophical hermeneutics need not lead to a paralysis of thought. Rather, it will be shown that it is an empirical

---

[28] See Löwith's detailed analysis (1984, 199ff.).
[29] See Gadamer's corresponding interpretation (GW 2, 331/1986, 379).

problem, which has long been studied using the tools of the empirical sciences.

I. Why the Hermeneutic Circle Is Not an Ontological Problem

According to Heidegger's own statements in his fundamental ontology, the circle of understanding is not an ontological *problem* that is to be solved. What is much more important here is that "[w]e must rather endeavor to leap into the 'circle' primordially and wholly, so that even at the start of the analysis of Dasein we make sure that we have a full view of Dasein's cicular Being" (*Being and Time*, 315/363). If it is then not an ontological *problem*, what is it concerned with? It is concerned with a further defining characteristic of the concept of 'Dasein' (e.g., of man). Within the description of the various characteristics of Dasein discussed earlier, the hermeneutic circle is one more on the list (in Heideggerian jargon, it is an 'existential'). "An entity for which, as Being-in-the-world, its Being is itself an issue, has ontologically a circular structure" (*Being and Time*, 153/195).[30] We are confronted with a *trivial description*, not a *problem* and unfortunately not even an *argument* that could lead us somehow to abandon the subject–object distinction.[31]

II. Why the Hermeneutic Circle Is Not a Logical Problem

While the reasons for denying that the hermeneutic circle is an ontological problem seem relatively clear, the question of its logical character is more complex. As Stegmüller (1986b/1988) noted in his classical article, logically the dispute about the hermeneutic circle runs up against a series of difficulties that burden all hermeneutic literature: the pictorial-metaphorical language, the blurring of object level and meta-level, the lack of clarity about the status of the key

---

[30] Here I would like to ignore the contradictory character of the whole because the sentence just following the text quotation maintains that we do need to avoid characterizing Dasein with the circle: "If, however, we note that 'circularity' belongs ontologically to a kind of Being which is present-at-hand (namely, to subsistence [*Bestand*]), we must altogether avoid using this phenomenon to characterize anything like Dasein ontologically" (153/195).

[31] Thus Heidegger's demand, without offering any argument ("Sein und Zeit," 315f./363f.). For a critique of the attempt to ontologize understanding and the circle of understanding, see Vossenkuhl (1998, 176ff.).

hermeneutic terms (above all, the ambiguity of the word 'understand-ing'), the merely apparent distance from psychologism, and, finally, the complete lack of the analysis of examples.

However, what in any case applies is that the phenomenon of the hermeneutic circle has nothing to do with a logical circle, despite fre-quent insinuations of hermeneuticists to the contrary. The relation-ship of the meaningful whole to its elements, and vice versa, is not of a logical nature. It is thus not concerned with circular *argumentation* in a deduction, which arises because in the process of proving something one falls back on a statement that one was supposed to prove. Nor is it related to a circular *definition*, which arises because the concept, which is still to be defined, has already unreflectively been used in the text beforehand.

It is nevertheless possible that the hermeneutic circle, while not being a case of circular logic, still presents another type of logical problem. In a detailed explication of the concept, Stegmüller (1986b) maintains that it constitutes a dilemma, or, more concretely, one of six specific forms of dilemmas, depending on what is meant by the hermeneutic circle in a particular case.[32] However, this transforma-tion of the phenomenon into different forms of dilemmas, namely, into the types of difficulties that force the researcher to choose be-tween two alternatives that are equally undesirable, does not seem to be correct.[33] In principle, Stegmüller's analysis attempts to show that the hermeneutic circle is not in fact a *logical* problem, but that it still can be interpreted as a *methodological* problem, which in some of its variations is by no means a narrow epistemological problem of the human sciences, but instead something that epitomizes all disciplines. This applies, for example, to what is known as the 'dilemma of con-firmation.' It also applies to the dilemma in distinguishing between background knowledge and facts. In a careful analysis based on exam-ples from both literature and astronomy, Stegmüller shows that, in test-ing the relative hypothesis, difficulties arise in precisely differentiating between background knowledge and facts. The testing of hypotheses requires a clear separation between hypothetical components in the observational data, on the one hand, and the theoretical background

---

[32] For an even more detailed explication of the concept, see Göttner (1973, 132ff.).
[33] This is also the view of Geldsetzer (1994, 137).

knowledge, on the other. As Stegmüller convincingly shows, by no means does this problem arise only in the humanities. It can be solved only through critical discussions and the agreement of those in the discipline in question about what are to be considered facts and what is to be considered background knowledge in connection with the specific hypothesis to be tested (1986b, 74 ff./1988, 145ff.).

Now, I have no objections to the treatment of the problem per se, except that it certainly is not concerned with a logical problem in any narrow sense, but rather with a methodological problem. I would, however, deny that the problem of the relationship between a meaningful whole and its elements can be plausibly transformed in this way. One central view that I share with Stegmüller is that, in the apprehension of the meaning of texts, interpretative hypotheses are to be tested; this will also play a significant role in the approach that I develop in Part II of the book. In testing such interpretative hypotheses, the methodological problems or the dilemmas that Stegmüller discusses will often, if not always, arise, especially the problem of distinguishing between facts and background knowledge. However, the problem of the relationship between the meaningful whole and its elements does not arise when *testing the interpretative hypotheses* but when *formulating them*. It is concerned with a special phenomenon that arises when one does not understand linguistic expressions (or other signs) immediately, that is, more or less automatically. It is then necessary to set up interpretative hypotheses, and it is in doing this that one runs up against the problem of the meaningful whole and its elements. I will subsequently deal with what this activity more concretely looks like and how it is to be explained.

In summary, it can be asserted that the way the hermeneutic circle is presented by representatives of philosophical hermeneutics does not suggest a methodological dilemma that can be solved by means of a decision or in any other way. Rather, the inevitability of the hermeneutic situation is pointed out and a 'circle' is spoken of in order to somehow dramatize the issue. Stegmüller denies the hopelessness of escaping this problem, and with the help of methodological considerations, he shows that there are rational ways to come to grips with this issue after all. I would like to admit this hopelessness but to play it down by showing that the hermeneutic circle is an empirical phenomenon.

III. Why the Hermeneutic Circle is an Empirical Phenomenon

"A person who is trying to understand a text is always projecting. He projects a meaning for the text as a whole as soon as some initial meaning emerges in the text. Again, the initial meaning emerges only because he is reading the text with particular expectations in regard to a certain meaning. Working out this fore-projection, which is constantly revised in terms of what emerges as he penetrates into the meaning, is understanding what is there" (GW 1, 271/2003, 267). This is how Gadamer, the most influential representative of philosophical hermeneutics, sketches out the process of understanding a text as a series of 'hermeneutic circles.' The reader or interpreter reads a text with preconceived expectations (preconceived opinions or prejudices) and, in his work, he makes revisions. The understanding of the text, however, remains "permanently determined by the anticipatory movement of fore-understanding" (Gadamer, GW 1, 298/2003, 293). When this activity has occurred, when understanding has already taken place, the circle of whole and parts is "not dissolved in perfect understanding," if you will, "but, on the contrary, is most fully realized" (ibid.). In this classical exposition[34] of the hermeneutic circle, it seems clear to me – in contrast to the view of most hermeneutic philosophers – that the phenomenon being described is empirical.[35]

What is, more specifically, the case? In the *Concept of Mind* (1949), Ryle makes the distinction between declarative and procedural knowledge, between 'knowing that' and 'knowing how': All of our knowledge of singular facts and causal connections is declarative knowledge. All

---

[34] Classic insofar as the present discussion continually refers to this depiction as *locus classicus*. See, e.g., more recently, Reale (2000, 96f.).

[35] It is characteristic of the prevailing confusion that, in diverse texts, Gadamer himself says different or contradictory things about the hermeneutic circle. So, he says in one text (GW 1, 298 f./2003, 293): "Thus the circle of understanding is not a 'methodological' circle, but describes an element of the *ontological structure of understanding*" (emphasis, added). But then, in a footnote, Gadamer reacts to the previously mentioned criticism of Stegmüller (GW 1, 271, Fn 187/2003, 266): "The objection raised from a logical point of view against talk of the 'hermeneutic circle' fails to recognize that this concept makes no claim to scientific proof, but presents a *logical metaphor*, known to rhetoric ever since Schleiermacher" (emphasis, added). Thus, it appears, it is supposed to be both an 'element of the ontological structure of understanding' and a 'logical metaphor', whereby it is completely unclear what is meant by a 'logical metaphor'.

of our skills are procedural knowledge. As is well known, Ryle postulates that this is a categorical difference between these two forms of knowledge and that it would be a category mistake to attribute a phenomenon that belongs to one of these categories to the other one. Since the publication of Ryle's book, it has become clear that the difference between knowing that and knowing how – which Ryle introduced into the philosophical discussion in order to assert an argument countering the doctrine of the 'ghost in the machine'[36] – is also empirically tenable.[37]

The question arises of whether linguistic understanding can be classified as knowing that or as knowing how.[38] Given that this cognitive activity is improvable with practice, one can become faster at it and can become more precise, it is clear that it is a skill,[39] that is, a form of knowing how. In general, acquiring skills is very different from learning facts. For example, a violinist learns to play pieces faster and to hold tones by practicing. A small child can only learn to brush his or her teeth by practice, etc. The investigation of learning processes that lead to the acquisition of these types of skills has long been an established branch of psychological research.

In our context, it is significant that in acquiring skills, one will not only become faster and more precise, but will also exercise them more easily; in fact, the skills will become automatic (Baron 1994, 85). In everyday life, an enormous number of skills are carried out in this automatized fashion. This means that they become routines, and no cognitive resources in the form of attention are required in performing them. The automatization of the skills implies that they are carried out without conscious effort. In the case of understanding language,

---

[36] See Ryle (1949), chapter I, especially pp. 17ff.

[37] Neurological studies of patients suffering from amnesia show that the difference between knowing how and knowing that is honored by the nervous system. In a classical study, for example, Cohen and Squire (1980) report on patients who were capable of acquiring a "mirror-reading skill," although they had a memory neither of the words they read nor even of being confronted with the task. Their amnesia in relation to knowing that (in this case, of the specific words and the fact that they dealt with them in a laboratory experiment) did not hinder the learning or the exercising of knowing how (in this case, the reading of words that were presented in mirror images).

[38] Knowing how need by no means be confused with what is known as 'tacit knowledge' For more on this distinction see Mantzavinos (2001, 31–4).

[39] For an analysis of the concept of 'skill' see Scholz (2001, 282ff.).

which is of interest here, the Stroop effect, named after its discoverer, Ridley Stroop (1935) is characteristic: If people are confronted with the names of colors that are printed in other colors – 'blue' printed in red, 'green' printed in black, and so on – and they are to name the colors in which the words are printed, then they tend to read the words, because reading is an automatized skill. We tend to pronounce the words unconsciously because we have practiced doing so for years.[40]

This automatization of learned skills is a general phenomenon that has already been empirically investigated and explained (although there is still no consensus about the neurophysiological processes that underlie it). It is known, for example, that in the middle phase of a game, a chess master needs five to ten seconds in order to propose a good move, which is often objectively the best move.[41] As Simon notes when referring to this explanation "[i]t does not go deeper than the explanation of your ability, in a matter of seconds, to recognize one of your friends whom you meet on the path tomorrow as you are going to class. Unless you are very deep in thought as you walk, the recognition will be immediate and reliable. Now in any field in which we have gained considerable experience, we have acquired a large number of 'friends' – a large number of stimuli that we can recognize immediately. [...] We can do this not only with faces, but with words in our native language. Almost every college-educated person can discriminate among, and recall the meanings of fifty to a hundred thousand different words. Somehow, over the years, we have all spent many hundreds of hours looking at words, and we have made friends with fifty or a hundred thousand of them. Every professional entomologist has a comparable ability to discriminate among the insects he sees, and every botanist among the plants. In any field of expertise, possession of an elaborate discrimination net that permits recognition of any one of tens of thousands of different objects or situations is one of the basic tools of the expert and the principal source of his intuitions" (Simon, 1983, 26).

---

[40] It is possible to experience the same difficulty in a similar way. Try to give the number of symbols in each group of symbols in the following list. For example, when you see YYY, answer with "three"; when you see 5555, answer with "four":

YYY YY 5555 33 444 22 222 3333 44444 3 11 222

[41] See Simon (1979, 386ff.).

It thus appears that texts are read not only against the background of readers' presumptions and prejudices, but also against the background of their own experience with the material. Because the corresponding skill has become routinized, the text is normally understood automatically, and not consciously. Thereby it is, of course, to be emphasized that, because it is a complex skill, all levels play a role in understanding language: the phonologic, semantic, syntactic, and pragmatic levels. One gains experience in all of these levels over time, so that sounds, words, sentences, and entire texts are automatically classified and therefore language processing under standard conditions takes place effortlessly.

If a difficulty arises in the language comprehension process and if one does not understand linguistic expressions immediately, then cognitive resources for solving the problem are activated. We focus our attention in order to consciously interpret an expression: An interpretative hypothesis is consciously generated.[42] In psycholinguistics this conscious comprehension of language is often modeled as an interactive process. The relevant levels of information processing – phonologic, semantic, syntactic, and pragmatic – are not sequentially activated, that is, one after the other. Rather, the information is processed in all of these levels in parallel and simultaneously. Our language comprehension system keeps all the information available so that it is possible to have recourse to all of the information categories at any time.[43]

The 'talk of a hermeneutic circle' does nothing more than imprecisely depict the search process that is activated if the interpreter of

---

[42] I believe that Schleiermacher saw this, although I grant that he did not treat it in a systematic way. See, e.g., Schleiermacher (1999, 333f.): "And for speaking and writing, it follows equably from the said that each initial interpretation is only provisional and imperfect, more or less a more measured and complete skimming, only sufficient and only up to the task where we find nothing at all unfamiliar and the understanding automatically understands itself, i.e. where there is no hermeneutic operation with determined consciousness. However, where it behaves differently, it is more often necessary at the end to return to the beginning and to supplement the interpretation by beginning again: the more difficult it is to comprehend the structure of the whole, the more one attempts to find it by examining the details; the more comprehensive and meaningful the details are, the more one attempts to understand in reference to the whole, with all of its relations" (trans. D. A.).

[43] This interactive approach of the language processing system has been experimentally studied, especially by Danks, Bohn, and Fears (1983).

a linguistic expression does not understand something immediately. Nowadays psycholinguistics not only offers more precise descriptions of the phenomenon, it also provides explanations of the underlying search processes or mechanisms of language comprehension. We know, for example, that language recognition results from the classification of patterns and that a considerable amount of data is necessary for this classification. The explanations that are offered from psycholinguistics are formulated in a testable form and have been tested in laboratory experiments, but care is taken here not to talk about hermeneutic circles.[44]

Finally, with respect to the completion of understanding in accord with the completion of the hermeneutic circle, I would like to point to the cognitive mechanism that lies at the basis of every "aha" experience. The aha experiences of diverse intensity, which an interpreter has when the process of comprehension is completed, are neither irrational nor apriori. The main argument for why a cognitive mechanism is at work in the phenomenon at hand is the fact that only people with the appropriate knowledge have aha experiences (Simon 1983, 27). People with no knowledge of ancient Greek cannot have an aha experience or fully comprehend the text at the end of the *Republic*. Without recognition based on previous experience, the process of comprehending new linguistic expressions cannot take place, and while performing this activity, our intuition exploits the knowledge that has been gained through past searches (Simon 1983, 28f.).

In summary, it is possible to assert that, up to now, it has not been possible to show that the hermeneutic circle constitutes an ontological or a logical problem. Rather, everything indicates that it depicts an empirical phenomenon, which can be studied within the framework of psycholinguistics and other empirical disciplines. It is thus not capable of serving as a legitimating argument for the separation between the natural and human sciences. It is even less capable of qualifying the current talk of representatives of philosophical hermeneutics, who use it as their main argument, as a hermeneutic, deeper philosophy.

---

[44] For an informative overview of linguistic understanding, with a further bibliography see Anderson (2002, ch. 12).

3

The Claim to Universality of Philosophical Hermeneutics

A Critique of Hans-Georg Gadamer's Hermeneutic Conception

3.1 HANS-GEORG GADAMER'S HERMENEUTIC CONCEPTION

Gadamer's hermeneutics is among the most influential philosophical conceptions of our time and has provoked lively discussions beyond the German-speaking world. It regards itself as philosophical hermeneutics and thereby differentiates itself from the general hermeneutics, for example, from the eighteenth and nineteenth centuries. Gadamer wants to build upon Heidegger's insights, especially upon his conception of understanding as "*the original form of the realization of Dasein*" (GW 1, 1960/1990, 264/2003, 259), as Heidegger worked this out in the "existential analytic of Dasein." Gadamer thus neither intends "to offer a general theory of interpretation and a differential account of its methods" (GW 2, 1986/1993, 441/2003, xxxi) nor "to produce a manual for guiding understanding in the manner of earlier hermeneutics" (GW 2, 1986/1993, 438/2003, xxviii). Nor is it his intention "to investigate the theoretical foundation of work in [the human sciences] in order to put [the] findings to practical ends" (ibid.). Gadamer's "real concern was and is philosophic: not what we do or what we ought to do, but what happens to us over and above our wanting and doing" (ibid.).[1]

This philosophical claim has a transcendental character. The question raised in *Truth and Method* is "by no means merely" aimed "at

---

[1] For an analysis of this claim see Graeser (2001, 88ff.).

the human sciences" (GW 2, 1986/1993, 439/2003, xxix). "Neither does it ask it only of science and its modes of experience, but of all human experience of the world and human living. It asks (to put it in Kantian terms): how is understanding possible? This is a question which precedes any action of understanding on the part of subjectivity, including the methodical activity of the 'interpretive sciences' and their norms and rules" (ibid./ xxx). As stated in the introduction of his main work, he "tr[ies] to develop [. . .] a conception of knowledge and truth that corresponds to the whole of our hermeneutic experience" (GW 1, 1960/1990, 3/2003, xxiii).

After such an elucidation, which broadens the question in this way, one would legitimately expect a general epistemological investigation to follow, which, in juxtaposition to other alternatives, would show what the conditions making understanding possible are. Because "the entirety of human experience of the world and life praxis" is at play here, a genuine general philosophy appears to be called for, which would be capable of giving a substantial transcendental foundation to hermeneutic experience. Instead of that, however, we receive a philosophy *more philologico*, which commences with the problem of understanding artistic works and texts and then applies the text metaphor to the world as a whole.[2] Thus, what is offered is a comprehensive investigation of the problem of text interpretation, the results of which are then generalized and provided with a claim to universality. Before asking whether this transference is plausible and whether the claim to universality is legitimate, however, I will discuss, the main features of Gadamer's theory of text interpretation.

Gadamer's starting point is the Heideggerean thesis of the historicity of understanding, which he raises to a general hermeneutic principle. The elements of the hermeneutic situation, that is, the interpreter and the text, are primarily to be grasped from an existential perspective, and Gadamer argues in Heideggerean jargon "that neither the knower or the known is 'present-at-hand' in an 'ontic' way, but in a

---

[2] Compare, e.g., Kempski (1992, 405): "One only need save the analogous word 'text' and to speak about the 'world' (or about Being or being) in order to get that form of truth-objectivism that hermeneutic philosophy so enthusiastically courts in all its existential and ontological shades. The secret of this philosophy *more philologico*, is namely, 'the world as a text'. But that is a metaphor, a hybrid metaphor" (trans. D. A.).

'historical' one – i.e., they both have the *mode of being of historicity*"
(GW 1, 1960/1990, 266/2003, 261). "[T]he historicity of human
Dasein in its expectancy and its forgetting" is thus constitutive of the
hermeneutic situation. It is "the condition for our being able to represent the past" (ibid/2003, 262). This thesis would have been innocuous
without the significant-sounding Heideggerean jargon: Who could object to the thesis that man is in history, that consciousness then is essentially shaped by the cultural environment? Gadamer, however, wants
to radicalize this thesis, and this leads him to a series of contradictions,
which we shall point out momentarily.

Gadamer specifies the general thesis of the historicity of man for the
case of textual understanding. As a consequence of man's historicity,
people always read and understand texts against the background of a
series of prejudices and preconceived opinions. The receptivity to the
meaning of the texts does not presuppose objective neutrality on the
part of the interpreter, but a certain way of dealing with his own preconceived opinions and prejudices. With this thesis – that every reader
or interpreter comprehends a text against the background of his own
learning history – Gadamer appears to offer a plausible description
of an empirical phenomenon. However, he introduces the concept of
prejudice in this context and maintains that prejudices are the *conditions of understanding* (GW 1, 1960/1990, 281/2003, 277). What does
this mean?

Gadamer points out that the Enlightenment did indeed discredit
the concept of prejudice, but he maintains that it was itself nonetheless
by no means without prejudices. "And there is one prejudice of the Enlightenment that defines its essence: the fundamental prejudice of the
Enlightenment is the prejudice against prejudice itself, which denies
tradition its power" (GW 1, 1960/1990, 275/2003, 270). The critique
carried out by philosophical hermeneutics thus aims to counter the
idea of absolute reason, which is itself supposedly capable of criticizing
the entire tradition. The overcoming of all prejudices proves itself to
be a prejudice; that is the point of the historicity of man or of Dasein.[3]

---

[3] See Gadamer (GW 1, 1960/1990, 281/2003, 276): "In fact history does not belong
to us; we belong to it. Long before we understand ourselves through the process of
self-examination, we understand ourselves in a self-evident way in the family, society,
and state in which we live. The focus of subjectivity is a distorting mirror. The self-
awareness of the individual is only a flickering in the closed circuits of historical life.

With that, Gadamer arrives at "the fundamental epistemological question for a truly historical hermeneutics [. . .]: what is the ground of the legitimacy of prejudices? What distinguishes legitimate prejudices from the countless others which it is the undeniable task of critical reason to overcome?" (GW 1, 1960/1990, 281 f./2003, 277).

Now, prejudices are nothing but opinions that are available in the tradition; and because people in general, and thus also text interpreters, are always socialized in a tradition, they also adopt the opinions prevailing in the tradition. To jump out of a tradition is certainly a utopian undertaking, and thus one should fully agree with Gadamer that there need be no necessary antithesis between tradition and reason (GW 1, 1960/1990, 286/2003, 281). However, one cannot agree with Gadamer's oveaccentuated view that understanding is an act of insertion in a tradition (*Einrücken in ein Überlieferungsgeschehen*), which is something specific to the human sciences. Rather, traditions also play a preeminent role in the natural sciences and, most importantly, also in everyday life.[4] The question is rather whether there is a selection criterion that makes it possible to clearly distinguish productive opinions – in Gadamer's terminology, the legitimate prejudices – from the rest. For understanding texts, Gadamer specifies one such criterion: the passage of time.

"Often temporal distance can solve [the] question of critique in hermeneutics, namely how to distinguish the true prejudices, by which we *understand*, from the *false* ones, by which we *misunderstand*" (GW 1, 1960/1990, 304/2003, 298f.). The passage of time is thus presented

---

That is why the prejudices of the individual, far more than his judgments, constitute the historical reality of his being."

4 For the role of tradition in science cf. Popper (1963/1989, (ch. 4). A very similar argument to Gadamer's, obviously in another context, can be found in Hayek's theory of cultural evolution. Hayek argues against 'constructivist rationalism' of the Cartesian variety (1973, ch. 1) and maintains the view that cultural rules, i.e., the norms, customs, traditions, and the entirety of human knowledge, evolves in a variation-selection process over time (1960, chs. 2 and 4). What Gadamer discusses as a problem of the 'insertion in a tradition' in the special case of textual understanding, Hayek analyses (1973, ch. 1, 1979, Epilogue and 1988, ch. 1) in a very general context, among other things, as 'the concurrent evolution of mind and society.' This basic idea is found in rudimentary form in his early philosophy, e.g., in his article "Individualism: True and False" (1948, ch. 1). A good overview of the role of tradition and culture in the epistemological process from the perspective of the modern cognitive sciences is provided by Sperber and Hirschfeld (1999).

as a selection criterion for those prejudices that are productive for the understanding. But that hardly seems to be a useful criterion, and Gadamer does not explain it in further detail. Were the appropriate passage of time very long, for example, then contemporary texts might be nearly incomprehensible.

Besides that, how is temporal distance related to other possible selection criteria? One can hardly find an answer in Gadamer's broad oeuvre. The only clarification is that the passage of time often helps us to separate the true prejudices from the false ones when questions are posed. "But all suspension of judgments and hence, a fortiori, of prejudices, has the logical structure of a *question*" (ibid.). But why is the temporal distance a prerequisite for asking questions? Or in the transcendental vocabulary: Why is the temporal distance the condition for the possibility of questioning? It is always possible to ask questions. Besides – and this is a fundamental problem – it is doubtful whether questions alone can lead to a correct understanding of a text. Instead, we can assume that the *critical analysis* of the prejudices is necessary in order to achieve a true understanding of a text. In Part II of this book, I shall attempt to show what this critical analysis might look like. In any case, it is questionable whether a process of understanding that is carried out only in the mind of the text interpreter and that in part takes on the form of questions need always lead to the clearing out of false prejudices.

Besides, Gadamer appears to advocate a peculiar theory of truth. With the help of the hermeneutic procedure, given a certain passage of time, the text interpreter is able to distinguish true prejudices from false ones. One can presuppose that he almost always succeeds in this, because questioning is able to suspend prejudices. But success cannot be measured or recognized on the basis of the fact that the interpreter achieves a somehow valid understanding, which could be juxtaposed to an invalid understanding. For one of Gadamer's basic principles is that "[I]t is enough to say that we understand in a *different* way, *if we understand at all*" (GW 1 1960/1990, 302/2003, 297).[5] The suspension of

---

[5] This sentence is found in the following context (GW 1, 1960/1990, 302/2003, 296): "Understanding is not, in fact, understanding better, either in the sense of superior knowledge of the subject because of clearer ideas or in the sense of fundamental superiority of conscious over unconscious production. It is enough to say that we understand in a *different* way, *if we understand at all*."

prejudices with the help of questioning always leads the interpreter to a different understanding of the text. This different, that is, individual understanding, has a claim to truth, according to Gadamer, namely, a truth that is allegedly specific to the human sciences. *In principle, this confounds meaning and truth.* Given a certain temporal distance, every interpreter manages, by posing questions in the hermeneutic process, to clear out the false prejudices and, by doing that, to achieve an idiosyncratic understanding of a text, which is also supposed to be true. *Identifying meaning and finding truth are accordingly identical processes.*

What we have here is a concept of truth and a theory of truth that are conceived especially for the human sciences. In the article "Truth in the Human Sciences" it is accordingly stated: "To stand in tradition and to heed it is clearly the way of truth that applies in the human sciences" (GW 2, 1986/1993, 40/1994a, 29). And in the article "What Is Truth?", which is dedicated especially to the problem of truth, Gadamer explains: "Thus the situation arises that there is something in the human sciences that is not thinkable in the same way in the natural sciences, namely that the researcher sometimes can learn more from the book of the dilettante than from the books of other researchers. Of course, this is confined to exceptional cases, but that such cases exist indicates that a relationship between recognition of the truth and effability [*Sagbarkeit*] discloses itself that cannot be measured in terms of the verifiability of propositions" (GW 2, 1986/1993, 50/1994b, 39f.). For Gadamer, truth is thus temporal and historical, and accordingly he pointedly notes, "I believe one can say in principle: There can be no proposition that is purely and simply true" (GW 2, 1986/1993, 52/1994b, 41). The various interpretations thus not only bring about a different meaning of the text, they even bring about a different true meaning. Truth, like meaning, is subjective. That is the main result of this transcendental analysis.

In Gadamer's transcendental analysis of understanding, the basic idea of historicity is further anchored in the principle of history of effect (*Wirkungsgeschichte*) and elaborated in the accompanying theory of the fusion of horizons (*Horizontverschmelzung*). The principle of history of effect is always at work "[i]f we are trying to understand a historical phenomenon from the historical distance that is characteristic of our hermeneutical situation" (GW 1, 1960/1990, 305/2003, 300). The hermeneutic situation is thus characterized by a consciousness of the history of effect, which has a certain inherent ambiguity: "This ambiguity is that it is used to mean at once the consciousness effected in the course of history and determined by history, and the very consciousness of being thus effected and determined" (GW 2, 1986/1993, 444/2003, xxxiv).

The way that this consciousness of the history of effect operates, which is always at work in the hermeneutic situation, is further specified in the theory of the fusion of horizons. "The horizon is the range of vision that includes everything that can be seen from a particular vantage point" (GW 1, 1960/1990, 307/2003, 302). Gadamer differentiates between two horizons that are at play in reading a text: that of the interpreter and that of the text. The horizon of the interpreter is the horizon of the present, which "is continually in the process of being formed because we are continually having to test all our prejudices. An important part of this testing occurs in encountering the past and in understanding the tradition from which we come" (GW 1, 1960/1990, 311/2003, 306). From this, Gadamer concludes that "the horizon of the present" is not formed "without the past" (ibid.).

It thus appears that there are fundamental difficulties in the process of understanding, because neither the horizon of the interpreter (i.e., the horizon of the present) nor the horizon of the text (i.e., the horizon of history) can be reconstructed or somehow appropriated. But following this, and indeed in the sentence directly after the preceding quotation, one finds what can fairly be called the *transcendental paradox of the fusion of horizons*: "*Rather, understanding is always the fusion of these horizons supposedly existing by themselves*" (ibid./306). How can two horizons be fused with one another if they cannot be reconstructed or somehow appropriated in the first place? Gadamer[6] appears to be aware of this paradox, for he asks: "If, however, there is no such thing as these distinct horizons, why do we speak of the fusion of horizons and not simply of the formation of the one horizon, whose bounds are set in the depths of tradition?" (ibid./306). His transcendental answer to the question touches on another fusion, namely, that of

---

[6] For this matter compare Hirsch (1967, 254): "Once again Gadamer's attempted solution turns out, on analysis, to exemplify the very difficulty it was designed to solve. How can an interpreter fuse two perspectives – his own and that of the text – unless he has somehow appropriated the original perspective and amalgamated it with his own? How can a fusion take place unless the things to be fused are made actual, which is to say, unless the original sense of the text has been understood?"

understanding, interpretation, and application. I would like to attempt to analyze this in more detail, turning to the role of understanding in Gadamer's work.

3.2 ON THE ROLE OF UNDERSTANDING

Gadamer criticizes the typical distinction of the early hermeneutics between *subtilitas intelligendi*, the understanding, *subtilitas explicandi*, the interpretation, and *subtilitas applicandi*, the application, and he maintains that all are integrated components of the hermeneutic procedure. "Interpretation is not an occasional, post facto supplement to understanding; rather, understanding is always interpretation, and hence interpretation is the explicit form of understanding" (GW 1, 1960/1990, 312/2003, 307). Besides, his reflections have led him to see "that understanding always involves something like applying the text to be understood to the interpreter's present situation" (GW 1, 1960/1990, 313/2003, 308).

The traditional differentiation between understanding a text, that is, identifying its meaning, and interpreting a text, that is, reproducing, deepening, and specifying its meaning, appears to have been plausible because normally it is necessary to identify the meaning of a text before it can be reproduced, deepened, and more clearly specified. For the same reason, a distinction between comprehension and application in a concrete situation appears to be plausible: It is necessary in the first step to derive the meaning of the text in order to be able to apply it in a concrete situation.[7] Whether the fusion of understanding, interpretation, and application is suitable in regard to other matters need not concern us here.[8] What is above all of interest here is that

---

[7] For a fuller treatment of this point compare Albert (1994, 56ff.).

[8] Grondin (2000, 16of.) speaks in this context even of a 'revolution of thought': "This emphasis on *applicatio* in fact characterizes pietistic hermeneutics. What is meant here is above all the 'application' of the text of the Bible, that the preacher is to carry out for the present situation of his community. It might be thought that this is concerned with a very remote case. But Gadamer will find it once again in the situation of the judge, who has to apply a legal text or a general law to a specific case. Beyond that, he will discover it in every form of understanding, not least in the historical-philological interpretation itself, insofar as the interpreter belongs to the texts and the events that he is able to announce in the present. Here, Gadamer paves the way for an unheard revolution of thought not dissimilar to a paradigm change, which allows the foundations of science (here hermeneutics) to be seen anew: Instead of beginning

Gadamer's confounding of the three moments of understanding is supposed to offer an answer to the transcendental paradox of the fusion of horizons.

It must, however, be stated that his proposed way out does not offer a convincing solution to the problem. It is difficult to see why the thesis that understanding, interpretation, and application constitute a unified process could eliminate or solve the paradox of the fusion of horizons. As has been shown in the previous chapter, a text is usually understood automatically and subconsciously because the appropriate skills have become routinized. Cognitive resources are activated only when a difficulty arises in the hermeneutic process and we do not immediately understand a linguistic expression. Our attention is then directed to a conscious interpretation. An interpretation could then be characterized, in accord with Gadamer, as a procedure in which the interpreter, in attempting to understand the (true) meaning of the text, must simultaneously interpret it and, beyond that, apply it to his own situation. This description would, however, only be a (partially incorrect) explication of what happens when the cognitive system of the interpreter is confronted with the text. It, however, offers no information about how the historical horizon of the text is created before it can be fused with the interpreter's horizon. Expressed in transcendental vocabulary: The fact that understanding is possible only in connection with interpretation and application does not explain why a fusion of horizons is possible when one of the horizons does not even exist at all.

The paradox of the fusion of horizons is, in my view only a consequence of the way that Gadamer conceives of understanding – above all, of his radicalization of the thesis of the historicity of man. Gadamer accepts the Heideggerean analysis of temporality as the meaning of the Being of Dasein and attempts to apply it to the case of textual understanding.[9] However, we saw in the previous chapter that the Heideggerean analysis of temporality brought only trivial results to

with a cognitive model of historical-philosophical interpretation, which attempts to understand an objective meaning, Gadamer refers to the practical model of legal and theological hermeneutics, in order to grasp the essence of the historical-philological interpretation from that starting point anew."

[9] See, for example Gadamer (GW 1, 1960/1990, 302/2003, 297): "For the hermeneutic productivity of temporal distance could be understood only when Heidegger gave understanding an ontological orientation by interpreting it as an 'existential' and when he interpreted Dasein's mode of being in terms of time."

light.[10] Thus, Gadamer's reference to the Heideggerean analysis cannot serve to legitimize his own conception of textual interpretation. Besides, the thesis of the historicity of man implies the thesis of the uniformity and permanence of human nature. For what else can the statement of the historicity of Dasein, formulated as a general principle, maintain other than that Dasein or man possesses a permanent characteristic, namely, this historicity?

I do not want to deny, of course, that the process of understanding when examined from an empirical point of view is influenced by history. I shall briefly review, in Part II of the book, empirical scientific results according to which the learning history of every interpreter decisively contributes, in interaction with other factors, to the way the interpreter understands a linguistic utterance. In this context, the 'historicity of understanding' entails the fully sensible view that, in the course of its cognitive development, the cognitive system of a reader or interpreter has produced an enormously large number of classifications; a linguistic utterance or a text is understood against this background at every given moment. The transcendental radicalization of this plausible thesis seems, however, to be less sensible. It is one thing to make the empirical claim that texts are understood in the light of certain background knowledge, and it is another thing to posit as an a priori postulate that the past meaning cannot be reproduced in the present because the past is ontologically foreign to the present.[11] In principle, this radical thesis questions the very possibility of communication, and not only the possibility of understanding the original meaning of a text from the past. That the past is ontologically fundamentally different from the present means that every point in time t_2 is ontologically fundamentally different from every point in time t_1, regardless of how large the time span is between t_1 and t_2. Since the performing of a linguistic expression always takes place over a certain period of time, the receiver – that is, the listener or reader – of the expression is in an ontologically different situation from the speaker or writer. Communication should thus be impossible.[12] Instead of offering us an explanation of the conditions for the

---

[10] See Section 2.1.
[11] See, for example, Gadamer (GW 1, 1960/1990, 301f./2003, 297f.).
[12] For a similar argument see Hirsch (1967, 256ff.).

possibility of understanding, Gadamer confronts us with the impossibility of understanding, indeed with the impossibility of any sort of communication.

In summary, it should be obvious that Gadamer's transcendental analysis is hardly useful for the interpretation of texts and that it is in part paradoxical. According to his conception, it seems impossible to grasp the author's intended meaning. The author's intention is disavowed as the criterion for a valid interpretation, but no alternative criterion is suggested. One understands *differently* if one understands at all, and that which one understands is also (subjectively) true: that is Gadamer's main message. However, the 'principle of history of effect' and the 'fusion of horizons,' which Gadamer's followers use as *termini technici* and which serve to support his main message, lead to paradoxes. It is difficult to see how this transcendental analysis might be able to offer any useful solution to the problem of the interpretation of texts. It is even more difficult to see how the generalization of this analysis, which was primarily conceived in order to solve the relatively modest problem of text interpretation, might prove to be fruitful for other issues.

3.3 THE PROBLEM OF HERMENEUTIC UNIVERSALITY

Many of Gadamer's interesting studies in the history of ideas must be ignored here. It is his claim to present his hermeneutic conception as a general philosophy and to expand his text model to the world as a whole that is of foremost systematic interest. In accord with my procedure in this first part of the book, I would like to concentrate on this claim to universality and discuss its plausibility.[13] This claim of universality is supported by three pillars: (I) the primacy of the phenomenon of questioning; (II) the language dependency of understanding; and (III) the orientation of hermeneutics on the rhetoric and the practical philosophy of Aristotle. In this section, I present these three main

---

[13] The discussion of the hermeneutic claim to universality is often fraught with controversy. But as Grondin rightly emphasizes (2001a, 168/ trans. D. A.): "It is not possible to say that the widespread controversies about this universality have brought about clarity. Gadamer, as is well-known, does not think much of precise explications of concepts, which at the same time pay tribute to the trend of propositional logic to fragment language into units of meaning."

arguments in support of the universality of hermeneutics in order to critically evaluate them in the following section.

I. The Hermeneutic Primacy of the Phenomenon of Questioning

In his article "The Universality of the Hermeneutical Problem" (1966), Gadamer formulates "[t]he hermeneutical *Urphänomen*: No assertion is possible that cannot be understood as an answer to a question, and assertions can only be understood in this way" (GW 2, 1986/1993, 226/Gadamer, 1976, 11). Already in *Truth and Method*, the hermeneutic primacy of the question is postulated with the argument that "we cannot have experience without asking questions" (GW 1, 1960/1990, 386/2003, 362). Since the structure of the question is presupposed in all experience, it is necessary to understand more deeply the essence of *questioning* (ibid.). In this way, appealing to Plato's dialectic, Gadamer places the hermeneutic phenomenon in the foreground (GW 1, 1960/1990, 374/2003, 368).

This means in concreto that every passed-on text that is to be interpreted ought to pose a question to the interpreter. "To understand a text means to understand this question. But this takes place," as Gadamer thinks he has shown, "by our attaining the hermeneutical horizon. We need to understand this as the *horizon of the question* within which the sense of the text is determined" (GW 1, 1960/1990, 375/2003, 370). These assertions suggest that it is possible to understand a text differently, depending on the questions one poses. This phenomenon thus seems to be able to serve as an argument for the universality of hermeneutics, because it presents a *logical phenomenon*. "Thus the meaning of a sentence is relative to the question to which it is a reply, but that implies that its meaning necessarily exceeds what is said in it. As these considerations show, then, the logic of the human sciences is a logic of the question" (GW 1, 1960/1990, 375/2003, 370; emphasis added).

II. The Language Dependency of Understanding

Gadamer's central argument in favor of the universality of hermeneutics is his thesis that understanding requires language: "This discussion shows how the claim to universality that is appropriate to the hermeneutical dimension is to be understood. Understanding is language-bound" (GW 2, 1986/1993, 230/Gadamer, 1976, 15).[14] According to Gadamer, "[t]o understand what someone says is [. . .] to come to an understanding about the subject matter" (GW 1, 1960/1990, 387/2003, 383). And "this whole procedure" is "linguistic" (ibid.). "*Language*" is "*the universal medium in which understanding occurs*" (GW 1, 1960/1990, 392/2003, 389), and the hermeneutic phenomenon proves to be a special case of the general relationship between thought and language. In principle, there is no thinking without language, and there is no understanding without the continual formation of concepts, an issue that has been obstructed by incorrect theories of language – for example, by instrumentalist semiotics (GW 1, 1960/1990, 407/2003, 403). "What is true of understanding

---

[14] Gadamer held this thesis until the end of his life: In his article "Geschichtlichkeit und Wahrheit" (1991), for example, he still maintains that "In my view this is the solid starting point of hermeneutic questioning – that the real essence of language lies in discourse. That means that we entrust language, which stands above all subjective consciousness, as our guide – language, which we are woven into, so to say, and which, through articulation and modulation, has long prepared and inspired us" (GW 10, 253/trans. D. A.). In the later Gadamer, however, the boundaries of language are recognized. So, he says in the article "Europa und die Oikoumene" (1993): "The highest principle of the philosophical hermeneutics, as I conceive of it (and that is why it is a hermeneutic philosophy), is that we can never entirely say what we want to say" (GW 10, 274/trans. D. A.). And in the presentation of his philosophy of listening, one of his last texts, he admits the *possibility of extralinguistic communication:* "Not only the speech sounds, but also the gesticulation of the speakers, this must all be joined in a convincing unity. Where this unity is lacking, understanding does not occur" (Gadamer, 2000, 50/trans. D. A.). In the same text, he even points to the possibility of prelinguistic communication, e.g. among animals (2000, 53). In principle, this recognition of the limits of language rebuts his thesis from *Truth and Method*, and one could simply accept that the claim to universality is no longer posed in the later Gadamer. Were this done, our further analysis would be superfluous. However, his followers maintain that the contradiction between the sentences "Hermeneutics is universal" and "Hermeneutics is not universal" can be eliminated, *somehow hermeneutically*. Thus Grondin, for example, who attempts to understand 'this turn,' says: "As a matter of fact both views are in an important and essential respect not only compatible, but complementary. For, what cannot be said or put in words is always what one wants to and must say, but simply cannot because the words fail. Words could only fail here because one searches for them insofar as one attempts to understand. That applies also for the faces of the unspeakable: the unspeakable – also the unutterable is always only the unexpressible because no word is capable of capturing what one would like to say. The later accentuation of hermeneutics thus indeed presumes the earlier view in accord with which understanding is essentially oriented on language" (Grondin 2001b, 104/ trans. D. A.). Since the claim to universality is held, if not by the later Gadamer himself, then by his followers, who refer to diverse textual passages of his work, I take it that the claim to universality still holds.

is just as true of language. Neither is to be grasped simply as a fact that can be empirically investigated. Neither is ever simply an object but instead comprehends everything that can ever be an object" (GW 1, 1960/1990, 408/2003, 404).

Thus no object can be constituted nonlinguistically, and this is the main argument in favor of the claim to universality. This thesis appears in Gadamer's expansive oeuvre in many variations – for example, in the well-known formulation that "Being, which can be understood, is language" or "Language is not just one of man's possessions in the world; rather, on it depends the fact that man has a *world* at all" (GW 1, 1960/1990, 446/2003, 443). The view that the world is only linguistically constituted is the main result of the transfer of the text metaphor to the world as a whole. Gadamer reaches the following conclusion: "Thus hermeneutics is, as we have seen, a *universal aspect of philosophy*, and not just the methodological basis of the so-called human sciences" (GW 1, 1960/1990, 479/2003, 476). It remains to be seen whether this conclusion is valid.

III. The Orientation of Hermeneutics on the Rhetoric and Practical Philosophy of Aristotle

The claim of the universality of philosophical hermeneutics does not rest only on the assumed plausibility of applying the text analogy to nature – that is, the view that nature can be read and understood as a text[15] – and the related assumption that the world is only constituted by nexuses of meaning that remain to be discovered and hardly, if at all, by causal nexuses. Beyond that, the universality of hermeneutics is justified by virtue of the fact that it is supported by alternative and superior disciplines, which enable it to help "guard us against the technological self-understanding of the modern concept of science" (GW 2, 1986/1993, 455/2003, 557). These disciplines are the rhetoric and the practical philosophy of Aristotle.[16]

---

[15] See, e.g. (GW 2, 1986/1993, 233/1997, 332 fn.1), "Thus [...] 'das Sein zum Texte' does not at all exhaust the hermeneutical dimension unless the word *Texte* is taken not in the narrow sense but as 'the text that God has written with his own hand,' i.e., the *liber naturae*, which consequently encompasses all knowledge from physics to sociology and anthropology."

[16] For an interpretation of both disciplines as a hermeneutic model, see Figal (2000, 388ff.).

Regarding the dependence upon rhetoric, the advantage consists in that fact that "from the oldest tradition, [it] has been the only advocate of a claim to truth that defends the probable, the *eikos* (verisimilar), and that which is convincing to the ordinary reason against the claim of science to accept as true only what can be demonstrated and tested! [...] Convincing and persuading, without being able to prove – these are obviously as much the aim and measure of understanding and interpretation as they are the aim and measure of the art of oration and persuasion [...]" (GW 2, 1986/1993, 236/1997, 318). Besides, the rhetoric is of significance because, in a certain sense, it is the transmission mechanism used to spread scientific results throughout society: *"What would we know of modern physics, which has so observably shaped our existence, from physics alone?* [All] the representations of science that are directed beyond the mere narrow circle of specialists [. . .] owe their effectiveness to the rhetorical element they contain" (GW 2, 1986/1993, 237/trans. D. A.).[17] And the third argument concerning why the rhetoric serves well as an orientation point for the claim to universality is obvious: "Clearly the ability to speak has the same breadth and universality as the ability to understand and interpret. One can talk about everything, and everything one says has to be able to be understood. Here rhetoric and hermeneutics have a very close relationship" (GW 2, 1986/1993, 305/1981, 119).

The relationship of hermeneutics to the practical philosophy of Aristotle appears to be more important than its orientation in reference to the rhetoric. The Aristotelian virtue of practical reason, phronesis, appears as the "hermeneutic basic virtue itself" (GW 2, 1986/1993, 328) and the practical philosophy of Aristotle as "the only sound model with which the human sciences can appropriately understand themselves" (GW 2, 1986/1993, 319/ trans. D. A.). If the hermeneutic orientation on the rhetoric legitimizes its *difference* from the sciences, the philosophy of science and logic, then the orientation on Aristotle's practical philosophy justifies its *superiority*. "So, too, the claim to universality on the part of hermeneutics consists of integrating all the sciences, of perceiving the opportunities for knowledge on the part of every scientific method wherever they may be applicable to given objects, and of deploying them in all their possibilities. But just as

---

[17] The lines in italics are missing from the Hess and Palmer English translation of Gadamer (1997) (D. A.).

[Aristotle's] *[P]olitics* as practical philosophy is more than the highest technique, this is true for hermeneutics as well. It has to bring everything knowable by the sciences into the context of mutual agreement in which we ourselves exist" (GW 2, 1986/1993, 318/1981, 137).

3.4 WHY HERMENEUTICS IS NOT UNIVERSAL

I. The Hermeneutic Primacy of the Phenomenon of Questioning

The first pillar upon which the claim to the universality of hermeneutics rests is the "primacy of the hermeneutic phenomenon of the question." As Keuth (1998) correctly notes, there is no proposition that cannot be understood as an answer; for every proposititon, a question can be formed, which is then answerable with the proposition itself or with its negation. Thus, it is possible, in reference to the proposition "The water is cold," for example, to ask "Is the water cold?" This question can then be answered with this proposition itself or with its negation: "The water is not cold." The same applies to the negation; and, as a result, every expression can be understood as an answer to at least two questions (in our example: "Is the water cold?" and "Isn't the water cold?"). But, of course, a much larger number of questions can be answered with the proposition "The water is cold." To offer three examples: "What's the water temperature?", "Why don't you get in the water?" and "Why won't your daughter drink the water?" To understand the proposition as an answer to one of these three questions, under certain circumstances, more information is needed, of course. But does the 'primacy of the hermeneutic phenomenon' mean to refer to such a simple logical characteristic of language? (Keuth, 1998, 79). If it was supposed to be something deeper or more important, it would have been necessary for Gadamer to demonstrate this.[18] In any case, the 'primacy of the hermeneutic phenomenon' is such a trivial logical characteristic of language that, if it were to function as an argument at all, this would favor the universality of logic more than the universality of hermeneutics.

---

[18] In an interesting article, Schwarz Wentzer (2000) attempts, in reference to Gadamer, to explain the basic provisions of the question. Although, after a critical discussion of logical positivism and the linguistic philosophy of Tugendhat, he rightly points to the difficulties of question-answer semantics, he himself does not offer a worked-out alternative.

II. The Language Dependency of Understanding

The idea that understanding presupposes language is, of course, an analytic sentence if understanding refers to linguistically coded facts, that is, texts. Insofar, the issue would be trivial. But obviously, the claim to universality is meant to allege that thought without language is impossible. Yet there is no doubt that we understand other living beings, especially other people, prelinguistically or extralinguistically (i.e., before language is employed or with means other than language),[19] and it appears that many animals do the same. The prelinguistic developmental psychology and the research on the social interaction of animals (above all, primates) offer very important empirically supported results, which seem to suggest that the claim to the universality of hermeneutics is illegitimate. In accord with the present stand of research, it is without doubt that babies and small children are able to understand and communicate before they have learned a language. So, for example, Acredolo and Goodwyn (1996) studied the prelinguistic communication of babies in a random sample of 140 families. Babies from eleven months to three years of age were studied. In tests with these children it was discovered, among other things, that children who were encouraged to communicate using symbols achieved higher-quality and more effective communication skills – including verbal skills – than children who were not similarly encouraged. Other developmental psychology studies have shown, for example, that the organization of the child's initial conceptualization system takes place in terms of event representations. The natural prelinguistic

---

[19] Habermas (1970/1982) and others were early to point to a prelinguistic experience of the world. Gadamer's answer to the empirical scientific results is formulated in the last sentence of the following quotation, which is characteristic of someone who does recognize a problem but who intends to avoid dealing with it scientifically: "Now it is certainly the case that our experience of the world does not take place only in learning and using language. There is prelinguistic experience of the world, as Habermas, referring to Piaget's research, reminds us. The language of gesture, facial expression, and movement binds us to each other. There are laughter and tears (Helmut Plessner has worked out the hermeneutics of these). There is the world of science within which the exact, specialized languages of symbolism and mathematics provide sure foundations for the elaboration of theory, languages which have brought with them a capacity for construction and manipulation which seems a kind of self-representation of homo faber, of man's technical ingenuity. But even these forms of self-representation *must constantly be taken up in the interior dialogue of the soul with itself*" (GW 2, 1986/1993, 204/2003, 547; emphasis added).

representation system of small children is based on an understanding of events in which social actors and asocial objects take part (Nelson, 1995).

The studies on the social interaction of animals, especially primate research, also offer insights into the possibility of extralinguistic communication. Tomasello and Call (1997, 243ff.), for example, document how primates, in their social communication, are able to infer the intention of their group members by drawing on specific gestures. Building on primate research and the results of cognitive archeology, Marlin Donald (1991, 1998a) points to the existence of a mimetic cognitive level that exists side by side with the symbolic level. In the course of the cognitive evolution from primates to humans, one of the greatest transitions was the development of a mimetic culture, which is also omnipresent in modern societies.[20]

It thus appears that the thesis that language is a prerequisite for understanding is either tautological, namely, if understanding refers to linguistically coded facts, or empirically false, namely, if it is generally alleged that there is no thought without language. Now, it is possible to counter that the dependency of understanding on language is meant to serve as a transcendental thesis. In the face of the mounting empirical evidence from an array of disciplines, such an attempt to present a thesis as an a priori is rightly suspected of serving, above all, to immunize the theory to criticism. And the legitimate question can be posed of why this statement itself, which is composed linguistically, and thus "is always already enclosed within the world horizon of language" (GW 1, 1960/1990, 454/2003, 450), is not subject to the general relativization to which other philosophical and scientific statements are supposed to be subject.[21]

---

[20] See Donald (1998b, 183): "Moreover, mimesis and language operate by different principles, the former by iconicity and analogy, the latter by explicit description and explicit denotation of relations. Even today, the user of material culture more often than not reflect these 'irrational' mimetic forms. The universal presence of fashion, music, custom, and ritual in popular culture, so apparently subversive of more formalistic and rational cultural institutions, testifies to this. Although apparently easy to acquire when young, such conventions are often difficult for adults – more difficult than languages, a lesson that many Western executives and diplomats have learned the hard way."

[21] Gadamer's followers appear not to want to take these simple questions seriously. See, for example, Fehér (2000), who in the article "Zum Sprachverständnis der

III. The Orientation of Hermeneutics on the Rhetoric and Practical Philosophy of Aristotle

The orientation of hermeneutics on Aristotle's rhetoric and practical philosophy must be seen as an attempt to elucidate the status of philosophical hermeneutics from the viewpoint of the philosophy of science. Since hermeneutics is an endeavor "to mediate between philosophy and the sciences" (GW 2, 1986/1993, 450/2003, 552), it is natural for hermeneutics to appeal to alternative theories of science in order to show that its intermediating contribution is both of systematic significance and universal validity. The orientation on the rhetoric is, however, by no means able to accomplish this. The primary argument in favor of rhetoric originates in a fundamental misunderstanding of modern science's claim to certainty. It is not true that scientific knowledge differs from other types of knowledge by being absolutely certain. This presupposes an ideal of science based on a justificationist model of knowledge that has long been rejected by modern philosophy of science. Above all, the works in the philosophy of science associated with critical rationalism have convincingly shown that the justificationist model of knowledge is untenable and that, instead, all of our knowledge is fallible.[22] Given this, it is no longer convincing that there should be a supposed preference for the field of rhetoric as a discipline, because it does not raise claims to certainty. The natural and social sciences no longer do either.

The second argument in favor of rhetoric, which emphasizes its significance as a mechanism for the diffusion of scientific results, is hardly convincing either. The implications of this argument show it to be false. For example, it would simply be false to maintain that generations of high school students need the help of rhetoric to learn the principles of modern physics and the other natural sciences. Neither the authors of school books nor high school teachers possess the necessary rhetorical abilities, and the transfer of knowledge functions reasonably smoothly nonetheless. But even if the quality of the

Hermeneutik Gadamers" points to the internal connection between language and objects and, while citing Gadamer with praise, wants to throw the philosophy of language overboard, because allegedly "the instrumental or merely conventional linguistic theory" would be unsuitable "because the word is grasped as a mere tool and thus initiates a debasement of language" (200).

[22] See especially Popper (1934/1971) and Albert (1968/1985).

transmission and the popularizing of knowledge could be improved with a special discipline, it remains to be seen how exactly this discipline should do this.

The third argument for why the rhetoric ought to serve as a point of orientation for the claim to universality is untenable. Since hermeneutics deals with the ability to understand and rhetoric deals with the ability to orate, there is – so goes the argument – a certain kinship or analogy between the two disciplines. This analogy is, of course, plausible. Only it is not clear how this analogy is able to support the hermeneutic claim to universality. In any case, it is false to claim (as I have shown in Section II) that "[o]ne can talk about everything, and everything one says has to be able to be understood" (GW 2, 1986/1993, 305/1981, 119). But even if this were true and it was possible to talk about everything, this would not legitimate the universal claim of rhetoric or of hermeneutics any more than the fact that all insects can fly might legitimate a universal claim from entomology.

If the orientation on the rhetoric is to justify the *difference* of hermeneutics from other disciplines, the orientation on Aristotle's practical philosophy serves as an argument for its *superiority*. The reliance on Aristotle's practical philosophy thus appears to be attractive, because it was conceived by the Greek philosopher himself as a guide for human action and simultaneously declared to be a science. As is well known, Aristotle (most systematically, above all, in the *Nicomachean Ethics*) developed a model of ethical action that enabled the actor to allow his action to be guided by knowledge provided by the dianoetic virtue of *phronesis*. *Phronesis* helps the actor to recognize how he ought to act in a concrete situation in a reasonable manner, both in the personal and the public spheres. In his description of this virtue, Aristotle did not tire of calling to mind the following principle: "Οὐδ' ἐστὶν ἡ φρόνησις τῶν καθόλου μόνον, ἀλλὰ δεῖ καὶ τὰ καθ' ἕκαστα γνωρίζειν· πρακτικὴ γάρ, ἡ δὲ πρᾶξις περὶ τὰ καθ' ἕκαστα" (Nic Eth. 1141b 17–19). ("Nor is phronesis concerned with universals only – it must also recognize the particulars; for it is practical, and practice is concerned with particulars" [trans. C.M.].)

The idea of applying practical knowledge in a concrete situation using phronesis thus appears to be a constitutive component of Aristotle's ethics.[23] As we have seen in the discussion in Section 3.2,

---

[23] See, for example, Höffe (1979/1992, 40ff.) and, in more detail, Höffe (1971/1996).

the conflating of understanding and application is a constitutive component of philosophical hermeneutics. But the existence of a distant analogy between the application of practical knowledge in a concrete action situation and the application of hermeneutic knowledge – whatever happens to be meant by that – in a concrete text to oneself can by no means accompany any transfer of legitimation.[24] Applying knowledge in action situations and applying knowledge gained in text interpretation are two completely different phenomena. Demonstrating an analogy of the type 'application here' and 'application there' is too simplistic to be convincing.

The flight into Aristotle's practical philosophy is by no means able to lend hermeneutics a scientific aura either. It is only a word game to maintain that hermeneutics assumes a place among modern scientific systems "that is more strongly tied to the earlier traditions of the concepts of science than to the notion of method proper to modern science" (GW 2, 1986/1993, 302/1981, 114f.). The search for legitimacy leads to the strange argument that, because of its general orientation on Aristotle's practical philosophy, today hermeneutics is somehow also to be classified as scientific, since in his systematization of the sciences 2,500 years ago, Aristotle also classified practical philosophy as ἐπιστήμη, that is, as science.

In any case, it is a misrepresentation of the development of the modern sciences for Gadamer and his followers to maintain that the *dissociation of theory and practice* is the result of this development and that practice is only conceivable as a direct application of science.[25] It is surely possible to bridge the gap between theoretical science and practical application without appealing to any allegedly existing hermeneutic knowledge. In modern philosophy of science it has been shown that a law can be formulated as a prohibition; if this is done, it can be technologically transformed without any problem.[26]

---

[24] This is what Gadamer claims in his essay "Hermeneutics as a Theoretical and Practical Task" (1981, 115): "Now there does exist at least one exemplar of the sort pertinent to the theory of science, which could lend a certain legitimacy to such a reorientation of the methodical heightening of awareness on the part of the Geisteswissenschaften. This is the practical philosophy established by Aristotle."

[25] See, for example, Gadamer (GW 2, 1986/1993, 314/1981, 131).

[26] See, for example, Popper (1957/1991, 58ff.) and Gemtos (2004, 105ff.). Unfortunately, I cannot go into the complex problem of the application of theoretical knowledge of the social sciences in political praxis. Herbert Keuth (1989) and Hans

In technologically transforming law-like sentences, no special logical problems arise. Applying nomological knowledge to practice is, of course, not just a matter of logic, because a series of other problems are always connected with it. But those applying knowledge usually use their imagination and their other cognitive abilities to solve these problems, and it is not clear how the transcendental theory of the fusion of horizons and of the history of effect might more clearly specify these abilities. It is hard to imagine how hermeneutic knowledge might simplify, for example, the work of a civil engineer who applies the law of statics in building a bridge. By contrast, research in cognitive science developed within the framework of the modern sciences – not highly esteemed by hermeneutic philosophy – offers at least some insight into the complex connections between declarative and procedural knowledge that are utilized in all applications.[27]

In conclusion, it is possible to see that the orientation on the rhetoric and the practical philosophy of Aristotle is hardly convincing, and it cannot establish the universal claim of philosophical hermeneutics. Transferring the text metaphor to the world as a whole has not proven to be frutiful. The three pillars of the claim to the universality of hermeneutics – (I) the primacy of the phenomenon of questioning in hermeneutics, (II) the language dependency of understanding, and (III) the orientation on the rhetoric and practical philosophy of Aristotle – are more shaky than supportive. Philosophical hermeneutics – whether striking out on a provincial or an urban path – leads in any case to a philosophical dead end.

Albert (1993b) have convincingly shown that the "Don Quijotesque" character of Max Weber's project (GW 2, 1986/1993, 165/in the English version of 1966, 582, this remark is missing) and the "notion of value-free enquiry" developed by him (GW 2, 1986/1993, 458/2003, 560) make complete sense and can simplify the application of social scientific knowledge to reality.

[27] See especially Anderson (1993).

PART II

HERMENEUTIC WAYS OUT

4

The Problematic of Meaning

The Naturalistic Way Out

4.1 WHAT TYPES OF NEXUSES ARE THERE?

Having presented and criticized three basic hermeneutic models in their systematic intention in the first part of the book, my goal of this second part is to highlight a naturalistic way of coping with the problematic of meaning. In this chapter, I will explain what types of nexuses there are before sketching out the naturalistic way of dealing with the problematic of meaning and plead for a unified approach to nexuses. In Chapters 5 and 6, I will then attempt to show that both human action in general and the results of such action, above all texts, can be easily grasped with a unified method.

Let's start with the plausible question concerning which types of nexuses can be apprehended. The answer to this question is simple: There are either nexuses of meaning or causal nexuses. A somewhat complex issue is which type of nexuses occur in which area of reality, or whether perhaps there are exclusively nexuses of meaning or exclusively causal nexuses.

Three positions are possible regarding this issue: One can argue that there are only causal nexuses or only nexuses of meaning in all areas of reality, or that there are certain areas of reality in which only nexuses of meaning arise and others in which only causal nexuses arise. It seems to me that no one today supposes that there are only causal nexuses; therefore, I ignore this view here and deal with the other two views. Because I dealt with these two philosophical positions in detail in the first part of the book, it is enough here just to sketch them out only with respect to how they treat the problematic of meaning.

I. In *the strong version*, when the *problematic of meaning* is overaccentuated, the thesis is that the world only consists of nexuses of meaning. In other words, all of the facts to be found in the world have a meaning that is to be grasped. This radical thesis implies that there are only nexuses of meaning to be discovered or experienced, not only in socio-historical reality but also in nature. According to this strong version, even when the natural scientific way of thinking usually attempts to specify causal nexuses, nexuses of meaning are to be sought. The text metaphor is applied to the world as a whole, and the text model is viewed as generally applicable. The dramatization of the problem of meaning in the strong version implies that the totality of knowledge from the empirical sciences no longer has a legitimate place. In accord with this position, the knowledge produced by the sciences that aim to study causal nexuses is hardly of any use, because it does not provide us with any information about nexuses of meaning that are supposed to be constitutive for the facts in the world.

II. In *its weak version*, the *problematic of meaning* is normally developed so as to admit causal nexuses for nature. Yet only nexuses of meaning are thought significant for the socio-historical world. This view is thus a variation of the old dualism between man and nature: Here it is expressed primarily in the fact that the data of the social sciences and humanities involve phenomena with internal meanings that cannot be grasped with natural scientific methods.[1] This is, in principle, nothing more than what Gellner fittingly characterized as a negative or defensive variety of anthropomorphism, to which we have bid adieu in the natural sciences.[2] Statements about the human world cannot be true,

---

[1] See Apel (1984).
[2] See Gellner (1968, 379f): "But within philosophy we find more commonly the negative, defensive versions, which defend a whole class of meaningful visions against a whole class of, as it were, inhuman ones. The 'meaningfulness' defended need not be a crude picture in which sinners are punished and virtue prevails. It is rather a world in which things happen and are understood in human terms, in some sense to be clarified further. These thinkers are not concerned or able to demonstrate that the human world is a *moral* tale, with justice and truth vindicated and some noble purpose attained: but they are concerned to show that it is, at least, a human tale. They wish to defend the anthropomorphic image of man himself."

nor can they offer a somehow successful description of it, if this world is presumed to be meaningless.

4.2 HOW IS IT POSSIBLE TO GRASP NEXUSES OF MEANING AND CAUSAL NEXUSES?

Accentuating the meaningful components of facts and events, and bracketing the possibility of reciprocal relations and causal processes among parts of the world, go hand in hand with the propagation of the idea that understanding is the adequate way of accessing these meaningful components. In the strong version, which, for example, is espoused in the conceptions of Heidegger and Gadamer that have already been discussed, understanding serves to identify meaning without being a concrete mental operation. Instead, it is interpreted as a concrete way of being in the world (*Seinsweise des Menschen*) or as a mode of human existence in general.[3] The understanding as an 'existential' thus serves to identify and grasp the meaning of the world.

In the weak version, of which, for example, the already discussed conception of Dilthey offers an archetypical explication, understanding also serves to identify meaning; however, it is typically interpreted as a mental operation. Grasping nexuses of meanings is directly contrasted with grasping causal nexuses, and the understanding is defended as the adequate means for penetrating nexuses of meaning. The characteristic ambivalence of the 'process' of understanding is once again to be recalled: Sometimes it is conceived of as a *type of knowledge* and sometimes as a *method*.[4] In any case, the hypothetico-deductive method, that is, the common method employed in the natural sciences, is strictly rejected as a method for apprehending nexuses of meaning. However, it is not claimed that the understanding can grasp causal nexuses at all. Thus Table 4.1 emerges, which is to be discussed further.

In the three columns of the table, three different interpretations of understanding are exposed: namely, it is portrayed as an existential (strong version), as a type of knowledge (weak version I), and as a

---

[3] See Section 2.2.
[4] See Section 1.2.

TABLE 4.1

	Understanding		
	(Strong Version) As Existential	(Weak Version I) As a Type of Knowledge	(Weak Version II) As a Method
Nexuses of meaning	Apprehensible: trivial desciption	Apprehensible: subjective mental process	Apprehensible: methodological antinaturalism
Causal nexuses	Not apprehensible	Not apprehensible	Not apprehensible

method (weak version II). In the rows, the two types of nexuses are then entered, forming a chart with six cells. First of all, it is to be emphasized that the bottom part of the table has to be kept empty, because understanding, regardless of its specification, cannot capture causal nexuses. The three cells on top succinctly display the ways that understanding is able to grasp nexuses of meaning. Understanding apprehends nexuses of meaning as *existential* by offering *trivial descriptions*; understanding apprehends nexuses of meaning as a *type of knowledge* by perceiving and processing meaningful material in the course of a *subjective* mental process; understanding apprehends nexuses of meaning as a *method* in a manner that *differs from the hypothetico-deductive method.*

In Chapters 2 and 3, we dealt in detail with the strong version of the problematic of meaning, and we investigated the way in which understanding can grasp nexuses of meaning as an existential. As we have seen, the fundamental-ontological analysis of Heidegger leads to a series of trivial descriptions of everyday phenomena. The transcendental excess baggage of understanding only smoothed the way to produce descriptions of nexuses of meaning with a certain aesthetic value but with little informative content. Something similar applies to Gadamer's analysis, which, although less radical than Heidegger's, still stakes a claim to universality. The transferral of the text metaphor to the world as a whole and the accompanying universalizing of the problematic of meaning have not proven to be successful. The upshot of our discussion of Heidegger and Gadamer in Part I is that the entire analysis of understanding as existential that is offered within the framework of philosophical hermeneutics is to be rejected on all grounds, except perhaps aesthetic ones, because it offers no satisfactory solutions to any problems, philosophical or otherwise. Thus the left column of Table 4.1 is hardly of any significance, and it will not be considered further in the following discussion.

In the conceptions that place the weak version of the problematic of meaning in the foreground, understanding is commonly admitted to have an eminent role, but unfortunately, its logical status is not explained more precisely; nor is the way that this process functions specified.[5] The lack of clarity is heightened by the fact that various authors use the concept of 'understanding' differently, and thus philosophers often talk at cross purposes when discussing understanding.[6] In addition, the term understanding used in the Anglo-Saxon discussion is a wide term, whose meaning overlaps more with *begreifen* than with *verstehen* in the German discussion. Be that as it may, in my opinion it is possible to do tolerable justice to the diversity of the use of the terms, and to the different conceptions, if one distinguishes between two very general uses of the concept of understanding (*verstehen*): namely, understanding as a type of knowledge and understanding as a method. In both cases, understanding is concerned with

[5] Abel's diagnosis from about a half a century ago thus also applies today (1948/1953, 678f.): "[T]here is no dearth of tradition and authority behind the idea of *Verstehen*. It is, therefore, surprising to find that, while many social scientists have eloquently discoursed on the existence of a special method in the study of human behaviour, none has taken the trouble to describe the nature of this method. They have given it various names; they have insisted in its use; they have pointed to it as a special kind of operation which has no counterpart in the physical sciences; and they have extolled its superiority as a process of giving insight unobtainable by any other methods. Yet the advocates of *Verstehen* have continually neglected to specify how this operation or 'understanding' is performed – and what is singular about it. What, exactly, do we do when we say we practice *Verstehen*? What significance can we give to results by *Verstehen*? Unless the operation is clearly defined, *Verstehen* is but a vague notion, and without being dogmatic, we are unable to ascertain how much validity can be attributed to the results achieved by it."

[6] See Strube's (1985) useful analysis of the concept of understanding, which shows that the concept is given different meanings, depending on the philosophical conception in which it is placed. See his conclusion (330): "The *cause* of the prevalent confusion regarding the philosophical use of the word *verstehen* can be characterized as follows: The philosophers who have used and defined the word *verstehen* have not recognized the systematic ambiguity of the concept, consequently they have not perceived the 'relativity' of the concept of *verstehen*, or not perceived it clearly enough" (trans. D. A.). See also Essler (1975) for an analysis of the concept of understanding in juxtaposition with his analysis of the concept of 'explaining.' See also Martin (2000).

objects that are meaningful, and thus, above all, with human action and the results of such action.

In the first case, the apprehension of this meaningful material constitutes a specific type of knowledge aiming at human action and the results of such action. Viewed from the vantage point of the history of ideas, since the eighteenth century, explications of the concept of understanding place emphasis on feeling and experience, so that a series of authors, including Dilthey, have conceived of understanding as immediate intuition or empathy (Bühler, 1995, 272ff.). This view of things is based on an (implicit or explicit) view of mind according to which feeling and reason, or emotion and cognition, portray distinct and even contrary cognitive abilities. From a contemporary point of view, this strict separation between cognition and emotions seems untenable. As, for example, the neurological studies of Damasio (1994) have shown, the damage to the part of the brain responsible for emotions can rob patients of the ability to make decisions that are clearly in their own interest, so that, over time, they lose the ability to lead their lives on their own. That occurs even though other components of the cognitive system remain intact, such as memory, concentration, language comprehension, and reasoning. As Damasio has convincingly shown, 'pure cognitive beings,' if one can call them that, cannot deal adequately with their social environment, because they lack the capacity to make decisions that are right for them, a capacity that exists, only if the emotions are interacting appropriately with the cognitive system. That points to the fact that the cognitive and the emotional systems, although in principle analytically separable and neurophysiologically distinct, are complementary and in constant interaction.[7]

---

[7] Special manifestations of feelings, which Damasio calls 'somatic markers,' are of service in this deliberation because they highlight either dangerous or favorable options and eliminate them rapidly from subsequent consideration. For details see Damasio (1994, ch. 8). For my discussion, it is mainly of interest that emotions that generate the special feelings called somatic markers are constantly interacting with the cognitive system. See Damasio (1994, 174f.): "The somatic-marker account is thus compatible with the notion that effective personal and social behavior requires individuals to form adequate 'theories' of their own minds and of the minds of others. On the basis of those theories we can predict what theories others are forming about our own mind. The detail and accuracy of such predictions is, of course, essential as we approach a critical decision in a social situation. Again, the number of scenarios under scrutiny is immense and my idea is that somatic markers (or something like them) assist the process of sifting through such a wealth of detail – in effect, reduce the need for sifting

For my discussion, it is important that conceiving of understanding as an act of immediate intuition or empathy is bound to appear implausible to us today. Building on modern findings, understanding as a type of knowledge can thus be plausibly viewed as a (subjective) mental process involving both cognitive and emotional components.

In the second case, understanding is interpreted as a method of apprehending meaningful material and indeed as a method specific to a group of sciences, namely, the social sciences and humanities. On this interpretation, understanding action and the results of human actions makes it possible to comprehend nexuses of meaning in delimitation from disciplines that are not directly related to human beings. With that, a claim to the autonomy of these disciplines is typically made. Important precursors of this position are the neo-Kantians, Windelband (1884/1907) and Rickert (1899/1926 and 1902/1929), and, most importantly, Dilthey, who was the most influential in defending this dualism at the beginning of the twentieth century. In the contemporary discussion, a whole series of approaches of diverse provenance refer implicitly or explicitly to the understanding (or *verstehen*) as a method of the social sciences and/or the humanities. A detailed presentation of these approaches would take us too far afield; thus, I shall only briefly mention those that have been given special attention in the literature.

In Habermas's *Theory of Communicative Action*, understanding is conflated with agreement such that the impossibility of a strict separation between questions of meaning and questions of validity can be postulated and normative consequences can be drawn from that.[8] Something similar applies to Karl-Otto Apel, who refers to the transcendental-pragmatic and onto-semantic presuppositions of a sophisticated philosophy of the social sciences and postulates that a speech community is a presupposition for all knowledge in the subject–object dimension.[9] Georg Henrik von Wright attempted to prove that explanations of human action do not follow what he calls

---

because they provide an automated detection of the scenario components which are more likely to be relevant. The partnership between so-called cognitive processes and processes usually called 'emotional' should be apparent." For the interaction between emotion and cognition see also Gazzaniga, Ivry, and Mangun (2002, 544f.).

[8] See especially Habermas (1981/1987, 152–203).
[9] See especially Apel (1979, 1984).

the 'subsumption model' of explanation, and consequently, the social sciences and the humanities are independent of the natural sciences.[10] Peter Winch's elaboration of the implications for the social
sciences that follow from Wittgenstein's late philosophy motivated him
to formulate the following central thesis: Since forms of life have to
be accepted as the givens, which cannot be criticized with external,
independent standards, all that remains for the social scientist is to describe the de facto practices that are constitutive of every form of life.[11]
Geertz more precisely specifies what such a description should look
like and what it should accomplish: The social scientist's task of offering
a thick description does not aim to codify abstract laws, or to generalize across cases, but to generalize within cases.[12] In Anthony Giddens's
'double hermeneutic' the social sciences are not concerned with interpretations of things, but with interpretations of interpretations; consequently, social scientific research results can only be as robust as these
interpretations themselves.[13] The influential work of Charles Taylor
offers an often cited plea for social scientific research, which aims
solely at producing studies that describe the intersubjective meanings
embedded in the social reality.[14] And in the presently much discussed
book of Bent Flyvbjerg, *Making Social Science Matter* the conclusion is
drawn – on the basis of an alleged impossibility to explain human
skills – that the social sciences should, leaning on the Aristotelian view
of *Phronesis*, be carried out as "phronetic disciplines."[15]

   This is not the place to offer a review of the literature on the issue. What is merely of interest here is the fact that all of these contributions, though entailing diverse arguments and diverse validity
claims, share a central idea, which has far-reaching methodological
consequences. They are facets and specifications of *antinaturalism*,

---

[10] See especially Von Wright (1971) and the edited volume by Apel, Manninen, and
   Tuomela (1978).
[11] See Winch (1958).
[12] See, for example, his classical methodological article "Thick Description: Towards
   an Interpretive Theory of Culture" in Geertz (1993).
[13] See especially Giddens (1993).
[14] See the article "Interpretation and the Sciences of Man" in Taylor (1985).
[15] See Flyvbjerg (2001), where, in the first part of his work, he discusses the epistemological difficulties of the social sciences, refering to Rorty, Giddens, Garfinkel,
   Foucault, Dreyfus, and Bourdieu before arguing, in the second part of the work, that
   the social sciences can make their greatest contribution as Phronesis.

the position, namely, that presupposes that occurrences in the socio-historical reality cannot be viewed in continuity with occurrences in the natural world, and that they therefore require entirely different research methods from that drawn upon in the natural sciences.[16] These methods are varieties of understanding, and in any case, they are not methods aiming at the nomological apprehension of phenomena.

In summary, it can be said that, leaving aside the view of understanding as existential, given its already criticized uselessness, understanding can be plausibly conceived in two other ways: either as a type of knowledge or as a method. In the former case, it is concerned with grasping meaningful material by means of a (subjective) mental process involving both cognitive and emotional components. In the latter case, it is concerned with grasping meaningful material by means of a method that, though variously specified, is in the last analysis antinaturalistic.

4.3 UNDERSTANDING VERSUS THE HYPOTHETICO-DEDUCTIVE METHOD

After this elucidation of understanding as a type of knowledge and as a method, it ought to be clear how meaningful phenomena are to be grasped in accord with the antinaturalistic position. This position is to be contrasted with *methodological naturalism*, which maintains that all empirical sciences, including the natural sciences, the social sciences, and the humanities, can and must employ the same method, regardless of the differences in object areas. In all areas in which increasing our knowledge about the real world can be presupposed as an aim, hypotheses can be formulated, consequences can be drawn by deduction, and these can be tested against empirical data. This operation, which, in the analytic philosophy of science, has been worked out in detail as the hypothetico-deductive method, is a methodological procedure, in principle, applicable to every subject matter, whether it be meaningful or not. This idea does not deny that different research styles and diverse research techniques dominate the various disciplines, nor does it deny the different structure of the object areas. As was shown more clearly in Chapter 1, the idea of the unity of method is to be confused neither with the demand for a universal language nor with the demand

---

[16] See the article by Axel Bühler (2003a), especially Section 2.

for a unified science; instead, it is a minimalistic requirement to set
up hypotheses whenever attempting to acquire knowledge and to test
them critically using empirical observations.

This method is characterized as *naturalistic* because it was successfully employed in the natural sciences before other disciplines came
to view it as necessary.[17] General methodological naturalism can be
characterized by the following three theses: (1) It is not the task of
philosophy to provide a foundation to the sciences (*antifoundationalist
thesis*). (2) Philosophy does not have a more epistemologically privileged position than the sciences; rather, there is a continuum between
philosophy and the sciences (*continuity thesis*). (3) The application of
scientific theses, research, and results are both acceptable and imperative for philosophy (*thesis of the scientific orientation of philosophy*).[18]

Of course, this does not constitute an exhaustive set of theses for
methodological naturalism; it is merely supposed to highlight that
no apriori foundation for the sciences is to be demanded from philosophy. On the other hand, continuity between philosophy and the
empirical sciences by no means implies the elimination of the traditional problems of epistemology, as is often suggested in the literature
based on Quine's naturalistic position.[19] The main point is rather that
the results from relevant empirical disciplines be used to treat traditional epistemological problems while *avoiding that, by virtue of this,
epistemology or the philosophy of science merges with empirical science.*

---

[17] See the fitting remark by Albert (1994, 97f.): "The individual sciences should not
be thought of as closed off and methodologically absolutely established areas of
knowledge with neatly delimited object areas, which have virtually nothing to say
to each other, that is, as sovereign petty kingdoms of knowledge. The development
of scientific knowledge has proceeded that far today, that the significance of the
theoretical empirical sciences for the historical human sciences has come under
broad discussion. Attempts to cope with this problematic by demarcating separate
areas do not merely contradict well-understood criticism, they probably also fail to
correspond to the internal stand of research that has long been achieved in the
individual sciences. The infiltration of theoretical thought into the domain of the
human sciences is not the phantasm of positivist philosophers, which came about
because of extraneous considerations; exponents of these areas have themselves seen
it to be necessary and have demanded it" (trans. D. A.).

[18] With this thesis I am especially following Koppelberg (1999), who differentiates
between a metaphysical, an analytical, and a methodological naturalism.

[19] Above all, as this is expressed in the classical article "Epistemology Naturalized,"
reprinted in Quine (1969). For an overview of the naturalized epistemology, see
especially the collection of articles by Kornblith (1994).

TABLE 4.2

	Understanding		Hypothetico-Deductive Method
	As a Type of Knowledge	As a Method	
Nexuses of meaning	Apprehensible: subjective mental process	Apprehensible: methodological antinaturalism	Apprehensible: methodological naturalism
Casual nexuses	Not apprehensible	Not apprehensible	Apprehensible: methodological naturalism

In sum, the positions can be most clearly represented in Table 4.2.

The first two columns in this table correspond to the two columns in Table 4.1, and they contain the already discussed views – that is, that understanding is a type of knowledge and that it is a method. In addition, there is a third column here, which illustrates the claim of the hypothetico-deductive method, namely, that both nexuses of meaning and causal nexuses can be grasped within the framework of methodological naturalism.

In the following two chapters, I will follow an argumentation strategy that aims at reaching a dual goal. On the one hand, I will attempt to show that, by explaining understanding with the help of nomological hypotheses, the hypothetico-deductive method is able to adequately grasp the understanding as a subjective mental process. On the other hand, I will try to show that, as a method, the hypothetico-deductive method is superior to understanding because it is capable of grasping both causal nexuses and nexuses of meaning. Since it is less controversial to maintain that causal nexuses can be adequately apprehended with the hypothetico-deductive method, I would like to focus on the more difficult claim here – namely, that it can also successfully grasp nexuses of meaning. This case will be made in the following two chapters. Since the problematic of meaning usually arises in human action and in the results of such action, especially in texts, in Chapter 5 I will apply the hypothetico-deductive method to the apprehension of the meaning of action, and in Chapter 6 I will apply it to the apprehension of the meaning of texts. Besides the teleological and semasiological views of meaning, which I will treat in more detail, there are, of course, other views of meaning, which, for example, arise in connection with institutions, works of art, and other cultural achievements. However, I will not deal with those here, because I have shown elsewhere what a general theory of institutions looks like that is able to analyze the action-relevant cognitive structures of agents without employing the concept of meaning.[20] Besides, it appears to me that human action and texts are the hardest cases. Hence, if the hypothetico-deductive method functions there, then it should also be possible to apply it to other manifestations of the human mind. The successful application of the hypothetico-deductive method in these two cases would not, of course, eliminate the different antinaturalistic variants of understanding, but it would imply that they are useless.

Before I begin with this task, it is important to clarify two questions that play an important role in the literature. The first question is related to the role of 'scientific understanding' and to the way that scientific explanation is connected to scientific understanding. In a classic article, Friedman (1974/1988) argued that every theory of explanation ought to show simultaneously how a scientific explanation effects scientific understanding. He conceived of his own theory of explanation as in fact connecting explanation and understanding. He claims that "this is the crucial property of scientific theories we are looking for; this is the essence of scientific explanation – science increases our understanding of the world by reducing the total number of independent phenomena that we have to accept as ultimate or given. A world with fewer independent phenomena is, other things equal, more comprehensible than one with more."[21] In connection with Friedman's idea of unification through explanation, a series of important contributions have appeared that connect scientific explanation with scientific understanding.[22]

The process by which scientific understanding comes about is important insofar as it aims to show that understanding can *also be objective.* In Friedman's formulation: "[A]lthough the notion of understanding,

---

[20] See Mantzavinos (2001).
[21] See Friedman (1974/1988, 195).
[22] See especially Kitcher (1981), Tuomela (1984), Schurz (1990), Lambert (1980/1990), Schurz and Lambert (1994), and Weber (1996). For a critique of the unification thesis, see Barnes (1992).

like knowledge and belief but unlike truth, just is a psychological notion, I don't see why there can't be an objective or rational sense of 'scientific understanding', a sense in which what is scientifically comprehensible is constant for a relatively large class of people. Therefore, I don't see how the philosopher of science can afford to ignore such concepts as 'understanding' and 'intelligibility' when giving a theory of the explanation relation" (190). Of course, it cannot be denied that understanding can also be objective if one is dealing with scientific understanding. That is the case if the communication of a scientific explanation causes intersubjectively the same mental process. However, the question of the effect of a similar process of understanding on different individuals who get additional information about the real world, which one could call the 'objectivity of understanding,' should be strictly distinguished from the question of understanding as a method.[23] Even if one has shown how the unification of laws reduces the number of independent phenomena in the world, and by so doing makes the world more comprehensible for all those who learn about these laws, one still has not said anything about understanding as a method. *For the proponents of understanding, however, the question of method is in the foreground.* I will consequently not follow the strategy of showing how scientific explanation increases our objective understanding of the world, because by so doing, the antinaturalistic objection could rightly continue to exist. In addition, as we have seen, the antinaturalists do not think it is possible to offer scientific explanation of nexuses of meaning; this means that for an entire class of explanations, it is not even sensible, in the view of the antinaturalists, to pose the question of the relation between scientific explanation and scientific understanding.

With that, a second important question arises, this time regarding the *character* of the hypothetico-deductive method. The basic characteristic of this method consists in the fact that scientific work is generally viewed as being related to hypotheses. Hypotheses can possibly explain phenomena, but the hypothetico-deductive method is not

---

[23] Popper also speaks of the 'objectivity of understanding,' but with this expression he refers to his method of situational logic. I will discuss this method at some length in Section 5.4.

identical to a model of scientific explanation (Føllesdal, Walløe, and Elster, 1988, 93ff.).[24] Popper and Hempel originally viewed it as a method that is directed toward deductive causal explanations in the sciences. *But there is no reason to presume that alleging the existence of individual facts is of less scientific interest.* Among others, historians are interested in such findings, and Popper (1947/1972) and Hempel (1942/1965) showed very early on how the hypothetico-deductive method might be successfully applied in historical research. The scientific disciplines that deal with meaningful material are, however, often somewhat neglected by analytic epistemology. It is thus important to work out the concrete application of the hypothetico-deductive method in this case, paying the due attention to the specific research techniques that are characteristic of this object area.

In conclusion, it should be emphasized that my intention is *neither* to show that the hypothetico-deductive method is the *only* method to be applied in the sciences *nor* to demonstrate that it is the *best.* Both of these claims would directly contradict a consistent fallibilistic position. Because all of our knowledge is fallible, our methods can in principle always be revised, and we cannot rule out the possibility that in the future we will succeed in developing a method that is better than the hypothetico-deductive one. Thus, here the claim is only made that the hypothetico-deductive method is a *comparatively better alternative* than understanding.

---

[24] In my opinion, this has very often led to unjustified criticism. For an exemplary case in point, see Nordenstam (1998), who attempts to show that explanation of the sort Hempel has in mind plays no role in art history. The hypothetico-deductive method can, however, also be used to identify matters of fact without at the same time offering explanations. This use of the method, which will be discussed in more detail in Chapter 6, may, for example, also be significant for art history.

5

The Apprehension of the Meaning of Actions

5.1 HUMAN ACTIONS AS MEANINGFUL EVENTS

There is a long tradition in philosophy and in the social sciences that systematically emphasizes the meaningfulness of human action. In Max Weber's classical definition, this is expressed characteristically: "We shall speak of 'action' insofar as the acting individual attaches a subjective meaning to his behavior – be it overt or covert, omission or acquiescence" (1922/1985, 542/1978, 4). Human behavior that is meaningful thus becomes human action. In accord with this, mere events, such as pure physiological reactions and bodily movements, are not in themselves actions: They can become actions only if the actor endows them with a subjective meaning.

What does it mean for an action to have meaning?[1] First of all, it certainly does not mean that an action is significant for the actor. The meaning of an action is to be strictly differentiated from its significance. An action is some human behavior that has meaning for the actor without necessarily also being significant. *Human behavior is bestowed with meaning when the actor engaging in this behavior interprets it against the background of his goals, his beliefs, and his other mental states*

---

[1] See also Gellner's comment (1968, 384): "What, incidentally, *is* it for an action to 'have meaning', or, in so far as this is meant to be a defining characteristic of an 'action', for an event to become an action through possessing meaning? I think it corresponds roughly to what we would, in unselfconscious unsophisticated moments, describe as 'being lived through consciously from the inside, as it were'."

while interacting with his natural and social environment; this is a complex process and can involve the conscious or unconscious use of symbols – though it need not.

The nexus of meaning that arises in connection with a human action can be accessed from two perspectives. From the first-person perspective, the nexus of meaning can be apprehended by the actor himself if the actor describes and reconstructs it. From the perspective of the observer, the nexus of meaning, which arises in connection with a human action, is apprehended by being externally described, reconstructed, and sometimes nomologically explained. The first-person perspective remains the privilege of the actor; consequently, the methodologically relevant question is how nexuses of meaning can be adequately apprehended from the perspective of the observer – also using information that the actor himself conveys, with the help of which the first-person perspective is described and reconstructed.

The hypothetico-deductive method can apprehend the meaning of an action in two ways: (i) by transforming nexuses of meaning that *repeatedly* occur in connection with certain actions into causal nexuses and nomologically explaining them, and (ii) by reconstructing the nexus of meaning of *a specific action* so that it is accurately depicted. We will analyze each of these areas of application of the hypothetico-deductive method in turn.

5.2 ON THE TRANSFORMATION OF NEXUSES OF MEANING INTO CAUSAL NEXUSES

One way to apprehend the meaning of an action is to identify the *motive* of the action. So, it could be assumed that the nexus of the meaning of an action is apprehended if the motive that prompted the actor to the action is specified (Weber, 1922/1985, 550).[2] This approach, however, obviously suffers from the fact that it implicitly presupposes

---

[2] See Weber (1922/1985, 550): "»Motiv« heißt ein Sinnzusammenhang, welcher dem Handelnden selbst oder dem Beobachtenden als sinnhafter »Grund« eines Verhaltens erscheint." The translation of the 1978 edition of *Economy and Society* is somehow confusing, because *Sinnzusammenhang*, which is of interest here, is not translated as "nexus of meaning" (11): "A motive is a complex of subjective meaning which seems to the actor himself or to the observer an adequate ground for the conduct in question."

that bestowing a given act with meaning is solely the function of the motivational system.

Instead, one often presumes that the meaning of an action can be revealed if its *intention* is apprehended. This somewhat more sophisticated theory postulates a conceptual difference between a purpose and an intention in the widest sense: A purpose is something that is seen as constitutive for an action (in the formulation of Frankfurt 1978, 158, for example, bodily movements constitute action when the movements *as they occur are under the person's guidance*). It is thus often maintained that there is a conceptual, logical relationship between purposes and actions, and that a statement about the purpose of a particular action only gives as much information about the action as, for example, the statement that Helmut is not married adds to the fact that Helmut is a bachelor.[3] That this is not true is easy to show – for example, by referring to purposes that have not been acted upon. Here it is merely important that one usually presumes that it is an *intention in the widest sense* that imposes meaning on an action. In Daniel Dennett's (1987) influential "Theory of Intentional Systems," the intentional stance is, for example, developed as a strategy according to which a system is described in reference to beliefs, desires, and other intentional states. In the case of human behavior, this theory points out that action should be presented with the help of an intentional vocabulary, that is, with the help of concepts that derive from folk psychology. Something similar applies to another influential theory, namely, that of John Searle. In this theory the concept 'intention' is conceived very broadly, such that a broad array of mental states can be characterized as intentional (Searle, 1983). For my line of reasoning, it is only significant that, according to this approach, the meaning of an action will be adequately apprehended only if the intentions behind it are specified. If one manages to apprehend the relevant intention or intentions, then one has grasped the nexus of meaning that is related to the action.

According to a third approach, it is above all the *reasons* for the action that are relevant for apprehending its meaning. As a rule, the beliefs and desires of the actor are highlightened as the reasons, and it is presumed that a clear specification of the beliefs and desires in

---

[3] For a discussion of this "logical-relational argument" see Greve (1997, 489ff.).

the respective cases makes it possible to reveal the relevant nexuses of meaning. Although this approach is sometimes argued for in connection with the intentionalist approach, as, for example, in Davidsons's classic article "Actions, Reasons and Causes" (1963/2001), specifying the actor's reasons remains an independent way of ascertaining the meaning of an action.

These three briefly outlined approaches, which appeal to the motives, intentions, or reasons for actions, are all variants of a *"one-to-one" theory of human action.* I use this term to characterize all approaches that offer a description of human action based on a few elements that stand in a one-to-one relationship to the respective action. Such approaches can depict the nexus of meaning of an action only in a primitive manner, because they do not specify a mechanism that would make it easier for the observer to better portray the complexity of the process of subjectively imposing meaning on an action. "The meaning of John's action – that he always comes to the office on time – is that John *wants* to be a good civil servant"; "The meaning of John's action – that he always comes to the office on time – is that John has the *intention* of being a good civil servant"; "The meaning of John's action – that he always comes to the office on time – is that John has the *belief* that this behavior makes him a good civil servant, and that he has the *desire* to be a good civil servant." Each of these statements captures the meaning of the fact that John always comes to work on time by appealing to John's mental states without specifying more clearly the mechanism by which these mental states lead to the subjective bestowal of a meaning on his action.

One approach that specifies such a mechanism, and that appears to be more fitting to the complexity of human action, places the *rationality* of the actor in the foreground. According to this approach, the meaning of an action can be apprehended if one presupposes that the situation of the actor has the following complex traits: The actor has numerous goals to begin with and numerous potential ways of realizing each goal. Thus, he has a whole series of preferences about the existing alternatives when he makes a decision, and he has a whole series of beliefs about the probability of achieving the existing alternatives. Beyond that, he also has, to a larger or smaller degree, an information-processing capacity, which leads him to choose the alternative that seems best to him relative to the situation he is in. Thus, with the help of a rationality hypothesis, convictions and desires are transformed into a concrete decision, which ends in action.

I will deal with the rationality model more extensively later; for the time being, it is sufficient to keep in mind that the nexus of meaning of an action can in principle also be apprehended with the help of a complex mechanism. "The meaning of John's action – that he always comes to the office on time – is that, while John would in fact rather sleep in or take his time while eating breakfast, these options appear less important to him in the face of his goal of being a good civil servant, and thus he has decided to come to the office on time – something that is a *rational decision* given his options, his preferences, and his knowledge of the circumstances." The theory of rationality is thus to be differentiated from the other three approaches, which we have called one-to-one theories of human action, because it specifies a more complex mechanism for apprehending the subjective meaning of an action.

The brief presentation of these four influential approaches serves to show that there are numerous possibilities for conveying the nexus of meaning from the observer's perspective. And now my main argument: Regardless of the approach and the descriptive means used in order to apprehend a nexus of meaning, there is always in principle the possibility that the *fundamental elements* of this nexus of meaning will also occur in connection with other actions of the same persons or of other persons. Here, by 'fundamental elements' I mean both all relevant mental states of the actor and all relevant mechanisms that are at work when an action is performed. Every time that one succeeds in identifying the same fundamental elements of a nexus of meaning in other nexuses as well, it is possible to view nexuses of meaning as causal nexuses. The key to transforming nexuses of meaning into causal nexuses is in demonstrating an *invariance* in the appearance of the fundamental elements in various nexuses of meaning. In those cases in which such a transformation is possible, nexuses of meaning can be nomologically apprehended, and thus their repeated appearance can be explained.

Let's take the example of an entrepreneur, X, who in a situation, S_1, undertakes the action to fire twenty employees of his firm. One can apprehend the nexus of meaning of this action by stating the motive of the action in this case, namely, that he wants to maximize his profit. The fundamental element in this nexus of meaning is the motive of profit maximization. If one succeeds in showing, that this element also appears in connection with other actions of the entrepreneur X in other kinds of situations, S_1, S_2, S_3, and so on, then one has discovered an invariance and therewith transformed the nexuses of meaning into a causal nexus. The way that the hypothetico-deductive method is applied to the explanation of human actions will be analyzed next.

5.3 THE HYPOTHETICO-DEDUCTIVE METHOD AND THE EXPLANATION OF HUMAN ACTION

There is neither in nature nor in the socio-historical reality a single repetition, B, of a process, A, which is absolutely identical to A. All repetitions are merely approximate repetitions, such that B can be more or less similar to A, depending on the standpoint from which A and B are viewed. Figure 5.1 illustrates this.[4]

In this diagram, it is possible to see that the similarity of certain geometric figures is based on the shading, the similarity of others on the interrupted lines that constitute the figues, and so on. These simple outlines illustrate that things can only be similar in certain respects: "Generally, similarity, and with it repetition, always presuppose the adoption of *a point of view*" (Popper 1959/2003, 442.).

Emphasizing the similarity between two or more things thus presupposes that one assumes a certain point of view. And for the case of interest here, namely, the transformation of nexuses of meaning into causal nexuses, this means that from a certain standpoint two nexuses of meaning can be dissimilar, while from another standpoint a similarity can be shown. Now, there may be numerous standpoints from which two nexuses of meaning are dissimilar. What is decisive for the validity of my argument, however, is that to transform a nexus of meaning into a causal nexus, it is sufficient for *just one* standpoint to exist from which two nexuses of meaning are similar.[5]

---

[4] For a similar diagram see Popper (1959/2003, 441).

[5] See the comment of Grünbaum (1953, 769): "[I]t must be pointed out that *all* particulars in the world are unique, whether they are physical objects like trees, physical events like light flashes, or human beings. The mere assertion that a thing is a particular, means that it is in one way or another unique, different from all other objects of its own kind or of other kinds. Every insignificant tick of my watch is a unique event, for no two ticks can be simultaneous with a given third event. With respect to

FIGURE 5.1

Now, there is a further problem: It is possible to reply to my argument that there may well be a standpoint from which the similarity between two nexuses of meaning can be demonstrated, but it is impossible to maintain such a standpoint permanently. The reason is that every standpoint, even if it is always assumed from the perspective of the observer, still remains a human standpoint, and because

uniqueness, each tick is on a par with Lincoln's delivery of the Gettysburg address! It is clear, however, that the uniqueness of physical events does not prevent them from being connected by causal laws, for present causal laws relate only *some* of the features of a given set of events with *some* of the features of another set of events. For example, frictional processes are accompanied by the development of heat in so far as they are frictional, whatever else they may be. A projectile fired under suitable conditions will describe a parabolic orbit regardless of the color of the projectile, its place of manufacture, and so on. Since the cause–effect relation is a relation between *kinds* of events, it is never necessary that all the features of a given cause be duplicated in order to produce the same kind of effect."

of the radical historicity of the human condition, it is thus not possible to maintain any standpoint permanently. This thesis of the radical historicity of standpoints dramatizes relative differences. In this, however, it implies the thesis of the uniformity and constancy of human nature. For what can the thesis of the radical historicity of standpoints mean other than that man and his actions possess a *constant* property, precisely this historicity?

Thus, for my argument, it is sufficient that there is at least one standpoint from which nexuses of meaning that arise in connection with two or more of a person's actions have a certain similarity. If this is true, then it is also possible to maintain that the nexuses of meaning are repeated over time. Such a similarity can also exist for nexuses of meaning that arise in connection with the actions of different persons. I call those fundamental elements that occur repeatedly – either in nexuses of meaning connected to numerous actions of a particular person or connected to the actions of different persons – the 'invariances' of human behavior.

These invariances can be of three different types, namely, *genetic, cultural,* or *personal.* If the fundamental elements of the nexuses of meaning that arise in connection with the action of all people are similar in certain respects, then one can speak of *genetic invariances.* If the similarities of the fundamental elements arise in respect to the action of agents in *a social group,* then one can speak of *cultural invariances.* If the fundamental elements of nexuses of meaning that arise in connection with a number of actions of *a particular person* are in a certain respect similar, then one can speak of *personal invariances.*

To offer an example: Person X drinks neither water nor anything else for thirty days and dies. The fundamental elements of the nexus of meaning of this action can be described with the help of the third approach as follows: Person X has the belief that this action will lead to her death, and she has the desire to die. If it can be shown that these fundamental elements appear in the nexuses of meaning for similar actions of all people, then one can speak of a genetic invariance.

Every time it can be shown that there is one of these invariances, nexuses of meaning are transformed de facto into causal nexuses. Statements whose content consist of a description of such causal nexuses are nomological statements. They describe laws and thus involve general limitations to what can possibly happen.[6] The precise nature of the law-likeness of statements presents a difficult problem, which is a topic of controversy in the analytic philosophy of science.[7] For the argument I am making here, however, it is only relevant that meaningful events can be apprehended nomologically as soon as there are invariances of one of the three types. The hypothetico-deductive method can then be applied in those cases by subjecting these invariances in human behavior to an explanation.

As mentioned in various passages of this book, hypotheses can be proposed in every area in which the expansion of our knowledge about the real world can be presumed to be a goal; consequences can be deduced from these hypotheses and then confronted with empirical data. This general hypothetico-deductive method finds its original and most frequent expression in the model of scientific explanation. In accord with this model, a procedure is causally explained in that the statement that describes it is logically deduced from the conjunction of general statements (hypotheses, laws) and particular statements (initial conditions). But not every deductive argument of the type portrayed that meets formal demands is an adequate explanation. Rather, the premises of the argument must also fulfill certain material conditions.[8] Most importantly, they must be empirically testable in order to be suitable to empirical-scientific explanation. Empirical testablity is not, however, to be equated with observability, mainly because, as a rule, in our explanations we use a number of hypotheses and a series of initial conditions; therefore, it is normally sufficient if only a few of them are observable.[9] In the following section we shall elucidate this

---

[6] For more, see Albert (1987, 104ff.). See also Mach (1917, 450): "A law always consists of a limitation of the possibilities, whether that be considered a limitation of an action, of the unalterable course of the occurrences of nature or of the guidepost for imagining and thinking, which complement the occurrences, occurring before them and hurrying them along." ("Ein Gesetz besteht immer in einer Einschränkung der Möglichkeiten ob dasselbe als Beschränkung des Handelns, als unabänderliche Leitbahn des Naturgeschehens oder als Wegweiser für unser dem Geschehen ergänzend vorauseilendes Vorstellen und Denken in Betracht kommt.")

[7] For a good overview of the present discussion, see Psillos (2002, chs. 5–7).

[8] See more in Keuth (2000, 67ff.).

[9] The issue of observability is treated in more detail in a discussion of the performative characteristics of theories in Albert (1987, 106f.).

procedure in more detail with the help of the 'Hempel–Oppenheim scheme.' Here it is only important that this model is compatible with the most diverse sorts of hypotheses, which can be formulated with the help of diverse conceptual apparatuses.[10]

In an explanation of events, and consequently also of human actions, a theory is normally found – that is, a set of nomological hypotheses, formulated with the help of a uniform conceptual apparatus and backed up with certain central theoretical ideas, rather than a mass of detached hypotheses. The application of the hypothetico-deductive method in the form of a scientific explanation thus presumes that a series of theories are enlisted to explain an action, and those are preferred that are provisionally viewed to be the best on the basis of a series of performative characteristics such as explanatory power, generality, precision, and depth (Albert 1987, 103ff.). In our context, it is important that *various sorts* of *hypotheses* can arise in explaining human activity, and they can be formulated with the help of various *conceptual apparatuses*. Earlier, I outlined four approaches that are often discussed in the literature. These describe the nexuses of meaning connected with a human action in very different ways. Besides, these four approaches view different elements of a nexus of meaning as fundamental: the motives, the intentions, the reasons, and the rationality of the action. From the standpoint of each approach, a causal nexus can arise – namely, if the respective motives, intentions, reasons, or the human rationality that is manifest in the different nexuses of meaning possess certain invariances. *These approaches*

---

[10] It should be noted here that there are, of course, *quite different views of causality*. In analytic philosophy the regularity view is dominant, which in essence goes back to the definition of cause that Hume introduced: "[w]e may define a cause to be an object, followed by another, and where all the objects similar to the first are followed by objects similar to the second" (Hume, 1748/1975, 76). The regularity view has been criticized from various vantage points; for a discussion, see Keuth (2000, 59ff.). Thus today, laws are often viewed as necessary relations among universals (Armstrong, 1983). According to another view, causality is explained with the help of counterfactuals (Lewis, 1973) or is clarified in connection with an elaboration of a mechanism (Salmon, 1984, 1997). In an important article, Heidelberger (1997) shows that the concept of action already presupposes the concept of causality. The differences among all of these views of causality – for a concise overview, see Kistler (2002) – are indeed important, but are negligible for the general argument in this book. My concern here is whether meaningful events can in principle be causally apprehended; thus, I would like to abstract from the debate about the appropriate definition of causality.

can thus be formulated as theories, which explain human action if the nexuses of meaning – described with the diverse conceptual apparatuses – can be transformed into causal nexuses. Accordingly, explanations based on motives, intentions, reasons, or rationality are possible, as are explanations of human action based on, at least in principle, an unlimited number of other theories.

5.4 THE STATUS OF THE RATIONALITY HYPOTHESIS

The three variations of the one-to-one theory of human action, which refer to the motives, the intentions, or the reasons of an action, all describe an action's nexus of meaning with the help of a few elements. These elements are supposed to portray mental states and to create a connection to the action under discussion. If the way in which these same fundamental elements occur is unchanged – be they motive, intentions, or reasons – it is possible to view nexuses of meaning as causal nexuses and correspondingly to apprehend them nomologically. The fundamental elements that show an invariant structure in each of these variations of a one-to-one theory are mental states. Their regular occurrence can be apprehended by law-like hypotheses, which, depending on the case, specify either the motives, the intentions, or the reasons.

In contrast to the variations of the one-to-one theory, the rationality theory of action describes nexuses of meaning with the help of a mechanism. Mental events are depicted as meaningful *processes*, and they are connected with the respective actions. The fundamental element that can be repeated in nexuses of meaning is the rationality of the actor, and correspondingly, it is a meaningful process that exhibits an invariant structure. The regular occurrence of such rational processes can be apprehended with a law-like hypothesis.

It is characteristic of the discussion in the past years in philosophy, psychology, and the social sciences that explanations of human action are normally offered in terms of the rationality of the actors. One-to-one theory appears either to have been surpassed or, in one way or another, to have merged with theories of rationality. Thus, in certain approaches, the intentions, the reasons, and the rationality of the actor all play a role, and an action is supposed to be explained not if the reasons and the intentions of the actor are identified, but only if an additional assumption about his rationality is made.[11] The increasing role that rationality is credited with in explanations of action should be positively assessed, because it specifies a *mechanism* that is supposed to transform mental states into actions. Insofar, it appears prima facie to be a theoretical improvement over the one-to-one theories: By specifying a mechanism, it is possible to connect diverse mental states with one another and to bring the complexity of the process more precisely to expression. Nevertheless, it is necessary to relativize the importance of this generally positive development, because the rationality discussion is quite confused at various levels.

I. Why a Rational Reconstruction Is Not an Explanation

It is characteristic of the prevailing situation that even thinkers who are otherwise quite clear, such as Karl Popper, have caused more confusion than clarity in discussing the status of the rationality hypothesis. The 'situational logic' propagated by him as the adequate method for the social sciences "consists in a sufficient analysis of the situation of the actor, in order to explain the action from the situation without the help of psychology" (Popper, 1969/1993, 120/trans. D. A.). Instead of suggesting that hypotheses on mental dispositions or mental states should be tested, Popper pleads to introduce a rationality principle on the basis of which the situation of the actor is more adequately apprehended. This rationality principle is in fact an almost empty principle[12] – albeit

---

[11] In this, it does not matter whether this explanation is viewed as causal or not. For an example, see Føllesdal (1982, 312): "In order for the intentional notions to make sense we must require enough rationality to let our pattern of explanation be reason explanation rather than merely causal explanation. We may permit all kinds of interferences of a merely causal kind, but in order to say that we deal with beliefs, desires, actions etc., rather than with mere physical phenomena, the underlying pattern of explanation must be reason explanation. That is, we must invoke rationality." See also, Searle (2001, 92) stated: "There is a special logical feature of rational action explanations. Construed as causal explanations, they do not work. The causes are typically not sufficient to explain the action. Yet they are perfectly adequate as they stand. Their intelligibility requires that we think of them not as citing causes that determine an event, but as citing the reasons that a conscious rational agent acted on. The agent is a self. Agency plus the apparatus of rationality equals selfhood."

[12] See Popper (1963/1994, 169): "Thus there is only one animating law involved – the principle of acting appropriately to the situation; clearly an *almost empty* principle. It is known in the literature under the name *'rationality principle.'*"

not a priori – and beyond that also false.[13] Nevertheless, one is bound
to adhere to this false principle with law empirical content for methodological reasons. Every time a theory is falsified, it is necessary to make
a methodological decision about which part of the theory is to be rejected or modified, and Popper's suggestion is to reject the other components of the theory and not the rationality principle. The reason is
that we are primarily interested in adequately apprehending the situation, and above all, we want to see whether the elements of the
actor's situation have been correctly reconstructed, not whether the
actor was rational or not.

To clarify Popper's thesis, keep in mind that an explanation is a
deductive argument of the following type:

$$\left.\begin{array}{ll} C_1, C_2, \ldots, C_n & \text{(Initial Conditions)} \\ L_1, L_2, \ldots, L_k & \text{(Laws)} \end{array}\right\} \quad \text{Explanans}$$

$$\frac{}{\quad E \quad} \qquad \text{Explanandum}$$

According to this model, the statement of the state of affairs to be
explained, that is, the explanandum, is explained by the fact that it
is logically deduced from the conjunction of singular statements (the
initial conditions) and from general statements (the laws).

In the case of situational logic, that statement that we call the explanandum describes human action. The situational elements serve as

---

[13] See Popper (1963/1994, 171): "You will remember my assertion that the rationality
principle does not play the role of an empirical or psychological proposition and,
more especially, that it is not treated in the social sciences as subject to any kind
of test. Tests, when available, are used to test a particular model, a particular situational analysis – but not the general method of situational analysis, and not, for
this reason, the rationality principle: to uphold this is part of the method. [. . .]
Thus, if a test indicates that a certain model is less adequate than another one, then,
since both operate with the rationality principle, we have no occasion to discard
this principle. This remark explains, I think, why the rationality principle has frequently been declared to be *a priori* valid. And indeed, what else could it be if it is not
empirical? This point is of considerable interest. Those who say that the rationality
principle is *a priori* mean, of course, that it is *a priori* valid, or *a priori* true. But it
seems to me quite clear that they must be wrong. For the rationality principle seems
to me clearly false – even in its weakest zero formulation, which may be put like
this: 'Agents always act in a manner appropriate to the situation in which they find
themselves'."

initial conditions, while the rationality principle plays the role of the general law.

$$SE_1, SE_2, \ldots, SE_n \quad \text{(Situational Elements)}$$
$$\underline{\ R\ } \quad \text{(Rationality Principle)}$$
$$A \quad \text{(Human Action)}$$

This deduction can also be conceived of as the following form of logical implication:

$$SE_1 \wedge SE_2 \wedge \ldots \wedge SE_n \wedge R \rightarrow A$$

The conclusion, A, is deducible from the conjunction of the premises, for example, from the situational elements and the principle of rationality. In case of a falsification, one can deduce from the negation of the conclusion the falsity of the conjunction of the premises such that the following applies:

$$\rceil A \rightarrow \rceil (SE_1 \wedge SE_2 \wedge \ldots \wedge SE_n \wedge R)$$

With the help of DeMorgan's law, one thus yields

$$\rceil (SE_1 \wedge SE_2 \wedge \ldots \wedge SE_n \wedge R) \rightarrow \rceil SE_1 \vee \rceil SE_2 \vee \ldots \vee \rceil SE_n \vee \rceil R$$

In other words, the falsification can affect either the situational elements or the rationality principle. Popper pleads for a methodological decision according to which one should modify the situational elements, not the rationality principle.

Two objections can be raised against Popper's situational logic: (i) It is unclear how exactly one is supposed to identify the situational elements. Regarding this point, Popper states: "[t]he situation is analyzed in such a way that, what appear to be psychological moments such as, for example, desires, motives, memories and associations are transformed into situational elements. An agent with such and such desires is replaced by an agent who finds himself in a situation in which he is following such and such *objective* ends. An agent with such and such memories and associations is replaced by an agent who finds himself in a situation in which he is objectively endowed with such and such theories or with such and such information. This enables us then, to understand his actions in the objective sense, that we can say: I do in fact have other ends and other theories (than, for example, Charles the Great), but had I or you been in such and such a situation – whereby the situation includes aims and knowledge – then I, as well as you, would have acted the same way." (Popper, 1969/1993, 120 f./trans. D. A.). It is clear that the term 'situation' applies both to all the social and individual conditions and to all the mental states of the actor. The technique that could render all of these situational elements objectively identifiable remains unclear, especially since Popper does not want to allow the formulation of empirical hypotheses about them. (ii) If the principle of rationality is almost empty and factually false, how then is it possible to apprehend human action nomologically and thus to explain it?[14]

The decisive weakness of the situational logic consists in the fact that it *confounds the explanation of an action with the rational reconstruction of an action*. It is one thing to apprehend an action nomologically and thus to explain it; it is another to reconstruct an action rationally ex post facto. In the first case, one develops law-like hypotheses to explain the action, because a nexus of meaning repeatedly appears in some invariable manner. In the second case, one is concerned with rationally reconstructing a unique nexus of meaning by specifying the relevant elements of the nexus.

In explaining an action according to the previously discussed schema, it is necessary that besides specifying the initial conditions, at least one or more law-like hypotheses is employed. The rationality hypothesis can be drawn on as one possibility. It is merely important that at least one general law be found in the explanans. According to the thesis of the structural identity (or the symmetry) of explanation and prediction, a scientific explanation differs from a scientific prediction in a pragmatic respect, not in its logical structure. In an explanation it is known that the action described in the conclusion has occurred, and one looks for the general laws and the special initial conditions needed to expain it. In predictions, the general laws and

---

[14] For an excellent treatment of Popper's situational logic, with extensive references to all the relevant passages in his opus, see Böhm (2002). The most ingenious attempt to make sense of Popper's use of the rationality principle that I know of is Latsis (1983).

the special initial conditions are given, and one deduces the statement about the action in question from these before the time of its
presumptive occurrence.[15]

A reconstruction of an action is to be differentiated from this sort of
genuine explanation of an action. In the reconstruction of an action,
the action is described with the aid of specific or singular statements.
These specific statements convey information about the mental states
of the actor – his desires, goals, beliefs, and so on. The reconstruction
of an action consists in formulating specific statements, which serve
to explicate the nexus of meaning that is connected with this action.
In other words, it involves the verbal representation of the event at
hand – in this case, the action, with the help of informative descriptive
sentences. The reconstruction of an action is of great scientific interest,
and I will show in the next section how the hypothetico-deductive
method is applied in reconstructing actions. For my argument here,
it is sufficient to call to mind that a reconstruction of an action is not
an explanation, because it contains no general law.

The *rational reconstruction* of an action is a subcategory of a reconstruction of an action. Not only does it contain specific statements
about the mental states of the actors; beyond that, it also employs statements that presume the rationality of the actors. The statements about
the rationality of the actors can, of course, be formulated in different
ways. In those cases in which the statements about the rationality are
formulated tautologically, in the rational reconstruction, besides the
specific statements about the mental states of the actors, one also finds
a tautology. That is the first characteristic of a rational reconstruction.
The second is this: A rational reconstruction is only possible ex post
facto. Hence, it is only possible to rationally reconstruct an action after
that action has already taken place. These two characteristics differentiate a rational reconstruction from a real explanation. The former
does not contain any law-like hypotheses, so naturally, the thesis of
the structural identity of explanation and prediction is not valid for it
either. To this extent, the rational reconstruction is simply a specific
type of a reconstruction of an action.

---

[15] For more details on the thesis of the structural identity of explanation and prediction,
   with a discussion of an array of objections, see Hempel (1965, 364–76), Stegmüller
   (1983, ch. II), and Gemtos (1987, 237ff.).

The basic idea of the situational logic, which is to be found in rudimentary form in the work of Max Weber,[16] consists in eliminating all mental phenomena from the explanation of an action. Introducing the rationality principle as a substitute for law-like hypotheses about mental phenomena, such as desires, beliefs, memory, and so on thus leads to tautologizing the rationality principle, and as a result, the action cannot be explained but only rationally reconstructed. The same applies to the rational model, which is now most often applied in the social sciences. In principle, it is only a refinement and a further development of the rationality principle, which Weber, Popper, and others introduced to the discussion. The most characteristic use of this rationality model is expressed in Gary Becker's theory of rational choice,[17] which in one form or another is applied not only to economics, but also to sociology, political science, legal studies, and other social scientific disciplines.

According to this theory, human action is understood to consist in a rational choice among alternatives. The decision-making situation of the actor is described in reference to two elements: his preferences and his constraints. Both elements are strictly separate. The preferences contain the notions of value of the individual that are presumed to be stable. The constraints limit the scope of action, so that alternative courses of action are possible only within the constrained choice space. In accord with his preferences, the actor evaluates the alternatives that are available to him, for example, he weighs the advantages and disadvantages, the costs and benefits of the alternatives, and decides for those that promise the highest net benefit. The claim of this model is thus that human action is explainable on the basis of the interplay among preferences, constraints, and the hypothesis of utility maximization. In the case of a rational choice under certainty, it is presumed that the agent knows all of the alternatives and all of the

---

[16] See Weber (1922/1985, 428ff.). The similarity to Popper's situational logic is well expressed in the following quotation: "Similarly the rational deliberation of an actor as to whether the results of a given proposed course of action will or will not promote certain specific interests, and the corresponding decision, do not become one bit more understandable by taking 'psychological' considerations into account" Weber (1922/1985, 559/ 1978/19).

[17] See Becker (1976) and the well-known article "De Gustibus Non Est Disputandum" from Stigler and Becker (1977), reprinted in Becker (1996).

conditions of his environment, as well as the whole range of the possible outcomes connected with his decision (assumption of complete
information). In the variant of the rational choice model under risk,
it is presumed that the agent knows all the alternatives open to him,
but has only a probability distribution over the possible outcomes of
his action (assumption of incomplete information).[18] All models presume that the agent is endowed with a perfect information-processing
capacity so that he can accurately carry out the (expected) utility maximization calculus.

For the purpose of my argumentation, it is possible to ignore these
and a series of other details of the model[19] and to concentrate on
essentials: All human action can – so runs the claim – be explained
by the interplay among a stable system of preferences, the prevailing constraints, and the hypothesis of utility maximization.[20] In my
view, this claim cannot be maintained. In the construction of the rational model, the actors' preferences are normally specified in a utility
function; and independently of which additional – in fact, very questionable – presuppositions are made about the more specific character of the preferences, preferences are clearly meant to serve as initial
conditions in the aforementioned schema. The same applies to the
prevailing constraints, which limit the actor's alternatives: They serve
to specify his environmental situation, and they are also clearly meant
to be initial conditions. To explain an action, at the very least one
needs one law-like hypothesis, and in the rational choice theory the

---

[18] I cannot consider the various models of what is known as the 'economics of uncer-
tainty' or the 'economics of information,' because only the principle is of concern
here. For a complete overview, see Wessling (1991, ch. III).

[19] For a complete presentation of the model, see Kirchgässner (1991, ch. 2).

[20] See Becker (1976, 14): "At the same time, however, I do not want to soften the im-
pact of what I am saying in the interest of increasing its acceptability in the short
run. I am saying that the economic approach provides a valuable unified framework
for understanding *all* human behavior, although I recognize, of course, that much
behavior is not yet understood, and that non-economic variables and the techniques
and findings from other fields contribute significantly to the understanding of human
behavior. [...] The heart of my argument is that human behavior is not compart-
mentalized, sometimes based on maximizing, sometimes not, sometimes motivated
by stable preferences, sometimes by volatile ones, sometimes resulting in an optimal accumulation of information, sometimes not. Rather, all human behavior can
be viewed as involving participants who maximize their utility from a stable set of
preferences and accumulate an optimal amount of information and other inputs in
a variety of markets."

utility maximization hypothesis can assume this role. "Man is eternally a utility-maximizer, in his home, in his office – be in public or private – in his church, in his scientific work, in short, everywhere" (Stigler 1981, 188) It is clear that in this and many other cases, the utility maximization hypothesis is formulated tautologically, for how could such a hypothesis be falsified? A statement can have empirical content only if it excludes at least one logical possibility. The utility maximization hypothesis, however, is usually treated in such a way that no logical possibility is excluded, and it thus ends up being a tautology. Such a methodological treatment of the interplay among preferences, constraints, and the utility maximization hypothesis can only result in the rational reconstruction of an action, and not in the explanation of an action.[21]

This thus presents us with a case analogous to that of the situational logic, only in a somewhat more refined form. The theory of rational choice leads to a *reconstruction* of the actor's situation with the help of preferences and constraints; beyond that, with the help of the utility maximization hypothesis, the theory leads to a *rational reconstruction* of the situation, albeit not to an explanation. For every conceivable action, it is possible to specify ex post the actor's preferences and constraints according to the available information, and then to postulate that the actor made the best of the situation, given his constraints and preferences.

One of the reasons this theory is so appealing is certainly that it entails a mathematical formulation of the theory that justifiably gives the view of theoretical precision (Latsis, 1972, 211).[22] The choice calculi that are part of the theory are deductively developed axiomatic systems. Such calculi can, of course, be interpreted in different ways – for example, also empirically. Thus, for example, Boolean algebra can be interpreted as a propositional logic and thus as logically true; that does not exclude, however, that it can also be interpreted empirically. Interpreting it as a circuit algebra – that is, as an algebra of certain electric circuits, which is the basis of computer technology – constitutes

---

[21] On the tautological danger, see Tietzel's (1988) important article. Becker (1976, 7) also discusses the tautological danger of his approach, but he makes the same mistake as Popper – namely, of equating a rational reconstruction with an explanation.

[22] A very good introduction for readers not versed in mathematics is offered in chapter 1 of Heap, Hargreaves, Hollis, Lyons, and Weale (1992).

one such empirical interpretation. Something similar applies to the action calculi: Their empirical import does not originate in the uninterpreted, deductively developed axiomatic system, but in the interpretation of this system, that is, in the propositions that bring the terms and postulates of the axiomatic system into connection with real objects and facts and specify them empirically.[23] The interpretation of the maximization calculus under constraints and the other calculi of choice that Becker, Stigler, and most rational choice theorists offer is, however, generally very narrow and thus only suitable for post hoc rationalizations.

In sum, it should be clear that in the rational-theoretical approach – both in the form of the situational logic and in the form of the rational choice model that dominates the social sciences today – no genuine theoretical development has occurred over the variants of the one-to-one theory. The reason is that the rationality principle is most often made completely untestable, and it is thus unable to capture human action nomologically. The rationality principle's only contribution is that it offers a special type of recontruction of a nexus of meaning, which arises in connection with an action – namely, a rational reconstruction.

II. Why the Normative Rationality Principle Cannot Explain Human Action

There is further confusion in the rationlity debate at another level. Namely, a whole series of influential approaches place the normative aspect of the rationality principle in the foreground and in one way or another argue for the use of a prescriptive rationality concept in explanations of action. This notion has played a prominent role in the discussion on the explanation of human action in the study of history. Dray (1957, 124 ff.), for example, holds that the goal of such an explanation consists in showing that what was done was the thing to have done for the reasons given. The reasons given thus possess a rational explanatory function if they are *good* reasons, at least in the sense that, if the situation had been as the actor envisaged it, then what was done would have been the thing to have done. Every rational

---

[23] See Hempel's (1952, 34ff.) remarks, which are still the most precise available.

explanation thus entails an element of *appraisal*, and thus a rational explanation does not refer to a general law, but to a principle of action: "When in a situation of type $C_1 \ldots C_n$, the thing to do is X" (Dray 1957, 132).[24] In accord with Dray's interpretation, a rational explanation looks like the following:

> A was in a situation of type C
>
> In a situation of type C, the appropriate thing to do is x
> _____
> Therefore, A did x.

As Hempel (1965, 470f.) accurately noted, the conclusion above is not a valid argument, because the conclusion cannot be deduced from the two premises. The information that A was in a situation of type C, and that the appropriate action in such a situation is x, affords grounds for believing that it *would have been rational for A to do x* in such a situation but no grounds for believing that A did in fact do x. Reasons can be "good reasons" in a normative sense without having de facto the slightest influence upon us. It is very possible that A either did not know the second premise or that she rejected it or consciously acted against it.[25]

It suffices, therefore, to repeat the obvious: A normative proposition, in this case the rationality principle, cannot explain an event, in

---

[24] For a detailed discussion of Dray's thesis, see Hempel (1965, 469ff.), Stegmüller (1983, 429ff.), and Gemtos (1987, 255ff.).

[25] See Passmore (1958, 275) and Stegmüller (1983, 438). I have related the discussion of the normative rationality principle to Dray's position, because it is the *locus classicus* in the literature. The thesis that it is necessary or at least possible to refer to a normative rationality principle is continually discussed in the philosophical literature. Recently it has also been taken up by John Searle, who views justificatory explanations as a subcategory of genuine explanations. See Searle (2001, 110ff.): "To take a case of more gravity much of the public discussion of whether Truman was justified in dropping the atomic bomb is not about the reasons he *acted on*, but about whether it was a *good thing* on balance. All reason statements are explanations, but the point I am making now is that the explanation of why *something should have been done is a good thing to have been done* is not always the same as *why it was in fact done*. In this book we are primarily concerned with explanations that state the reasons that the agent acted on or will act on. We are interested in justifications only insofar as they also explain why the agent acted or will act. Therefore I will distinguish between justifications and what I will call 'justificatory explanations.' Justification does not always explain why something in fact happened, but an explanation of its happening, whether justificatory or not, has to explain why it happened. A subclass of genuine explanations, therefore, are justificatory explanations."

this case a human action, in conjunction with positive, specific statements, because it is not a law-like hypothesis.

III. Why a Law-Like Rationality Hypothesis Is Unsuitable to Explain Human Action

In accord with what has been said previously, it appears that human action is explainable neither with a tautologically formulated rationality principle nor with a normative one. The only remaining possibility is to introduce a rationality hypothesis in the explanans of a human action, which constitutes a law-like statement, such as in the following formulation from Hempel (1965, 471):

> A was in a situation of type C.
> A was a rational agent.
> In a situation of type C, any rational agent will do x.
> Therefore, A did x.

In comparison to the schema of rational explanation, which involves a normative rationality principle, here the explicit assumption is added that A was a rational agent. Besides that – and this is the most significant point here – the normative rationality principle is replaced with a general empirical statement about what rational actors do in situations of type C.

I want to provide two arguments to counter the thesis that a law-like rationality hypothesis in the form introduced by Hempel, or in any other form, can correctly explain human action. I shall start with the first argument, which is easier to formulate and should in fact be the more powerful of the two: There is a lot of empirical evidence showing that a general rationality hypothesis is false, regardless of its form. In a very common formulation, the rationality hypothesis is specified as a maximization of the actor's self-interest. This formulation avoids the tautology charge that I raised earlier, because it specifies the concept of utility maximization more closely, namely, as the maximization of self-interest. Here, self-interest is normally meant in a substantial sense, and not in a formal sense, so that altruistic elements are excluded. (If the concept of self-interest were so broadly conceived as to include altruistic elements as well, as is common enough in the literature, then the rationality principle is tautologized in another way: Every conceivable action, whether selfish or altruistic, would then be self-interested, such that the concept of self-interest would only be another definition of the concept of action.) The rationality hypothesis in the sense of the maximization of self-interest has been repeatedly falsified in numerous experiments, a fact that prompts us to look for alternatives.[26]

The same applies to other dominant formulations of the rationality hypothesis, namely, as consistency in decision-making behavior. Here too, a whole series of experiments have shown that phenomena such as loss aversion,[27] the endowment effect,[28] and preference reversals[29] systematically arise in people's decisions, such that it is also untenable to hold to this formulation of the rationality hypothesis.[30]

A further argument that speaks against the law-like rationality hypothesis is more complex than the first: The heuristic potential of a theory of human action that is based on a descriptive-psychological concept of rationality is very low, and thus we should – as far as possible – look for explanations of human action that do not refer to rationality hypotheses. The main reason for the very limited heuristic potential of the rationality principle lies in the fact that using it gives rise to the false impression that a simple law-like hypothesis is sufficient to explain human action. As already pointed out, the theory of the rational actor prima facie represents an advance over one-to-one theories,

---

[26] It is hardly possible to survey the literature. See, for example, Kagel and Roth (1995), Conlisk (1996), Gigerenzer (2000), Gigerenzer, Todd, and the ABC Research Group (1999), Gigerenzer and Selten (2001), Güth and Kliemt (2003), and Kahneman and Tversky (2000). For an excellent discussion of the problems of the theory of rational choice in the case of political decisions of ordinary citizens, see Sniderman (2000).

[27] See, for example, Kahneman, Knetsch, and Thaler (1990) and Tversky and Kahneman (1991).

[28] See, for example, Thaler (1980) and Kahneman et al. (1990).

[29] See, for example, Tversky and Thaler (1990).

[30] The argument concerning the empirical falsification of the rationality hypothesis can, however, be rejected on other grounds. Namely, one could point to the necessity of upholding the rationality hypothesis in the social sciences given the fact that there the primary aim is not to explain individual human actions, but to explain *types* of actions. The discussion of this argument would lead to complex problems of theory building in the social sciences, which are irrelevant for the context of interest here: Here the concern is whether and to what extent a rationality hypothesis that is empirically formulated is able to explain *concrete* human action.

because it describes a nexus of meaning with the help of a mechanism. Mental states are depicted as meaninful *processes* and connected with the action under consideration. A meaningful process can be shown to have an invariant structure, and the regular appearance of such a meaningful rational process can be apprehended with a law-like hypothesis. However, the desire to maintain the rationality hypothesis results de facto in an attempt to observe and describe this meaningful process as rational in one way or another. There is, nonetheless, no reason to view the mechanism by which mental states are transformed into actions from the perspective of the rationality of this mechanism. There are in principle an unlimited number of hypotheses that can be formulated to explain this mechanism, and the dogmatic adherence to specific criteria of rationality, which are supposed to oblige this mechanism, can only lead to the a priori ruling out of a large number of theoretical possibilities for studying this mecahnism. What we need are both diverse conceptual apparatuses, with the help of which specific mechanisms are described, and diverse law-like hypotheses, which show, with the help of these conceptual apparatuses, the way that nexuses of meaning that arise in connection with human actions are invariant.

The desire to adhere to the rationality hypothesis is connected to the fact that rationality is a prescientific concept, and it is common that in the early phases of the development of a scientific discipline, the first systems of statements are constructed primarily with the help of everyday concepts. However, the more mature a discipline becomes, the rarer the use of such everyday concepts. In addition, developed empirical scientific systems do not consist of a singular hypothesis, but rather of an entire hierarchy of hypotheses of various levels of generality. Beyond all that, a whole array of mechanisms have been specified in the disciplines known as 'cognitive sciences' that explain aspects of human action in detail without employing rationality hypotheses in doing so. Today, for example, perception is described as a complex process that unfolds in constant interaction with memory and that possesses a specific neurological basis.[31] It is even claimed that both the genesis of intentions and their realization in programs of action are to be

---

[31] See, for example, Farah (2000) and Kosslyn and Thompson (2000).

explained with the help of neural nets.[32] In other words, the rapid advancement in the cognitive sciences has come about as researchers have looked for alternative explanatory patterns to the rationality of action. Also, independently of how the explanations produced by brain and cognitive research are to be assessed, it is in any case clear that the rationality hypothesis does not do justice to the complexity of the mechanism that transforms mental states into actions.

This is, I think, also the reason that Hempel so broadly interprets the concept of rationality in his classical discussion of rational explanation (1965, 472): "By whatever specific empirical criteria it may be characterized, rationality in the descriptive-psychological sense is a broadly disposititonal trait; to say of someone that he is a rational agent is to attribute to him, by impication, *a complex bundle of dispositions*. Each of these may be thought of as a tendency to behave – uniformly or with a certain probability – in a characteristic way under conditions of a given kind [...]" (emphasis added).

Conceiving of rationality with the help of dispositions may seem useful prima facie, because it makes it possible to grasp the rational explanation as a broadly dispositional explanation.[33] Although postulating dispositions has the advantage of making it possible to show invariances in behavior, it neither specifies a mechanism for transforming mental states into behavior nor says anything *about how dispositions arise in the first place*. Thus, in my opinion, the retreat to dispositions is not a satisfactory solution. In contrast, what we should seek are law-like hypotheses that are not to be interpreted a priori as 'rationality,' 'disposition,' and so on. Just as we generally speak about *natural laws* in the natural sciences, which unveil the invariances that occur in nature,

---

[32] See, for example, Dehaene and Changeux (1997). See also Singer (2002): "The neuro-psychological findings and above all results from developmental biology impressively show that mental functions are very closely connected with the function of neural nets. It is possible to duplicate step by step how in the process of brain development increasingly complex structures emerge from the aggregation of simple elements of matter and how the degree of complexity of the system achieved in each case is related to the complexity of its performance" (39/trans. D. A.).

[33] One could say that Hempel's argumentation strategy consists in giving Ryle's well-known analysis of dispositions a methodological twist (1949, ch. V). By conceiving the rationality of the actors as a complex bundle of dispositions, in a second step he is able to adopt Ryle's analysis of dispositional concepts and then, in a third step, present the rational explanation as a broad dispositional explanation. For a detailed treatment of dispositions, see Mumford (1998).

we ought to speak about *behavioral laws* that unveil the invariances that occur in human action. Just as it would be absurd to try to explain all natural phenomena in their diversity on the basis of a single hypothesis, it is also absurd to attempt to explain all human actions in their entire diversity on the basis of the principle of rationality.

As already mentioned, such *behavioral laws* can apprehend either genetic, cultural, or personal invariances, whereas one should keep in mind that laws that disclose genetic invariances have more explanatory power than those that disclose cultural invariances, and that laws disclosing these latter invariances, in turn, possess greater explanatory power than those that capture personal invariances. In the philosophy of mind there is, however, a discussion about whether statements that have personal invariances as their content are to be viewed as laws at all. Davidson (1973/2001, 250; 1976/2001 265), for example, disputes that propositions that express regularities in the behavior of a person can be plausibly characterized as laws.[34] It appears to me, however, that if we know a regularity in the behavior of an individual, then in any case, our information about the facts of the world has been increased. Besides, it is to be emphasized that in general, behavioral laws have less empirical content than natural laws, above all because of the creativity of human action. Since the creative element is omnipresent in human praxis, it should be more difficult for us to discover regularities in human action than regularities in nature.

Besides, the creativity of human action has further consequences that are of great methodological significance: There is a whole array of nexuses of meaning that cannot be transformed into causal nexuses, and that consequently cannot be nomologically apprehended. This is true for those cases in which there is no standpoint from which two or more nexuses of meaning show a similarity. This is the case when the actor is confronted with a new problem and, as a result of the creativity of his cognitive system, acts novelly. Nexuses of meaning that arise when such actions are carried out are characterized by the fact that the actor signifies his natural or social environment against the background of his mental states in a novel way. Given his current stand of knowledge, the respective mental processes constitute genuinely new nexuses of meaning. Such new nexuses of meaning mostly arise

---

[34] For a critical appraisal of Davidson's theory, see Føllesdal (1980).

in connection with the mental process of decision making. In contrast to what is maintained by the theory of rational choice, it is only in situations in which people are confronted with genuinely new problems that the cognitive system searches for new problem solutions and the phenomenon that we call decision making takes place.[35] A decision and a respective new problem solution thus result in an action that is not predictable. In other words, there is no standpoint from which the nexus of meaning that arises in connection with a new action can be transformed into a causal nexus.

In none of these cases are nexuses of meaning nomologically apprehensible. This, however, does not mean that they do not constitute scientific problems. If one shares the view that sciences are characterized by the formulation and solution of problems rather than by the existence of specific object areas (as the proponents of the autonomy of the human sciences tend to think), then it seems consistent to maintain that such nexuses of meaning also need to be treated scientifically. However, treating them scientifically does not consist in subjecting them to a nomological explanation, but in reconstructing them as accurately as possible. In such reconstructions the same method can be used, namely, the hypothetico-deductive method, but in a specific application, as I shall show.

5.5 THE HYPOTHETICO-DEDUCTIVE METHOD AND THE RECONSTRUCTION OF HUMAN ACTION

On 11 September 2001, two hijacked airplanes were flown into the twin towers of the World Trade Center in Manhattan, New York. In the collision, 3,000 people died. It is suspected that Osama Bin Laden initiated this act, and I presume that this is the case. Naturally, this event is a very complex matter that did not come about on the basis of

---

[35] For a more detailed treatment, see Mantzavinos (2001, ch. 4). As far as I know, the first one to emphasize and offer a detailed treatment of the creativity of decision making was Shackle (1972/1992, 1979). See also Hesse (1990), who speaks about the "principle of cognitive creation." The main message of this literature from political economy and the social sciences can be summarized in Buchanan's (1979, 40) aphorism: "Choice, by its nature, cannot be predetermined and remain choice." Of course, creativity has always been a research area within psychology, but to my knowledge, it was never explicitly connected with decision making. For a good overview of the psychological research on creativity, see Sternberg (1999), and for a philosophical treatment of creativity, see Lenk (2000).

a single action. Of interest here, however, is only the original action, which gave impetus to the development that then led to the collision of both planes with the two towers. This action was Bin Laden's order to his collaborators to begin the action.

First, it is to be observed that there is no explanation for the action. The present stand of psychology and cognitive science does not offer us law-like hypotheses – either in the form of strict deterministic laws or in the form of statistical laws – that are able to explain this action. (Precisely this expresses the significance of such laws: If we had such laws, then – on the basis of the structural identity of explanation and prediction, and assuming that the relevant initial conditions of this action were available to us – we would be able to predict Bin Laden's behavior.) However, it is obvious that this action is of great scientific relevance for the disciplines of history, law, political science, and religious studies, and perhaps for studies of an array of other scientific disciplines. The scientific problem consists in reconstructing this action accurately, and my claim is that the hypothetico-deductive method is at work in such a reconstruction.

The problem that the pertinent disciplines are confronted with consists in accurately reconstructing the nexus of meaning that has emerged in connection with Bin Laden's action. It is thus a matter of adequately reconstructing the nexus of meaning that arose in connection with the following action: "Bin Laden gave the order to topple the towers." The hypothetico-deductive method is to be applied here by formulating a hypothesis regarding the fundamental elements of the nexus of meaning and testing it on the basis of the empirically available material. Bin Laden's problem is to be analyzed by apprehending the motive of the action, the intentions of the action, the reasons for the action (one-to-one theories), or the rationality of the action or, beyond that, by attempting to reconstruct the fundamental elements of the action using other description systems. These hypotheses can then be tested with the help of empirical material – for instance, of statements that Bin Laden himself made about the action and that were recorded in videos or writings. Empirical material can also be drawn on with the help of natural scientific techniques: If, for example, a clinical examination of Bin Laden were available, it could possibly show that a certain type of brain damage played a role in a number of his actions, including the action that is of interest here.

I have taken the example of Bin Laden because it seems to me to illustrate well the great scientific importance that a reconstruction of action can have. Besides, this example also shows that scientific problems of this sort are not about explanations, but about ex post facto reconstructions.[36] These reconstructions can be developed with the help of rationality principles, and the result is rational reconstructions of the type discussed earlier. However, reconstructions can involve different conceptual apparatuses, and thus the fundamental elements of the nexus of meaning can be expressed with different natural or artificial linguistic means.

Since the concept of reconstruction is thematized differently within the different approaches in philosophy of science,[37] I want to point out here that I hold reconstruction to be an attempt to describe, that is, an attempt to accurately depict singular events. I presume that two sorts of objectives in the human sciences play a role: on the one hand, explanations that answer "why" questions and, on the other hand, the identification of individual facts that answer questions of the type "what is the case?" or "what was the case?".[38] The answers to questions of the second type allege the existence of individual facts or occurences. They are singular desriptive sentences about individual events and are temporally and spatially determined (Bühler 2003b, 28). In other words, they are descriptive attempts.[39] The reconstruction of an action is thus

---

[36] In my opinion, the decisive weakness of the analysis of the original proponents of the hypothetico-deductive method lies precisely here. Both Popper (1949/1972) and Hempel (1942) always portrayed scientific activity as explanatory activity. This rightly led many representatives of scientific disciplines such as history, law, and so on to protest. Therefore, it should be emphasized that here we are dealing with a scientific task that accords with the hypothetico-deductive method but that is not explanatory in nature.

[37] For a history of the use of the concept of 'reconstruction,' see the informative article by Scholtz (1998).

[38] Here I follow Bühler (2003b, 22f.): "We thus see that two types of goals play a role in the social sciences and the humanities: for one, the answer to 'why'-questions, i.e. the provision of explanations; for another, the ascertainment of individual facts, i.e. answers to questions concerning 'what was the case'. Since examples of both types of goals could be multiplied at will and since [. . .] goals that appear to be different in kind can be connected to these two types, it is justified to say that answering the 'why'- questions and ascertaining individual facts are two *central* epistemological goals of the social sciences and the humanities" (trans. D. A.).

[39] See Stegmüller (1983, 114): "In the simplest case, descriptions take the form of narrative reports in which either one's own observations are outlined or the perceptions

always the answer to a question of the sort "What was the case?" and it is especially relevant if the action cannot be explained.

Reconstructions have a hypothetical character, and they must thus be tested empirically. How can this testing be carried out, and what kinds of research techniques are available for checking such reconstructions? And by which criterion is it possible to distinguish between a good and a bad reconstruction?

I shall start with the first question. There are two types of research techniques with the help of which reconstructions of nexuses of meaning can be tested: (i) Research techniques from the humanities and social sciences. The statements of the actors themselves belong to this category, as well as what is known in the humanities as 'source criticism.'[40] It must be emphasized immediately that there is no guarantee that the empirical material that is gathered with the help of such techniques is reliable. In their statements about their actions, the actors can purposefully attempt to deceive, or, for psychological reasons, they may not be able to accurately express their mental states, such as their motives, intentions, and so on;[41] the statements of witnesses

of others are presented. Descriptions can however also be more ambitious and they can contain stronger or weaker hypothetical components, about which there can be no absolute certainty, but which are treated in the description 'as if' they were settled facts. Thus, for example, we also say that an astronomer *describes* the structure of a star cloud or that a historian offers a precise *description* of the course of the French Revolution. [...] The common element of all descriptions is that they can be apprehended as an answer to a certain type of questions, namely to questions of the form 'what is the case?' or 'what was the case?'" (trans. D. A.).

[40] For the testing of hypotheses from the human sciences by means of source criticism, see Bühler (2003b, 181ff.).

[41] See, for example, Singer (2002, 79): "That which can be perceived from moment to moment is even more restricted by the limited capacity of those processes upon which conscious perception is based. There are constantly many more signals from the sense organs that reach our brains than we are conscious of. Many of these signals are also processed, but the result of these analyses does not reach consciousness. And this is the reason that when asked about the motives for certain behavior – the real motives being related to such unconscious processes – people offer newly made up motives, without being aware that the reasons they are giving are incorrect. Two conclusions important for our problem result from this: First, the reasons given for the motives of actions must be mistrusted, not because those questioned might intentionally lie, but because they can have no complete conscious control over their motives. Second, people have the irresistible need to find causes and justifications for what they do" (trans. D. A.).

can be biased for various reasons;[42] and it is possible that the sources are not well preserved. The scientific achievement of the experts in the humanities and the social sciences consists precisely in testing the hypotheses regarding the nexus of meaning to be reconstructed on the basis of the existing empirical material, which is itself fallible. (ii) Experimental or natural scientific research techniques. Protocols that are carried out in psychological laboratory experiments and videos that are recorded during game-theory experiments are examples of techniques that belong to this category.[43] So are DNA analyses of the actors and techniques that are applied in the cognitive sciences, such as magnetic resonance imaging and other brain-imaging techniques.[44] Above all, the cognitive sciences have made great progress in this respect over the past few years, so that today even the effects of the meaning of actions can be exactly represented. For example, with the help of a positron emission tomography scanner, Decéty et al. (1997) have registered the brain activities that occur if a subject observes gestures, depending on whether they are meaningful for the subject or not. The cerebral activity of the subject who observes hand movements that have a meaning for him (the opening of a bottle, the sewing of a button, etc.) looks different than the cerebral activity that occurs if the subject observes hand movements that are not meaningful for

---

[42] See the comments by Gomperz (1939, 32f.): "In the first place the witness [...] may have possessed direct or indirect knowledge concerning statements made by the agent himself, or may have had access to letters, documents, diaries, memoires, or other autobiographic material on which we have no other information. This is, for instance, the chief basis for the historian's claim to know more about the matter than the layman: he is supposed to have looked into the evidence which is, in most cases, practically inaccessible to the latter. And the position of the 'source' with respect to the historian is very frequently precisely the same. [...] But it must never be forgotten that, on the other hand, a man is not at all an ideal witness, merely because he was closely associated with the agent. Close association with the agent, friendly or unfriendly, is in itself a source of bias and may prompt the witness to give a distorted account, from a desire to make the agent appear either better or worse than he was. Neither a devoted friend nor a malicious foe is the kind of witness the historian ought to be looking out for. But unfortunately it will be a rare piece of luck should he dispose of the testimony of one who was close enough to know and yet was above all temptation either to idealize or to slander. It is, among other things, because we suppose Thucydides to have almost perfectly fulfilled these requirements that we feel inclined to view him as the most outstanding of the guild."

[43] See Bosman, Hennig-Schmdt, and van Winden (2002).

[44] For an overview, see chapter 4 of Gazzaniga et al. (2002).

him (the gestures of American body language). In other words, today we have exact brain images of an array of mental activities that –
independent of the problem of translation or of the correspondence
of the relevant descriptive systems – do provide additional empirical
material.[45]

On the basis of such empirical material, hypotheses – in this case,
the reconstructions – are tested. Here, however, the second of the preceding questions arises, namely, how good or bad reconstructions are
to be differentiated from one another. Reconstructions aim at providing an accurate depiction of a nexus of meaning, and it is consequently
clear that the activity of reconstructing is or can be oriented on the
idea of truth. Now, we know from the discussion of the correspondence theory of truth that one has to differentiate between *definitions*
of truth and *criteria* for truth (Keuth 1989, 164ff.). Although attempts
to formulate truth criteria have admitedly failed thus far, we do at least
have adequate definitions of truth, such as, for example, Tarski's. In
any case, the idea of truth is easy to understand without necessarily using the conception of a *criterion* and even without the need of a formal
definition (Albert 1982, 16). Truth, as the *idea* of the accurate depiction
of facts with the means of language, is sufficient to serve as a regulative
principle for scientific activity.

An orientation on the idea of truth is also possible in the case of interest here. In reconstructions, as in identifications of individual facts
in general, certain singular descriptive statements serve as hypotheses precisely because one looks for reasons for their truth or falsity
(Bühler, 2003b, 28). The diversely offered reconstructions of nexuses
of meaning are thus to be compared to each other with respect to
truth. Those that are most accurately able to reconstruct the nexus
of meaning are to be preferred. The regulative idea of truth in the
more specific sense, as entailing the accuracy of a reconstruction, can
be further specified in the disciplines that deal with this type of scientific problem. It is also possible to develop more specific standards
for the purpose of evaluating the reconstructions offered. It is in any
case important that the respective decision regarding the accuracy of
a reconstruction be made on the basis of the empirical material.

[45] On the problem of the correspondence between systems of description see Keuth
(1990) and Kim (1989/1997).

5.6 ON THE EXPLANATION OF THE UNDERSTANDING OF ACTIONS

Thus far, I have attempted to show that the hypothetico-deductive method can successfully grasp nexuses of meaning, and thus, no autonomous method is needed for apprehending material that possesses meaningful components. Methodological antinaturalism, the doctrine that maintains that understanding is the adequate method for apprehending the meaning of human action, must be rejected, primarily because it is useless. Now, it still must be shown that the hypothetico-deductive method can adequately apprehend understanding as a subjective mental process. In other words, if understanding is conceived as a type of knowledge, then it is important to show how the hypothetico-deductive method can plausibly be applied to this process. Because we are dealing here with human action in particular, this is concerned in concreto with the understanding of human actions.

The focus is on the mental process that can be referred to as 'understanding persons' or 'understanding actions.' If one attempts to understand the action of another person, then a nexus of meaning arises, because the action of the other person is interpreted. The fundamental elements of this nexus of meaning repeatedly occur, so that it can be transformed into a causal nexus. The hypothetico-deductive method can thus be applied in its standard way: namely, by subjecting the respective invariances to a nomological explanation. *The mental process of understanding human actions can thus be explained by showing the laws to which this process is subject.*

But what exactly is to be explained? In 'understanding' other persons and their actions, an entire bundle of mental processes occur, and in each case the issue consists in specifying the respective regularities. I would like to briefly outline two of these processes. To begin with, other persons are perceived, so understanding is to be viewed as a special case of *perception*. It is a commonplace view in psychological research on perception that the cognitive system of the perceiver actively interprets both natural and social events. The question consists rather in how these interpretive components of the perception process are to be modeled. For this purpose, an array of models have been developed in cognitive psychology that, for example, explain the process of perception with the help of a neural net (McClelland

and Rumelhart, 1986) or with the help of mental models (Holland, Holyoak, Nisbett, and Thagard, 1986, ch. 2). One important result of this research is that there is a range of standard mistakes that arise in the perception of other people. One very well-known mistake of this sort is for example, that people systematically overestimate the consistency of the social behavior of others.[46] Empirical evidence thus supports the existence of some systematic differences between the process of the perception of persons and the process of the perception of objects or natural events, although the fundamental mechanism of perception can in principle be modeled in the same way.

The attribution of mental states is the second process at work when persons or their actions are understood. An important aspect of the mental process that we call 'understanding action' consists in attributing desires, opinions, expectations, emotions, moods, decisions, and other mental states to actors. This practice of attributing mental states can occur at either a *symbolic* or a *mimetic* level. In understanding actions, various sorts of mental predicates are attributed to other people – for example, predicates about desires, opinions, expectations, perceptions, feelings, and so on. This presupposes the existence of symbolic cognition, and there is no doubt that this is consistent with the architecture of the human mind. But people possess a more differentiated practice of attributing characteristics to others, which is related to the evolutionary development of the human brain: They are also capable of attributing mental states to others without using symbols. It is possible to understand other organisms prelinguistically or extralinguistically, and this is connected to the existence of a mimetic cognitive level, which arose earlier in evolution and which coexists with the symbolic level.[47] Attributing mental states thus occurs in parallel at both the

---

[46] Cf. the remark of Holland et al. (1986, 214): "The corollary of assuming great consistency within individuals is assuming much more diversity across individuals than actually exists. This encourages people to model events at the level of 'Joe' even when there is little diagnostic information available about Joe, rather than modeling events at the level of 'college students' or perhaps even at the level of 'people'".

[47] See Donald (1998a, S. 14): "Early hominids, possibly Homo habilis, but certainly Homo erectus, must have had the ability to rehearse and evaluate, and thus refine, their own actions. The implication of such a supramodal capacity to review and rehearse action was that the entire skeleto-motor repertoire of hominids became voluntarily controllable under the supervision of conscious perception, an ability I call non-verbal action-modelling, or mimesis. This greatly increased the morphological

symbolic and mimetic levels, and the question is, which regularities are relevant in this?

It is not possible here to offer an overview of the research results and the controversies related to this in the relevant disciplines. It is only to be pointed out that understanding persons, like understanding language, is a skill. In general, we acquire skills completely differently than we learn facts or statements.[48] In acquiring skills, three stages are distinguished: the cognitive stage, during which a declarative encoding of the skill occurs; the associative stage, during which the individual elements that are necessary for successfully practicing the skill become more closely related to each other; and the autonomous stage, during which the procedure occurs increasingly fast and increasingly automatized, and it is only necessary to pay a little attention to what is being done (Anderson 2002, ch. 9). After the skill that underlies the understanding of people or the understanding of actions is acquired, it becomes automatized, so that the respective communication between people often occurs unconsciously.

It can thus be stated that numerous aspects of the understanding of actions are the object of empirical scientific analysis. Above all, processes of perception and the attribution of mental states appear to be relevant, and the question is not *whether* but *how* these processes can be explained. The current discussion focusses on the appropriate form of folk psychology.

An important thesis that often appears in the literature maintains that the layman's understanding of persons necessarily presumes the rationality of human action, be that in the form of a presumption of coherence, of truth, or of something else. In this context, it is emphasized that folk psychology does not merely consist of empirical hypotheses – that is the attribution of mental states is not a purely descriptive task – but that normative elements such as various sorts of presumptions of

---

variability of explicitly retrievable, conscious hominid action. The result was, I believe, the rapid emergence of the non-verbal background of human culture, a layer of 'mimetic' culture, that still persists in the form of numerous cultural variations in expression and custom (most of which people are unaware of and cannot describe verbally), elementary craft and tool use, pantomime, dance, athletic skill, and prosodic vocalization, including group displays. The mimetic dimension of human culture is still supported by a primarily analogue mode or representation."

[48] See the discussion in Section 3.4.

rationality are imperative (Scholz 1999, 87ff.). But there are a series of cases in which a person, *A*, must attribute false beliefs to another person, *B*, in order for *A* to be able to understand *B* at all – for example, if *B* has received misleading instructions or information. In addition, it is hardly possible to understand the actions of pathological personalities with the help of presumptions of rationality. Finally, it is once again to be emphasized that understanding actions is not always a conscious cognitive act: If the respective skill has been acquired, then it is usually performed unconsciously, and consequently, no conscious fomulation of presumptions of rationality is nomally taking place.

Simulation, as a folk psychology approach, also seems to be afflicted with problems. The basic idea of the simulation approach is that we understand the psychology of other people not by applying some sort of theory but by using our own mental processes to simulate the processes of others (Goldman 1990, ch. 1).[49] Although the proponents of simulation theory do not advocate "putting oneself in another's shoes" as the exclusive mechanism for understanding others, they do view it as the mechanism that people most often use to understand the mental states of others.[50] This special skill of mental simulation is thus introduced as an alternative to the existence of knowledge or commonsense theories, on the basis of which people are able to understand and predict the behavior of others. However, the idea that simulation can function without any theoretical components whatsoever is difficult to defend. How can an American, on the basis of a simulation process, which has one's own mental states as the input, without any knowledge, understand someone from China? Besides, in many cases, simulation is not necessary to understand something: People who are congenitally blind or deaf can largely understand other people (Churchland 1989, 119).

It thus appears that folk psychology is fundamentally of a theoretical nature, and that it therefore need not entail the thesis of the rationality of action or employ the thesis of an autonomous simulation mechanism. While interacting with their social environment, laymen

---

[49] Grandy's (1973) 'principle of humanity' is also along these lines.
[50] See e.g., Goldman (1990, 18): "In any case there is no assumption here that people are always successful or optimal simulators. What I do conjecture is that simulation – whether explicit or implicit – is the fundamental method used for arriving at mental ascriptions to others."

learn how other people behave, and they accumulate knowledge about this, which is activated when understanding the actions of others. This knowledge is acquired in the form of skills and it makes it possible to attribute mental states to other actors.

As Churchland (1979, 114; 1989, 6f) has emphasized, there are great gaps in folk psychology. For a whole array of phenomena, such as mental illness, memory, creativity, differences in perception, and others, it offers no explanation whatsoever; for others, the explanations that it offers are empirically false. For its part, this fact itself requires an explanation, which has to be based on scientific theories. From the numerous theories developed, I just want to refer to the research on autism, which shows that, if not a special module of knowledge, then there is at least a domain-specific knowledge, which contains the theory of mind. Baron-Cohen's experiments with autistic children (1995) show that these children perform very badly on what are called 'false belief tasks.' This finding mainly supports the hypothesis that the communicative incompetence of autistic individuals is to be traced back to their lack of ability to ascribe mental states to others.[51]

In sum, it can be stated that the special mental process that is known as 'understanding persons' or 'understanding actions' is underlied by an array of regularities that are connected both with perception and, more generally, with the attribution of mental states. As is usual in the sciences, we have better explanations for some phenomena of folk psychology than for others, and there are an array of controversies regarding the quality of the existing theories. For us, however, what is of primary importance is that *this particular type of understanding can be explained, and thus that the hypothetico-deductive method can be applied to it without any difficulty.* It remains to be demonstrated how this method can be applied to the apprehension of the meaning of texts.

[51] For an informative discussion of the relevant experiments as well as of the theoretical positions, see Hughes and Plomin (2000).

6

The Apprehension of the Meaning of Texts

6.1 LINGUISTIC EXPRESSIONS AS MEANINGFUL EVENTS

Besides languages, there is a whole array of symbolic systems that one encounters in everyday life, such as gestures, pictures, chess notes, music notes, and so on. The historically developed, natural languages may, however, be the most expressive symbolic systems, and they play an eminent role in our lives. Linguistic expressions, oral or written, are the result of human actions, and thus they are meaningful objects. Since spoken utterances and written texts, being human productions, are nothing other than meaningful events, I will treat them analogously to the way I treated human action in the previous chapter.

The most obvious question in the analysis of linguistic expressions is undoubtedly this: What is the meaning of a linguistic expression?[1] Yet there are as many answers to the question of the 'meaning' of linguistic expressions as there are theoreticians of meaning. In order to presume as little as possible in my treatment of the problematic of meaning, I start with the following definition: *Linguistic expressions are bestowed with meaning when, in producing them, the author construes them against the background of his goals, his beliefs, and his other mental states while interacting with his natural and social environments; such a construal*

---

[1] Künne (1981, 1) even views this as a fundamental question of analytic philosophy. Hogan (1996, 9ff.) correctly argues for the obvious: This question can only be answered by a stipulation.

of meaning is a complex process, and it involves the conscious and unconscious use of symbols.

From the perspective of the observer, the nexus of meaning that arises in connection with a linguistic expression can be apprehended by being externally described and, if necessary, nomologically explained. The methodologically relevant question thus concerns the way that the nexuses of meaning are to be adequately apprehended – naturally also with the help of information that the speaker or writer herself conveys. In what follows, I will attempt to show that the hypothetico-deductive method can apprehend the meaning of a linguistic expression in two ways: (i) by transforming nexuses of meaning that *repeatedly* arise in connection with certain written expressions into causal nexuses and nomologically explaining them and (ii) by accurately determining the nexus of meaning that is connected with a *specific* text. I shall analyze both of these areas of the application of the hypothetico-deductive method successively.

6.2 ON THE TRANSFORMATION OF NEXUSES OF MEANING INTO CAUSAL NEXUSES

In the previous chapter, I discussed three approaches of the one-to-one theory of human action that describe the nexus of meaning of an action with the help of a description of the motive, the intentions, or the reasons for the action. Something similar applies to linguistic expressions. We often describe their meaning on the basis of a few elements, which are placed in a one-to-one relationship to the respective statements. In particular, it is often presupposed that the meaning of a linguistic expression can be disclosed if one can apprehend its underlying intention (e.g. Grice, 1989, Searle 1983, ch. 6). All variants of the one-to-one theory appeal to simple mental states of the speaker or writer without more precisely specifying the mechanism on the basis of which these mental states lead to the subjective imposing of meaning on the statements.

One approach that attempts to specify such a mechanism more precisely points to the rationality of the authors (e.g., Livingston, 1993). According to this approach, it is possible to apprehend linguistic expressions only if one assumes that the situation of the speaker or writer has more complex features, which can be dealt with by imputing a mechanism, namely, the rationality of the author. Above all, deductive rationality plays a role here: One presumes that in bringing about linguistic expressions, the rules of inference of propositional and predicate logic are observed. Linguistic expressions are imbued with meaning when, among other things, a valid logical deduction occurs when producing them. The role of the presumption of rationality will be dealt with in more detail later. For my argumentation here, it is only important to keep in mind that a linguistic expression can also be apprehended with the help of a more complex *mechanism*.

This very concise reference to various approaches merely serves to show that there are numerous possible ways *to describe* the nexus of meaning from an observer's perspective. My main argument is parallel to that of human action: Regardless of the approach and the descriptive means used in order to apprehend a nexus of meaning, it is in principle possible that the fundamental elements of this nexus of meaning will also occur in connection with other linguistic expressions of the same person or of other persons. By 'fundamental elements' I mean both all relevant mental states of the speaker or writer and all relevant mechanisms that are at work in bringing about a linguistic expression. Every time one succeeds in identifying the fundamental elements of a nexus of meaning in other nexuses as well, it is possible to view nexuses of meaning as causal nexuses. Just as in actions, here, too, the key to transforming nexuses of meaning into causal nexuses lies in showing an *invariance* in the appearance of the fundamental elements in various nexuses of meaning. In those cases in which it is possible to make such a transformation, nexuses of meaning can be nomologically apprehended and thus their repeated occurrence can be explained.

Let us take the example of a one-year-old child, X, who, in the presence of her mother, points to a ball and says the word 'ball.' The meaning of this expression can be apprehended by identifying the intention of the expression – in this case, that the child wants to communicate to her mother that the object in front of her is called that. The fundamental element in this nexus of meaning is the intention of giving the object a name. If one can show that this element arises in connection with other expressions from other children in similar situations, then one has discovered an invariance and thus has transformed the nexus of meaning into a causal nexus. This type of invariance does in fact arise in the process of language acquisition of children, a phenomenon known as 'fast mapping' in developmental psychology.[2] I will now attempt to show how the hypothetico-deductive method is applied in explaining linguistic expressions.

6.3 THE HYPOTHETICO–DEDUCTIVE METHOD AND THE EXPLANATION OF LINGUISTIC EXPRESSIONS

As shown in detail in Section 5.3, a nexus of meaning can be transformed into a causal nexus if there is at least *one standpoint* from which two nexuses of meaning are similar. If one succeeds in showing that from one standpoint the fundamental elements of several nexuses of meaning show a similarity, then it is possible to maintain that the nexuses of meaning occur repeatedly over time. Just as there are three types of invariances in human action, so too there are three types of invariances in linguistic expressions: namely, *genetic, cultural,* or *personal.* If the fundamental elements of nexuses of meaning that arise in connection with the linguistic expressions of *all people* are similar in certain respects, then one speaks of *genetic invariances.* If the similarities of the fundamental elements arise in respect to the linguistic expressions of agents in *a social group,* then one speaks of *cultural invariances.* If the fundamental elements of the nexuses of meaning that arise in connection with a number of linguistic expressions of *one person* are in a certain respect similar, then one speaks of *personal invariances.*

Every time one manages to reveal invariances of the sort just mentioned, nexuses of meaning can de facto be transformed into causal nexuses. The corresponding statements that describe such causal nexuses are nomological statements. Meaningful events of this sort, namely, linguistic expressions, are thus also nomologically apprehensible as soon as invariances of one of the three types are detected. The hypothetico-deductive method can then be applied in those cases by subjecting these invariances in linguistic expressions to an explanation. The hypotheses that are found in the explanation of

---

[2] On 'fast mapping' see Gopnik, Meltzoff, and Kuhl (1999, 115f.). See also Pinker (1994, 269ff.).

linguistic expressions can, of course, vary greatly, and they can be formulated with the help of *various conceptual apparatuses*. The variants of the one-to-one theory or of those approaches that place the rationality of the authors in the foreground merely represent *some* possible ways of describing and explaining the respective nexuses of meaning. Although these possibilities can be fruitful, it is certainly unproductive to insist that all hypotheses about linguistic expressions ought to be formulated with the help of descriptions of the intentions or the rationality of the writer or speaker. In contrast, what ought to be looked for instead are law-like hypotheses, which do not refer a priori to the rationality of the author. In the past decade theoretical linguistics has specified a whole array of mechanisms, which explain *aspects* of the generation of linguistic expressions in detail without calling on rationality hypotheses in doing so and without referring to intentions.[3] Whether the respective mechanisms are to be interpreted as 'rational' or not plays no role whatsoever in explaining the respectively specified aspects.

It thus appears that just as there are *natural laws*, which disclose the invariances that arise in nature, and *behavioral laws*, which disclose the invariances that arise in human action, there are also *linguistic laws*, which disclose invariances in the production of linguistic expressions. As an example, reference should be made to Humboldt's classical

---

[3] See Chomsky's interesting remarks (2000, 49f.) in his critique of the prevailing conception of Anglo-Saxon philosophy of language, in which the phenomenon of language is often discussed in very general terms, such as, for example, in Dummett's (1986) approach, where language is generally viewed as a "social practice": "In this connection, it is perhaps worthwhile to recall some further truisms; in rational inquiry, in the natural scieces or elsewhere, there is no such subject as the 'study of everything.' Thus it is no part of physics to determine exactly how a particular body moves under the influence of every particle or force in the universe, with possible human intervention etc. This is not a topic. Rather, in rational inquiry we idealize to selected domains in such a way (we hope) as to permit us to discover crucial features of the world. Data and observations, in the sciences, have an instrumental character. They are of no particular interest in themselves, but only insofar as they constitute evidence that permits one to determine fundamental features of the real world, within a course of inquiry that is invariably undertaken under sharp idealizations, often implicit and simply common understanding, but always present. The study of 'language' in Dummett's sense verges on the 'study of everything,' and is therefore not a useful topic of inquiry, though one might hope, perhaps, to build up a study of *aspects* of such questions in terms of what comes to be understood about particular components of this hopeless amalgam" (emphasis added).

formulation that language involves "the infinite use of finite means" (1836/1998, §13, VII 99/ trans. D. A.). This refers to the ability to form a principally unlimited number of sentences. Everyone who masters a language possesses this ability – a matter that is treated in theoretical linguistics under the facets of the productivity and regularity of language: The productivity of language refers to the fact that an unlimited number of utterances are possible in every language; the regularity refers to the fact that these utterances exhibit similarities in many respects and are systematic in many ways. One elementary insight of theoretical linguistics, for example, is that there is no natural language without a grammar, that is, that in the production of linguistic expressions *all* speakers observe syntactic, semantic, and phonological rules *of one sort or another.* Insofar, this fact presents an invariance. What precisely these rules are, how their use can best be modeled, and whether the respective invariances are genetic or cultural in nature is the object of scientific discussions. But *that* all speakers use some form of grammar is an invariance that can be nomologically apprehended.[4]

---

[4] It is well known that Noam Chomsky advocates the controversial thesis that language acquisition is based on special inborn mechanisms; by this, he maintains that the respective invariance is genetic. See his commentary (2000, 60): "As is agreed on all sides, without innate structure there is no effect of the external environment in language (or other) growth; in particular, without innate structure Jones could not have developed in a specific way from embryo to person, and his language faculty could not have assumed the state of mature competence that underlies and accounts for Jones's behavior. The child is endowed with this innate structure and therefore grows to maturity along a course that is largely inner-directed; the task of the scientist is to discover what the innate endowment is and what is the nature of the state attained. Currently, the best theory is that the initial state of the language faculty incorporates certain general principles of language structure, including phonetic and semantic principles, and that the mature state of competence is a generative procedure that assigns structural descriptions to expressions and interacts with the motor and perceptual system and other cognitive systems of the mind/brain to yield semantic and phonetic interpretations of utterances. A vast range of empirical evidence is relevant in principle to determining just how this proposal should be spelled out in detail. Again, all of this is normal science, yielding theories that are true or false regarding Jones's competence and his initial state, part of the human biological endowment. Perhaps this approach should be abandoned in terms of some other conception, now unavailable; however, to establish this conclusion it does not suffice to demand that the linguist abandon the methods of the sciences." For an overview of some recent research results on the production of linguistic expressions, including the neurological basis of language processing, see the Annual Report (2002) of the Max Planck Institute for Psycholinguistics.

6.4 THE HYPOTHETICO-DEDUCTIVE METHOD AND THE INTERPRETATION OF TEXTS

In the previous section, I attempted to show that, with the help of the hypothetico-deductive method, nexuses of meaning that *repeatedly* occur in connection with certain written expressions can be transformed into causal nexuses and nomologically explained. There is, however, a whole array of nexuses of meaning that cannot be transformed into causal nexuses and thus are not nomologically apprehensible either. This is the case where two or more nexuses do not show similarities from any standpoint. One reason for this may be, by analogy to the more general case of human action, that written expressions are very often the result of creative activity and constitute therefore genuinely new matters of fact. But there can also be many other pragmatic reasons that a nexus of meaning is not nomologically apprehensible – for example, if written expressions or texts are handed down historically and one does not know the author or, as is common for law texts, they are the product of numerous unknown authors.

In all of these cases, the respective scientific problem is not best characterized as a search for an answer to a "why"–question, but as an attempt to answer a "what is the case?"–question or a "what was the case?"–question.[5] In the case of interest here, the scientific problem consists in identifying individual facts, and thus in accurately determining a nexus of meaning that is connected with a *specific* linguistic expression or a specific text. The aim of identifying the meaning of a spoken or written expression can be reached with the help of interpretation. Because I do not want to allow the treatment of the theme to run wild, in what follows I shall concentrate on interpretations of written expressions, above all, texts.

Now, there are many philosophical and methodological conceptions that focus on the problem of interpretation, and in the first part of the book we examined the role assigned to interpretation within the framework of philosophical hermeneutics. Given this,

---

[5] The scientific problem in these cases does not consist, thus, in seeking an explanation. I think therefore that Livingston (1988, 232ff.) is wrong when, in his otherwise very interesting book, he portrays the scientific problem in the case of literary research as the search for "literary explanations."

a few things are to be clarified before the problematic is in fact treated:

(i) *Interpreting* a text and *applying* a text are two distinct activities. In different disciplines there are very heterogeneous applications of textual content, depending upon the difference in the problems that those disciplines deal with (Bühler, 1999a, 128f.). Thus, in applying a legal text in the field of jurisprudence, one is concerned with regulating concrete social problems. The application of literary texts, on the other hand, consists in the reader's adoption of a particular view of life (ibid.). In our context, it is only important that, irrespective of how the application of textual content is thematized, this activity is not to be confounded with interpretation.[6]

(ii) *Interpreting* a text and *criticizing* a text are also two distinct activities. Interpretation, as we will see in a moment, is an activity that aims at ascertaining the *meaning* of a text, while textual criticism is an activity that is concerned with the *significance* of a text according to diverse evaluative standards.[7] Although textual commentaries often consist of a mixture of interpretation and textual criticism, it is nonetheless advisable to emphasize that these are two distinct activities. In textual criticism, evaluations and value judgments are in the foreground; in interpretation, the formulations of interpretive hypotheses.[8]

---

[6] See Section 3.2 for a more detailed treatment of this confusion.

[7] See the fitting commentary of Hirsch (1967, 7f.), who has rightly insisted on the distinction between meaning and significance: "Probably the most extreme examples of this phenomenon are cases of authorial self-repudiation, such as Arnold's public attack on his masterpiece, *Empedocles on Etna*, or Schelling's rejection of all the philosophy he had written before 1809. In these cases there cannot be the slightest doubt that the author's later response to his work was quite different from his original response. Instead of seeming beautiful, profound, or brilliant, the work seemed misguided, trivial, and false, and its meaning was no longer one that the author wished to convey. However, these examples do not show that the meaning of the work had changed, but precisely the opposite. If the work's meaning had changed (instead of the author himself and his attitudes), then the author would not have needed to repudiate his meaning and could have spared himself the discomfort of a public recantation. No doubt the *significance* of the work to the author had changed a great deal, but its meaning had not changed at all."

[8] See Hirsch (1967, 141f.): "The distinction between interpretation and criticism, meaning and significance, points to a phenomenon that is not limited to textual commentary. It represents a universal distinction that applies to all fields of study and

Having clarified this, it is now important to show that the activity of text interpretation does not involve an independent method, but that the hypothetico-deductive method applies here, too. Textual interpretation is about correctly identifying the meaning of a text. The scientific problem consists in accurately *reconstructing* the *nexus of meaning* that has arisen in connection with the text to be interpreted.[9] The nexus of meaning can be reconstructed either with the help of some variant of the one-to-one theory – for example, by indicating the author's intention – or with the help of principles of rationality, and these are in fact the descriptive systems that are often used in everyday research. In principle, however, reconstructions can be carried out with the most diverse conceptual apparatuses, and therefore the fundamental elements of the nexus of meaning can be expressed with quite diverse natural or artificial linguistic means.[10]

A reconstruction is an attempt to describe, that is, an attempt to accurately depict an individual event, and it is an answer to the question of the sort "what was the case?" As already emphasized, answers to questions of this sort assert the existence of individual facts. They are singular descriptive statements about individual events and are spatially and temporally determined. A reconstruction of the meaning

all subject matters. In the field of biography, for example, interpretation corresponds to the understanding of a man's life as it was lived and experienced, while criticism corresponds to the placing of that life in a larger system of relationships. It is one thing to trace the life of the Duke of Marlborough and another thing to discuss the significance of his life with respect to European political history in the seventeenth and eighteenth centuries, or to such exemplary moral values as prudence and patience, or to the development of constitutional monarchy. Biography would be a poor thing without such criticism, but everyone would agree that there is a difference between a man's life on the one hand, and its significance within various historical, moral and social contexts, on the other. Similarly, if one subject's matter is a still wider domain such as the English party system in the seventeenth century, it is one thing to describe that system, another to relate it to later developments in English politics. One's subject matter can be as large or as small as he likes, but the distinction between understanding the subject matter and placing it in some context or relationship will always be a viable one that will help him to keep in mind just what his subject matter is and just what aspects of its significance he wishes to lay bare."

9 Eugenio, Coseriu (1994, 124ff.), in his own theory, which builds on the classic Organon Model of Karl Bühler (1934/1999), denotes what I here call 'nexus of meaning' as 'Umfeld,' the scientific task being in his case to grasp the meaning taking into consideration the different 'Umfelder.'

10 Therefore, reconstructions are not to be confused with *rational* reconstructions, which are often developed in studies in the history of ideas. For the latter, see Bühler (2002).

of a text is thus an attempt at description, and it aims to correctly depict the act that produced the particular text in question. Because a text is bestowed with meaning when the author construes it against the background of his goals, his beliefs, and his other mental states by means of symbols, the point is to identify this meaning by correctly reconstructing the fundamental elements of this nexus.

In order to achieve this, one establishes interpretive *hypotheses*, and this is the first step in applying the hypothetico-deductive method. The system of propositions that constitutes these interpretive hypotheses is in principle hypothetical, because it is not certain whether it is apt to meet the epistemological goal or not, that is, if it is apt to identify the meaning of the text. In contrast to the prevailing opinion, there are no particular algorithms underlying the process of formulating interpretive hypotheses to elicit the meaning of the text.

In the discussion on what is known as 'radical interpretation' in the Anglo-Saxon world, one presupposes that the interpretation of written expressions must follow some specific interpretive principles. Quine (1960, 59) and Davidson (1984, 27) propose, for example, the 'principle of charity' as the general interpretive principle, which is supposed to be an imperative instrument for correct interpretation. In two of the most common versions, this principle requires that the interpreter assume that the conditions under which the author holds the sentences to be true are largely conditions under which these sentences are in fact true (the presumption of truth in general). Alternatively it requires that the interpreter presume that the sentences of the author are, in general, internally consistent and consistent with one another (presumption of consistency). Grandy (1973, 443) views the 'principle of humanity' as a guide – that is, the requirement that the pattern of relations among beliefs, desires, and the world ascribed to the author be as similar to our own patterns as possible.

The logical status of the principle of charity, the principle of humanity, and all the other principles of interpretation that were proposed in the older hermeneutic tradition or that are currently discussed in analytic philosophy of language[11] remains largely unaddressed. But in

---

[11] For a very informative overview of the general interpretive principles proposed since classical antiquity, see Scholz (2001, 17ff.). See also the interesting discussion in Bühler (1987) regarding interpetive maxims as technological rules for achieving

general, they are felt to be indispensable rules that must be used in every interpretation that strives to be correct. As Scholz (2001, part II) has convincingly elaborated, however, whether these principles are indispensable or not, they are in any case to be viewed as presumptive rules, that is, as empirical rules that can fail to stand up to experience.[12] So, every presumption can break down in the light of experience, a view that – interestingly enough – is already to be found in Meier's (1757/1996, §39) formulation of the principle of charity: "The hermeneutic equity (aequitas hermeneutica) is the tendency of the interpreter to hold that meaning for hermeneutically true that best comports with the flawlessness of the originator of the sign, *until the opposite is shown*" (emphasis added).[13] Whether the usage of those presumptive rules is constitutive for the practice of interpretation can be left undecided. It seems to me in any case that their apparent indispensability is to be traced to the fact that they have been particularly well corroborated, because they have often been employed with success. It is thus only their higher degree of corroboration that disposes one to presume that they are indispensable for every interpretation.[14]

knowledge. Sinclair (2002) discusses the radical interpretation from a naturalistic perspective. See also the interesting overview article by Føllesdal (2001).

[12] See Scholz (2001, 239): "What remains decisive for the empirical character is that the proposed interpretations can be thwarted by experience. Every individual presumption also remains open to correction, or even refutation by emprical knowledge; in every individual case the presumed matters of fact can turn out not to be the case. The general interpretation principles are, as we have continually emphasized, presumptive rules, with refutable presumptions." (trans. D. A.)

[13] See also Gomperz's fitting remarks (1939, 74f.): "If we were justified in assuming that context is *always* unobjectionable and that, therefore, we are justified in 'correcting' a text, or in forcing an artificial interpretation upon it, as soon as it seems to lack perfect congruity, connectedness and consistency, there could, *by definition*, be no such thing as a fault in grammar, desultory thinking, and fallacious reasoning. We may go further and ask the question: Do people never talk or write nonsense? If they do, can it be right to follow a method according to which we should be warranted in rejecting any interpretation, or even the traditional wording, of a text, solely on the ground that it 'does not make sense'?"

[14] It is interesting to note that Hirsch emphasized the heuristic character of interpretive rules and maxims in his classical monograph. See Hirsch (1967, 203): "What then is the status of the many traditional canons and maxims of interpretation, and what is their purpose? Clearly, they are provisional guides, or rules of thumb. In the absence of compelling indications to the contrary we follow them because they hold true more often than not. [. . .] More often than not a legal text will mean the same thing when it uses the same words – and there are very plausible reasons why this should be so. [. . .] two consequences follow with regard to their intelligent application. First, the canon

After the interpretive hypotheses are formulated, they must be empirically tested. They are tested on the basis of the available evidence, which is primarily made accesible with the help of research techniques from the social sciences and the humanities.[15] This evidence can be drawn from what the author says about his own work, but it can also encompass anything else that the author has ever written. Besides that, the details of rhyme, rhythm, or other literary stylistic means can be taken into consideration, as can the frequency with which words occur in the text and similar such evidence.[16] In any case, it is important to

is more reliable the narrower its intended range of application. Practical canons that apply to a very strictly limited class of texts will be more reliable for those texts than canons which lay claim to broader application. Second, since any interpretive canon can be overturned by subsuming the text under a still narrower class in which the canon fails to hold or holds by such a small majority that it becomes doubtful, it follows that interpretive canons are often relatively useless baggage. When they are general, they cannot compel decisions, and even when they are narrowly practical, they can be overturned. The important point about a rule of thumb is that it is not a rule." Regarding the heuristic function of interpretive principles, see also Scholz (2001, 163).

[15] It ought to be clear that the development of such research techniques is, of course, based on nomological knowledge. Insofar, in testing interpretive hypotheses, nomological knowledge is drawn upon implicitly, if not explicitly. What is decisive is only that this knowledge, i.e., the respective law-like statements, have been tested in contexts other than the one under consideration, that is, independently, and have been validated. The law-like statements can be rather trivial – for example, that every written document is written by a person – but that is not to say that they play no role whatsoever.

[16] In his famous article "What Is Stylistics and Why Are They Saying Such Terrible Things About It?" Stanley Fish (1980, ch. 2) launched a much-cited attack on the use of formal features in determining the meaning of a text. In the process of unfolding his influential argument, he pleaded for a shift of the focus of attention "from the spatial context of a page and its observable regularities to the temporal context of a mind and its experience" (91). In his supposedly improved version of stylistics that he called 'affective stylistics,' "[t]he demand for precision will be even greater because the object of analysis is a process whose shape is continually changing. In order to describe that shape, it will be necessary to make use of all the information that formal characterizations of language can provide, although that information will be viewed from a different perspective. Rather than regarding it as directly translatable into what a word of a pattern *means*, it will be used more exactly to specify what a reader, as he comes upon that word or pattern, is *doing*, what assumptions he is making, what conclusions he is reaching, what expectations he is forming, what attitudes he is entertaining, what acts he is being moved to perform" (91f.). His argument seems to be confused, however, because it does not distinguish between the formulation and the testing of interpretive hypotheses. In his conception, stylistics are used in order to somehow describe the process of the generation of interpretive hypotheses; in the conception defended in the text, stylistics are, to the contrary, used as (one among other pieces of) evidence in the process of testing interpretive hypotheses.

emphasize that in listing the various features that are supposed to support the respective interpretive hypothesis, it is not only the number of features that is important; so are the types of features that we are dealing with (Føllesdal et al. 1988, 114).[17]

On the basis of such empirical material, the interpretive hypotheses are checked; the question then arises of how good interpretations are to be differentiated from bad ones. The concern in these interpretive hypotheses, as already emphasized, is with correctly depicting the nexus of meaning that has arisen with a given text. Like every other scientific activity, interpretation can also be characterized as an enterprise that can in principle be oriented on the idea of truth.[18] In the case of interpretation, truth, as the accurate depiction of facts, can also serve as a regulative idea, on the basis of which interpretative hypotheses can be evaluated. Interpretations, as reconstructions of nexuses of meaning, are hypotheses precisely by virtue of the fact that one searches for reasons for their truth or falsity.[19] The various

---

[17] For more on evidence in the establishment of interpretative hypotheses, see the still relevant study by Gomperz (1939, 59ff.). See also Føllesdal (1979, 327): "[W]hen one interprets a text [...] one proceeds hypothetico-deductively. We set forth an hypothesis concerning the text or possibly the work as a whole and test this hypothesis by checking how its consequences fit in with the various details in the text. These details may be rhyme, rhythm and other literary devices. If, for example, a work is kept strictly in a rhythm that suddenly is broken, a satisfactory interpretation of the text, together with a stylistic theory of rhythm, should enable us to derive a conclusion which fits in with the break in the rhythm." See also Rescher (1997, 200f.): "For text interpretation is clearly an evidential exercise where one has to make the best possible use of the relevant data over a wide range of information because a wide variety of hermeneutical factors must come into play:

    – What the text itself explicitly affirms.
    – Other relevant discussions by the author bearing on the issues that the text addresses.
    – Biographical evidence regarding the author's education, interests, contacts, relevant interactions with contemporaries, and the like.
    – Considerations of 'intellectual history' regarding the state of knowledge and opinion in the author's place and time, and the cultural translation within which the text originated.
    – Philological data regarding the use of terms and expressions in the time and place where the text was produced."

[18] The *possibility* of orienting the activity of interpretation on the idea of truth can serve as a bridge between the 'two cultures' whose existence Snow diagnosed so accurately in his famous Rede Lecture in 1959. See Snow (1993).

[19] The provision of sufficient empirical evidence is the condition sine qua non for establishing claims to truth. See the engaging and convincing critique of Tallis (1999)

reconstructions of nexuses of meaning offered are to be compared to each other with regard to their truth, and those to be preferred that most accurately reconstruct the respective nexuses of meaning.

In order to substantiate these claims, I would like to provide two examples: one of a popular text and one of a scientific text.[20] First, consider the following text taken from the Yahoo travel guide describing the Acropolis in Athens:

A splendid religious complex, the Acropolis consists of several temples, which were built by the world's first democracy during the 5th century B.C. The most majestic building of all is the Parthenon, a temple dedicated to the goddess Athena. The Parthenon became the paragon of classical Greek architecture, and has suffered serious damage over the years, though a renovation is underway and construction may limit access to some portions. A small museum features an outstanding collection of ancient Greek sculptures.

Here are three concise interpretive hypotheses of this text:

1. The text deals with the soccer game of Germany versus Brazil. This was the Final match in the 2002 World Cup championship, which took place on June 30, 2002. Brazil captured its fifth World Cup championship with a 2–0 win over Germany in Yokohama, Japan. (South Korea and Japan hosted the fifth World Cup championship, the first time in history that such an event took

showing how a series of postmodernist theorists seem to favor, on the contrary, "evidence-free generalizations" that are usually of colossal scope.

[20] For examples of the testing of interpretive hypotheses in literary studies, see Føllesdal (1979) and Göttner (1973, ch. 1). In connection with the detailed discussion of a very interesting example, Göttner sums up her conclusions as follows (60): "We come to the upshot of this analysis of argumentation in the field of literary studies: We could not find any place where literature scholars have argued in accord with a dfferent method than that described by general empirical methodology. We noticed a particularity of argumentation in literary studies in that there is hardly a single argument that is posed without a series of related sub-hypotheses – something that makes the process of validation somewhat complicated. This fact may have contributed to the hermeneutical misunderstanding, i.e. that because of the existence of, in principle, untestable presuppositions, no interpretation can achieve a form of 'scientific objectivity.' By contrast we saw that, despite the complex validation process in literary studies, there are, in principle, no untestable presuppositions. In the worst case they are practicaly untestable. (Perhaps hermeneuticists falsely hold this virtual untestability for untestablity in principle.) In better cases the sub-hypotheses are not even untested, and in the best case they are directly confirmed by observations. 'Scientific objectivity' is thus possible for interpretations precisely to the degree that the hypotheses that occur in them are confirmed."

place in Asia.) The World Cup championship is a clear case of a democratic institution conceived in the Parthenon, a temple dedicated to Athena, the goddess who was born from the head of Zeus.

2. The meaning of the text is that the customer of the café in the small museum of the Acropolis can choose among twenty-three different sorts of ice cream. This great variety of flavors includes chocolate, vanilla, strawberry, mango, and caramel. Besides, one can order Coup Denmark, a banana split, and a Chicago. On hot summer days, the café is very crowded by tourists exhausted after climbing the Acropolis hill, the most important site of the city of Athens. Ice cream was dedicated to the city's patron goddess, Athena, during the four-day festival of the Panathenea.

3. This text provides a short description of the Acropolis in Athens, where a number of buildings of a religious character can be found, built during the fifth century B.C. The most important one is the Parthenon, a temple dedicated to Athena, the goddess who was born from the head of Zeus and was the city's patron. The Parthenon remains the main symbol of classical architecture as well as of the first democratic regime in the world, though damaged – most severely in an explosion in 1687 caused by a bomb during the siege of the Acropolis by the Venetians. Renovations are taking place, and thus some parts of the monument may not be open to the public for some time. The museum of the Acropolis contains a series of impressive Greek sculptures from different historic periods, the relief of the Mourning Athena among others.

If one compares these three interpretations, then I think that it is obvious – even without a meticulous consideration of the empirical evidence – that the first and second are false interpretations of the text from the travel guide, whereas the third is a true one. This simple example demonstrates that an evaluation of interpretive hypotheses with respect to their truth is possible: even when one lacks standardized truth criteria, reconstructions of nexuses of meaning can be compared to each other with regard to truth as a regulative idea.

There are, of course, harder cases. I would like to discuss such a case with the help of an example from a scientific work. The example that I want to refer to is the interpretation of the invisible hand in Adam Smith's work *An Inquiry into the Nature and Causes of the Wealth of Nations* (1776/1976). I choose this example because of its salience in the social sciences. Book IV, Chapter II of this classic work (477f.) is as follows:

But the annual revenue of every society is always precisely equal to the exchangeable value of the whole annual produce of its industry, or rather is precisely the same thing with that exchangeable value. As every individual, therefore, endeavours as much as he can both to employ his capital in the support of domestic industry, and so to direct that industry that its produce may be of the greatest value; every individual necessarily labours to render the annual revenue of the society as great as he can. He generally, indeed, neither intends to promote the public interest, nor knows how much he is promoting it. By preferring the support of domestic to that of foreign industry, he intends only his own security; and by directing that industry in such a manner as its produce may be of the greatest value, he intends only his own gain, and he is in this, as in many other cases, led by an invisible hand to promote an end which was no part of his intention. Nor is it always the worse for the society that it was no part of it. By pursuing his own interest he frequently promotes that of the society more effectually than when he really intends to promote it. I have never known much good done by those who affected to trade for the public good. It is an affectation, indeed, not very common among merchants, and very few words need be employed in dissuading them from it.

This passage was the focus of interest of many scholars in the twentieth century, and there has been much discussion about the meaning of the invisible hand. I would like to distinguish among three interpretations of this passage:

1. There is the standard interpretation of the invisible hand, that is, the interpretation that is usually found in most histories of economic thought and that most students of markets and political systems seem to endorse: A society of self-interested people constrained by criminal law and law of property and contract is capable of an orderly disposition of its economic resources; such a society need not be anarchic and is indeed coherent with order (Hahn, 1982, 1). The order of the economic system of such a society is usually conceptualized as a system of a general equilibrium that can be shown to prevail in an economic system if a series of assumptions are made.

This reconstruction of the nexus of meaning of this specific passage is supported by evidence usually drawn from the general argument of

Adam Smith's book concerning the merits of "the obvious and simple system of natural liberty" (Bk. IV, Ch. IX, 208) as well as his elaboration on the theory of price (Bk. I, most importantly Ch. VII). This standard interpretation is supported by further evidence drawn from another famous passage to be found in his other major work, *The Theory of Moral Sentiments* (1759/1976, 184):

> The capacity of [the proud and unfeeling landlord's] stomach bears no proportion to the immensity of his desires, and will receive no more than that of the meanest peasant. The rest he is obliged to distribute among those, who prepare, in the nicest manner, that little which he makes use of, among those who fit up the palace in which this little is to be consumed, among those who provide and keep in order all the different baubles and trinkets which are employed in the economy of greatness; all of whom thus derive from his luxury and caprice, that share of the necessaries of life which they would in vain have expected from his humanity or his justice. The produce of the soil maintains at all times nearly that number of inhabitants which it is capable of maintaining. The rich only select from the heap what is most precious and agreeable. They consume little more than the poor, and in spite of their natural selfishness and rapacity, though they mean only their own conveniency, though the sole end which they propose from the labours of all the thousands whom they employ, be the gratification of their own vain and insatiable desires, they divide with the poor the produce of all their improvements. They are led by an invisible hand to make nearly the same distribution of the necessaries of life, which would have been made, had the earth been divided into equal portions among all its inhabitants, and thus without intending it, without knowing it, advance the interest of the society, and afford means to the multiplication of the species.

The standard interpretation of the invisible hand is supported further by the analysis of works of other authors of the Scottish Enlightenment who held similar views (e.g., Starbatty, 1985) and by the analysis of the ideas prevailing in France, especially among the so-called Physiocrats of the eighteenth century (Ott/Winkel, 1985, 46ff.).

2. Alec MacFie (1971) was the first to draw attention to a third locus in the Smithian opus where the invisible hand is mentioned: In his *History of Astronomy*, originally published in the *Essays on Philosophical Subjects* (1795/1980), Adam Smith in a section dealing with the "Origins of Philosophy" refers to the savage "in the first ages of society" (p. 48) and points out (p. 49):

> With him, therefore, every object of nature, which by its beauty or greatness, its utility or hurtfulness, is considerable enough to attract his attention, and whose

operations are not perfectly regular, is supposed to act by the direction of some invisible and designing power. [. . .] Hence the origin of Polytheism, and of that vulgar superstition which ascribes all the irregular events of nature to the favour or displeasure of intelligent, though visible beings, to gods, daemons, witches, genii, fairies. For it may be observed, that in all Polytheistic religions, among savages, as well as in the early ages of Heathen antiquity, it is the irregular events of nature only that are ascribed to the agency and power of their gods. Fire burns, and water refreshes; heavy bodies descend, and lighter substances fly upwards, by the necessity of their own nature; nor was the invisible hand of Jupiter ever apprehended to be employed in those matters. But thunder and lightning, storms and sunshine, those more irregular events were ascribed to his favour, or his anger. Man, the only designing power with which they were acquainted, never acts but either to stop, or to alter the course, which natural events would take, if left to themselves. Those other intelligent beings, whom they imagined, but knew not, were naturally supposed to act in the same manner; not to employ themselves in supporting the ordinary course of things, which went on of its own accord, but to stop, to thwart, and to disturb it.

MacFie notes that the function of the "invisible hand of Jupiter" in the *History of Astronomy* appears to be exactly the reverse of that of the Christian deity of the *Moral Sentiments* and the *Wealth of Nations* (p. 595): "In the *Essay*, the regular 'orderly course of things' by which 'fire burns and water refreshes' is capriciously stopped, thwarted, and disturbed so as to satisfy the god's 'favour' or 'anger'. In the two books, on the contrary, the Deity acts to preserve and develop the purposes of 'Nature' when they are disturbed by men – the only other 'designing power' which, in Smiths description (the 'savage' here, but obviously men at any time) can disturb them."

What we have before us, thus, is a new piece of evidence, that is, a passage of another work of the same author where the meaning of the invisible hand seems to be a different one. The scientific problem consists in accurately reconstructing the nexus of the meaning that has arisen in connection with the notion of the invisible hand in the *Wealth of Nations*; MacFie establishes the following interpretive hypothesis, aiming at an accurate reconstruction using the principle of charity (p. 596):

Perhaps it should be stated here that while the *capricious* role of the "invisible hand of Jupiter" is quite different from that of the order-preserving "invisible hand" in the two books, there is no inconsistency. The explanation is the view of history typical of the Enlightenment. In the *Essay* Jupiter represents the ignorant "savage's view", long before the seventeenth- and eighteenth-century understanding of the divine order, mainly preserved through social individuals, had been worked out. The invisible hand passages of the two books in fact describe Adam Smith's interpretation of how the natural order of "providence" animates and directs the orderly development of these societies (as well, of course, as the physical universe). One is reminded of the first and third ages of Vico – the age of the gods and the age of men. But similar interpretations of history were common in the Scottish eighteenth-century school.

It is obvious that this interpretive hypothesis is constructed following the principle of charity: The interpreter, MacFie, presumes that the sentences of the author, Adam Smith, are in general internally consistent and consistent with one another. This allows him to set forth a hypothesis concerning the invisible hand that provides a unitary interpretation and makes a number of different and specific features of the work all fit into place.

3. Emma Rothschild has proposed a novel interpretative hypothesis of the invisible hand according to which Smith did not particularly esteem the invisible hand and thought of it as an ironic though useful joke (1994, 319). Rothschild (1994; 2002, ch. 5) tries to reconstruct the nexus of meaning, drawing on four sorts of evidence: (i) One reason to suspect that Smith was not entirely enthusiastic about theories of the invisible hand is that these theories are condescending or contemptuous about the intentions of individual agents. Smiths three uses of the phrase have in common that the individuals concerned are quite undignified; they are silly polytheists, rapacious proprietors, disingenuous merchants" (1994, 320). For an author such as Smith who is otherwise known to be a defender of individual liberty and of the independence of individuals, such an account of the invisible hand seems to be contradictory, if seriously meant. (ii) The invisible hand presupposes the existence of a theorist who can view what the rest cannot; this knowingness of the theorist is characteristic of eighteenth- and nineteenth-century doctrines of unintended consequences but is quite unlike Adam Smith. (iii) The invisible hand should not be viewed as the expression of Smith's religious (or, more specifically, deistic) beliefs, that is, as the hand of the Christian deity. Smith was in fact quite critical of established religion throughout his work, and his comments on religion, like Hume's, are often ironic and also conscious of pious public opinion. Hence, other passages in his work are

also ironic rather than pious, as when he, for example, speaks of the "all-wise Being, who directs all the movements of nature; and who is determined, by his own unalterable perfections, to maintain in it, at all times, the greatest possible quantity of happiness" (Smith, 1759/1976, 235). (iv) Since Smith's criticisms of government and institutions are central to his political economy, and since he has himself proposed an institutional design for consciously influencing the economic life of a nation by way of appropriate political institutions, it is rather improbable that he would simply forget this when presenting the merits of the functioning of an invisible hand.

Rothschild's interpretive hypothesis, thus, based on different sorts of evidence, provides an interpretation of the invisible hand that is contrary to the standard interpretation and different from the interpretation of MacFie.

The evaluation of these three interpretive hypotheses with respect to their truth is, of course, much more difficult than in the first example. All three of them are based on deductions of a number of consequences from them that, along with other empirical evidence, are shown to fit in with the passage of the invisible hand in the *Wealth of Nations*. Especially in the case of the standard interpretation, there is evidence not only from other similar passages of the same author but also from other authors and from the intellectual environment that Smith was part of. This interpretation is thus founded on solid empirical evidence.

In MacFie's interpretation, on the other hand, there is only consideration of the three passages in which Smith mentions the invisible hand. He deduces from its use in the *Wealth of Nations* and in the *Theory of Moral Sentiments*, along with the premise that Smith endorsed Deism, the consequence that the function of the invisible hand was to preserve the purposes of "Nature" in the social realm and thus to help bring order in a society of self-interested individuals. From the use of the "invisible hand of Jupiter" in the *Essay*, along with the premise that the lecture notes on which the *Essay* was based stem from his juvenile work (MacFie, 1971, 598), he draws the conclusion that the function of the invisible hand was not to maintain order, but rather to disturb it according to god's "favour" and "anger." In order to deal with this contradiction, he proposes that the change in the role of the invisible hand is a matter of literary taste. "Throughout his works, Smith employed and enjoyed pithy, forceful phrases" and simply "remembered the 'invisible hand of Jupiter' [b]ut he inevitably reversed its relation to the natural order" (p. 598). This is not very convincing, however. Taking also into consideration that only the three passages are used as evidence, it seems that this interpretation is the least valid of the three.

For Rothschild's interpretation speaks the solid evidence based on the consideration of a large amount of relevant material. On the other hand, it seems to be the case that there is something crucial that is not adequately considered by Rothschild. In the passage of the *Wealth of Nations*, one very important sentence is the following: "By pursuing his own interest he *frequently* promotes that of the society more effectually than when he really intends to promote it" (emphasis added). This seems to weaken Rothschild's evidence referred to especially under (i) and (iv).

Concluding, it seems to be the case that the second interpretation should be disregarded and that there is enough evidence to support both the standard interpretation and the interpretation of Rothschild. As is common in science, the empirical evidence does not allow one in this case to clearly favor one interpretive hypothesis, and the only rational attitude is to abstain from a judgment regarding the truth of the respective hypotheses.

Let me summarize the argument: Like every scientific activity, interpretation is primarily concerned with generating hypotheses and testing them on the basis of evidence. Generating hypotheses is normally a creative act, which, precisely like the generation of other scientific hypotheses, hardly follows an algorithm: There is no procedure, logical or otherwise, there are no principles that necessarily lead to the generation of a correct interpretation of a text.[21] But, by requiring that

---

[21] See Coseriu (1994, 150): "Verschiedene Linguisten sind offenbar der Ansicht, daß es Ziel der Bemühungen um die Textlinguistik sein müsse, ein allgemeingültiges Verfahren für die Textinterpretation zu entwickeln, eine Art von 'Entdeckungsverfahren', das uns – etwas überpointiert formuliert – die 'richtige' Interpretation jedes beliebigen Textes liefert, wenn es nur 'wissenschaftlich korrekt' angewendet wird. Das ist gerade nicht möglich. Wir können nie im voraus wissen, welche Zeichenrelationen in einem bestimmten Text fertiggestellt werden können, wenn wir diesen Text in seiner Individualität betrachten wollen. [...] Es gibt kein mechanisches Verfahren, alle denkbaren Möglichkeiten 'aufzuzählen' oder gar 'vorauszusagen.'" See also Hirsch (1967, 203): "The notion that a reliable methodology of interpretation can be built upon a set of canons is thus a mirage. [...] No possible set of rules or

the interpreters test their interpretations on the basis of the data, the hypothetico-deductive method ensures that the problem of validity is solved.[22]

6.5 THE RECONSTRUCTION OF A NEXUS OF MEANING AND THE AUTHOR'S INTENTION

Since the publication of Wimsatt and Beardsley's (1946) classical article and their formulation of the intentional fallacy, which states that "the design or intention of the author is neither available nor desirable as a standard for judging the success of literary work of art" (468),[23] an intensive discussion about the methodological role of the author's intention in interpretation has been carried out at many levels. This discussion has, above all, shown that the intention of the author can be conveyed. In principle, it is possible to identify the author's intentions as long as the sources and the transmission of the text allow this (Bühler, 1999b, 62ff.), and it is even possible to specify the (communicative) intention of the author in fictional texts in highlightening how he moves those he is addressing to "act as if" the contents of fictional speech were real.[24] Besides, the debate concerning the conception of Hermeneutic Intentionalism (*Hermeneutischer Intentionalismus*) has shown that the intention of the author is

rites of preparation can generate or compel an insight into what an author means. [...] The methodical activity of interpretation commences when we begin to test and criticize our guesses. These two sides of the interpretive process, the hypothetical and the critical, are not of course neatly separated when we are pondering a text, for we are constantly testing our guesses both large and small as we gradually build up a coherent structure of meaning. [...] But the fact that these two activities require and accompany one another in the process of understanding should not lead us to confuse the whimsical lawlessness of guessing with the ultimately methodical character of testing. Both processes are necessary in interpretation, but only one of them is governed by logical principles."

[22] Insofar as the validity of the interpretation results from the criticism that relies on empirical means and is oriented on the idea of truth, the principle of critical examination is manifest in this application of the hypothetico-deductive method. In this context, it is to be pointed out that the principle of critical examination is broader than the falsification principle. Insofar the requirement of "criticizability" does not share a number of weaknesses of the requirement of falsifiability – primarily the fact that the latter is not applicable to itself. See Vollmer (1999, 119ff.).

[23] In later publications Wimsatt formulated the intentional fallacy differently. For a discussion see Hermerén (1975, 6off.)

[24] For a more detailed discussion of the literature, see Bühler (1999b, 66ff.).

a completely desirable interpretive objective (Bühler, 1993a, 1993b, 1995b). Insofar, the intentional fallacy is not a real fallacy; the intention of the author is in fact a possible and desirable objective of interpretation.

Whether conveying the intention of the author is the *only* legitimate objective of an interpretation is a different question. The fierce controversy that periodically rearises about this question seems to me to be resolvable if the technological character of hermeneutics is borne in mind.[25] As a technological discipline, hermeneutics does not need to commit to a particular goal of interpretation; it only needs to presume its *hypothetical* validity. The objectives connected with the scientific activity of textual interpretation need not be reduced to a common denominator; nor need some of them be sacrificed for the sake of others. Although a discussion about the significance of the various objectives of interpretation can, of course, be carried out with the help of rational arguments, it must not necessarily end up with results that are binding for everyone. Rather, it is sufficient to presuppose the hypothetical validity of a certain objective of interpretation and then to formulate and test alternative hypotheses in relation to this objective. The standards for the comparative evaluation of interpretive hypotheses can be oriented on various regulative ideas. For example, above we

---

[25] A controversy about this issue took place in recent volumes of the journal *Poetics Today*, dedicated to the fruitfulness of the cognitive sciences for literary theory. Some parties to the debate were against using the recent findings of cognitive science for the study of literature, some parties were in favor of it, but most parties seemed to be confused regarding this question. It is apparent, I think, from the two quotations that follow that the authors, among other things, refuse to commit themselves to specific objectives of (literary) interpretations. Adler and Gross, in their critique of cognitivism in the study of literature, point out (2002, 214): "Note that the category of truth does not enter into the equation; the issue is one of adequacy of approach, and that in turn depends on one's view of the subject in question. Literary analysis is much less predicated upon correctness or probability of findings or the incontrovertibility of evidence. Instead, its 'success' relies on such parameters as originality, appropriateness, inventiveness, or 'insight value': it may be measured by our degree of satisfaction with what is revealed or illuminated about a text." The editors of the original volume, Alan Richardson and Francis Steen, in their reply to the criticism of Adler and Gross, note (2003, 155): "It is our firm conviction that science will not and cannot provide authoritative answers to the meaning and significance of literary works.[. . .] Taking a vital interest in the models, theories and findings emerging from work in the cognitive science and neurosciences does not commit one to a scientific methodology, any more than taking an interest in psychoanalysis commits Freudian or Lacanasian literary critics to a therapeutic discipline."

have seen that the interpretive hypotheses about the meaning of a text can be assessed in relation to the idea of truth. But it is also possible to interpret a text in reference to other objectives – for example, aesthetic ones.[26] And when this is done, other standards and regulative ideas such as beauty, would be applicable. The correspondent technological systems can be designed with regard to these ideas without necessarily viewing the respective objectives as binding.

Besides, it is also to be emphasized that, from the perspective argued for here, what is called the 'identity thesis' – in accord with which the author's intention constitutes the text's meaning (Danneberg and Müller, 1983, 118) – seems one-sided. It *may* well be that the specification of the author's intention proves to be adequate for the description of the nexus of meaning, but the reconstruction of the nexus of meaning can also be more complex than that. As was shown earlier, in reconstructing the nexus of meaning, it is not necessary to comply with a certain descriptive system; consequently, the process of reconstruction is not committed to the concept of intention. Since what is to be constructed is a whole nexus of meaning, a completely different descriptive system can be used, which makes it possible to grasp the meaning more adequately. Or it is possible to use the intention of the author and, in addition, to incorporate an analysis of the grammatical elements, or some other elements, in order to make a correct reconstruction.

It is thus obvious that interpretation is a process of reconstructing nexuses of meaning, serving purposes diametrically opposed to those of deconstruction – the philosophical school, which, following Derrida, appears to be quite well received in some quarters.[27] And it is,

---

[26] There is a common claim in the literature that texts should be interpreted with reference to other objectives than truth, a claim that is both plausible and correct. However, in hermeneutics as a technological discipline, the same set of interpretations can be evaluated with respect to different standards or criteria and found to be fulfilling some of them while not fulfilling others. An interpretation can be, for example, original but at the same time false.

[27] As Rescher (1997, 201) has appropriately noted in this context: "The crucial point, then, is that any text has an envisioning historical and cultural *context* and that the context of a text is itself not simply textual – not something that can be played out solely and wholly in the textual domain. This context of the texts that concern us constrains and delimits the viable interpretations that these texts are able to bear. The process of *deconstruction* – of interpretatively dissolving any and every text into a plurality of supposedly merit-equivalent constructions – can and should be offset by

of course, to be emphasized that reconstructions are procedures that can be oriented on the idea of truth; or in other words, it is possible to differentiate fitting reconstructions from unfitting ones.[28] Stressing the fact that every interpreter understands every text differently and that what he understands is also (subjectively) true – a message that, as we have seen, Gadamer also wants to convey – confounds the process of conveying meaning with the process of finding truth. It is one thing to claim that every interpreter who is confronted with a text can, in principle, interpret it differently; it is another thing to find out which of the interpretive hypotheses is true and which is false. The first case deals with a mental process that takes place in the brain of the interpreter; the second, with the question of the validity of the interpretation. Thus far, I have concentrated on the second case and have attempted to show how the hypothetico-deductive method can be applied in this context. Now I would like to

---

the process of *reconstruction* which calls for viewing texts within their larger contexts. After all, texts inevitably have a setting – historical, cultural, authorial – on which their actual meaning is critically dependent."

[28] This task is, of course, burdened with many difficulties, but that does not mean that skepticism is justified, such as Rorty (1992, 102f.) argues for, which doubts that there are good reasons for or against the truth of a textual interpretation: "The thought that a commentator has discovered what a text is really doing [. . .] is, for us pragmatists, just more occultism." Cf. Bühler's commentary (1998, 94f.) on arguments against such skepticism: "According to the skeptical thesis, the various tasks that are assigned to the research in the human sciences cannot be fulfilled. Observe, for example, one of the tasks, namely that of determining the communicative intentions of the author. Applying the skeptical thesis to this task, one must deny that good reasons can be offered for identifying the communicative intention of other persons. – *For* this standpoint it is often advanced that we can have no certainty about the thinking of others and that there is thus no means to determine what others think. From the fact that there is no certainty about a state of affairs, however, it does not follow that there is no means to determine the characteristics of a state of affairs, and above all, that no good reasons can be given for beliefs about states of affairs. Besides: that it is impossible to attain certainty with respect to a hypothesis holds for all knowledge, especially for knowledge about empirical reality. It is not only in interpersonal understanding, not only in the social sciences and the humanities that we cannot attain certainty, but also in the natural sciences. – *Another* justification of the skeptical denial that there are good reasons for hypotheses about the thinking of others runs into special difficulties that are connected with the identification of the mental states of other people. 'We can indeed sensually perceive the behavior of others. However, we have no access to the mental states of others, because their mental states are not the object of sensual perception'. This argument ignores the fact that knowing of every kind includes inferences about not directly perceptible entities. This also applies to knowing the mental processes of others" (trans. D. A.).

turn to the first case and show that the hypothetico-deductive method can also adequately apprehend understanding as a subjective mental process.

6.6 ON THE EXPLANATION OF THE UNDERSTANDING OF TEXTS

If understanding is interpreted as a subjective mental process, that is, as a form of knowledge, then the issue that we must deal with *in concreto* concerns the understanding of texts. When one attempts to understand a text, a nexus of meaning arises, since a series of signs and sentences are construed by the reader. The fundamental elements of this nexus of meaning occur repeatedly, so that a transformation into a causal nexus is possible. The hypothetico-deductive method can thus be applied in the most common way, namely, so as to nomologically capture the corresponding invariances. *The mental process of understanding texts can thus be explained by showing which regularities underlie this process.*

But what precisely is to be explained? In 'understanding' texts, a whole array of mental processes occur, and, as in understanding persons, in each case the specific problem consists in identifying the corresponding regularities. I would like to address three such mental processes here. First, given that symbols or sentences are perceived, understanding is to be viewed as a special case of *perception*. I need not work out *in extenso* the commonplace view in the research on the psychology of perception that the cognitive system of the perceiver actively interprets the objects that confront it, in this case the texts. The more interesting question is rather how the interpretive component of the perception process can be modeled. Since the perception of signs is nothing more than a subcategory of the perception of objects, the mechanisms underlying the perception of signs, such as, for example, the classification of patterns, can in principle be modeled in the same way as in the general case of the perception of objects (Anderson 2002, ch. 2).

It is important in this context to emphasize that in the perceptual process, first, the written expression is encoded before, at a second stage, the syntactic and semantic analysis known as *parsing* can follow. Parsing is the process by which the words in the expression are transformed into a mental representation with the combined meaning of the words. During this procedure, the meaning of a sentence is processed phrase by phrase, and the exact formulation of the phrases is accessed only while processing its meaning (Anderson 2002, 392). People integrate both semantic and syntactic cues in order to achieve an understanding of a statement or text. As Steven Pinker (1994, 227) has correctly noted: "Understanding, then, requires integrating the fragments gleaned from a sentence into a vast mental database. For that to work, speakers cannot just toss one fact after another into a listener's head. Knowledge is not like a list of facts in a trivial column but is organized into a complex network. When a series of facts comes in succession, as in a dialogue or text, the language must be structured so that the listener can place each fact into an existing framework."

It thus appears that in understanding, the principle of the immediacy of interpretation is at work. In accord with this principle, as soon as a word occurs, people attempt to extract as much meaning as possible from it: They do not to wait until a sentence is completed to decide on how to interpret a word – a finding brought to light by the experiments of Just and Carpenter (1980), among others.[29] If a sentence contains unfamiliar words that cannot be understood immediately, then one spends additional time at the end of the phrase or the sentence to integrate the meaning. This principle of the immediacy of interpretation appears to be closely related to the problematic of the hermeneutic circle, which I treated in detail in Section 2.4. As has been shown there, the problem of the relationship between the meaningful whole and its constitutive elements, and vice versa, does not arise when testing interpretive hypotheses but when generating them. It refers to a phenomenon that arises when it is not possible to understand linguistic expressions immediately, that is, more or less automatically. This problem thus appears to arise *both for words and sentences and for entire texts.* To resolve it, cognitive resources are activated. We focus our attention to

---

[29] Just and Carpenter (1980) studied the movement of the eyes during the reading of a sentence, and since in reading a sentence subjects typically fixate on almost every word, they found out that the time that the subjects spend fixating on a word is proportional to the amount of information the respective word contains. If a sentence contains a relatively unfamiliar word, the eye movement pauses longer at this word. Besides, at the end of the phrase in which the unfamiliar word is found, there are longer pauses as well.

consciously interpret an expression, and interpretive hypotheses are consciously generated.[30]

A second procedure that is especially relevant for textual understanding refers to the information processing taking place after the processes of syntactic and semantic analysis have occurred. Kintsch and van Deijk (1978) have developed a model that concentrates on the further development of the text after the initial set of propositions have been identified and after parsing processes have been applied to their analysis. They presume that there is a capacity limit, a limitation on the number of propositions that can be kept active in working memory. One consequence of this is that only those propositions are kept active that are relevant – in accord with the criteria of temporal proximity and importance of the information – for conveying the meaning of the entire text. In accord with what is called the 'leading-edge strategy,' subjects keep active the proposition that has most recently been processed and the propositions that, in the hierarchical representation of the text, have priority over the rest. They do this under the presupposition that there is a hierarchical relationship between the propositions in the text. What is important here is that there is also a parallel process of elaboration during which, on the one hand, 'bridging inferences' are made in which the comprehender adds inferences in order to relate otherwise unrelated terms and, on the other hand, 'macro-propositions' are established that contain a summary of the gist of the text. During this process of elaboration, the interpreter actively construes the meaning of the whole text and thus understands it.[31]

---

[30] For more details, see Section 2.4.

[31] See also the summarizing description of the model, which Kintsch (1998, 119) called the 'construction-integration model': "A process model of text comprehension attempts to describe the step-by-step processes by which written or spoken language is transformed into a mental representation in the reader's or listener's mind. The construction-integration (CI) model assumes that this process involves two phases: a construction phase, in which an approximate but incoherent mental model is constructed locally from the textual input and the comprehender's goals and knowledge, and an integration phase that is essentially a constraint satisfaction process that rejects inappropriate local constructions in favor of those that fit together into a coherent whole. The construction rules in this model can be relatively simple and robust because they have to take into account only the local context. The global context becomes important only in the integration phase, when the tentative, incoherent network that has been formed by the context-free construction rules settles into a stable state."

Finally, Mark Turner's theory is to be considered. It is important because it deals with the *creativity* of understanding – something emphasized by all of the postmodern hermeneuticists. The fact that a human cognitive system permanently creates new meanings – as soon as it is confronted with signs and words – is to be traced back to the mental ability of imagination. The well-known motto of Gadamer – that one understands differently if one understands at all – presents a fact that is an object of empirical studies showing that complex mechanisms are at work.

It is first to be emphasized that the mechanisms responsible for the fact that new meanings are developed do not operate at the level of consciousness, but instead through what is called 'backstage cognition' (Turner 2001, 67ff.). That the most relevant mental processes take place unconsciously is one of the main findings of modern cognitive science. In accord with this, in their most recent book, Fauconnier and Turner (2002, 33f.) emphasize: "Our major claims in this book are radical but true: Nearly all important thinking takes place outside of consciousness and is not available on introspection; the mental feats we think of as the most impressive are trivial compared to everyday capacities; the imagination is always at work in ways that consciousness does not apprehend; consciousness can glimpse only a few vestiges of what the mind is doing; the scientist, the engineer, the mathematician, and the economist, impressive as their knowledge and techniques may be, are also unaware of how they are thinking and, even though they are experts, will not find out just by asking themselves. Evolution seems to have built us to be constrained from looking directly into the nature of our cognition, which puts cognitive science in the difficult position of trying to use mental abilities to reveal what those very abilities are built to hide."

If they are right, and their position seems to be the *opinio communis* in the cognitive sciences, then introspection is not even available as a heuristic for formulating hypotheses. Rather, the naturalistic path seems to be the only viable way to discover the relevant mental mechanisms that are constitutive for 'understanding.' Thus, for example, the constitutive principles of the mechanism of 'conceptual blending,' which lead to the production of new meanings, can only be investigated from an external perspective (Fauconnier and Turner, 2002, ch. 3). In accord with this mechanism, mental representations (which also possess a neural basis) are used as input. After the complex process of combining elements of these representations is completed, emergent structures are formed that are constitutive for new mental representations. This unconscious mechanism of conceptual blending creatively produces new meanings, which are only recognized as such by interpreters after they have been generated in their cognitive system – without the help of consciousness. Only by viewing the cognitive system as a constitutent part of nature is it thus possible to discover this and other mechanisms.

In sum, it can be stated that there is a series of regularities underlying the mental procedure known as 'understanding a text': regularities with regard to perception and other cognitive processes. As usual in science, there is better explanations for some of these processes than for others, and there is a series of debates about the quality of the existent explanations. What is of primary importance for us, however, is that *this particular type of understanding can also be explained and thus that the hypothetico-deductive method can be applied to it without any difficulty.*

Epilogue

The arguments investigated in this book have shown that the philosophical hermeneutics so predominant in the German-speaking world
is afflicted with many grave deficiencies and contains little of use. In
particular, the hermeneutic views of Heidegger and Gadamer offer no
satisfactory solutions – either to the problem of text interpretation or to
any other problems. Heidegger's philosophy, developed with impressively formulated, excessive claims, in principle offers nothing more
than a series of trivialities that are practically devoid of information.
Gadamer's conception, although more closely connected with the traditional hermeneutic questions, possesses a very low problem-solving
capacity: The transcendental vocabulary and the claim to the universality of the approach are not sufficiently substantiated, and they offer
neither a correct analysis of the process of understanding nor a useful methodological guide for interpretive praxis. Notwithstanding the
fact that philosophical hermeneutics is a source of inspiration for the
work of many contemporary authors, it remains essentially misguided.

The naturalistic approach to the problematic of meaning pleads for
a unified treatment of nexuses, maintaining that it is possible to apprehend causal nexuses and nexuses of meaning with the same method.
Despite being meaningful, both human action in general and the results of such action – above all, texts – can be apprehended sufficiently
with the hypothetico-deductive method. Hence, the second part of
this book consists of an attempt to show that nexuses of meaning
can very often be transformed into causal nexuses, and thus can be

nomologically explained. Even in those cases in which, for whatever reasons, this transformation is not possible, the hypothetico-deductive method can still be applied: It is possible to formulate hypotheses, which serve to reconstruct the respective nexus of meaning, and then to test them, on the basis of the available empirical information, in order to find out which hypotheses are true. In reconstructions, as in identifications of individual facts in general, certain singular descriptive statements serve as hypotheses precisely by virtue of the fact that one looks for reasons for their truth. Thus those disciplines that deal with the scientific problems associated with reconstructing nexuses of meaning can be oriented on the idea of truth and need not orient themselves on other regulative ideas.

References

Abel, Theodore (1948/1953) "The Operation Called *Verstehen*," in *American Journal of Sociology*, vol. 54, and reprinted in Herbert Feigl and May Brodbeck: *Readings in the Philosophy of Science*, pp. 677–87. New York: Appleton-Century-Crofts.

Acredolo, Linda, and Susan Goodwyn (1996) *Baby Signs: How to Talk with Your Baby before Your Baby Can Talk*. Chicago: Contemporary Books.

Adler, Hans, and Sabine Gross (2002) "Adjusting the Frame: Comments on Cognitivism and Literature," *Poetics Today* 23:2: 195–220.

Adorno, Theodor W. (1964) *Jargon der Eigentlichkeit. Zur deutschen Ideologie*. Frankfurt am Main: Suhrkamp.

Albert, Hans (1968/1985) *Treatise on Critical Reason*. Princeton, NJ: Princeton University Press.

Albert, Hans (1978) *Traktat über rationale Praxis*. Tübingen: J. C. B. Mohr (Paul Siebeck).

Albert, Hans (1982) *Die Wissenschaft und die Fehlbarkeit der Vernunft*. Tübingen: J. C. B. Mohr (Paul Siebeck).

Albert, Hans (1987) *Kritik der reinen Erkenntnislehre*. Tübingen: J. C. B. Mohr (Paul Siebeck).

Albert, Hans (1993a) "Die Einheit der Sozialwissenschaften," in Ernst Topitsch (ed.): *Logik der Sozialwissenschaften*, 12th ed., pp. 53–70. Frankfurt am Main: Neue Wissenschaftliche Bibliothek.

Albert, Hans (1993b) "Wertfreiheit als methodisches Prinzip. Zur Frage der Notwendigkeit einer normativen Sozialwissenschaft," in Ernst Topitsch (ed.): *Logik der Sozialwissenschaften*, 12th ed., pp. 196–225. Frankfurt am Main: Neue Wissenschaftliche Bibliothek.

Albert, Hans (1994) *Kritik der reinen Hermeneutik*. Tübingen: J. C. B. Mohr (Paul Siebeck).

Albert, Hans (1998) *Marktsoziologie und Entscheidungslogik: zur Kritik der reinen Ökonomik*. Tübingen: J. C. B. Mohr (Paul Siebeck).

Anderson, John R. (1993) *Rules of the Mind.* New Jersey and London: Lawrence Erlbaum Associates Publishers.

Anderson, John R. (2002) *Cognitive Psychology and Its Implications,* 5th ed. New York: W. H. Freeman.

Anz, Heinrich (1982) "Hermeneutik der Individualität. Wilhelm Diltheys hermeneutische Position und ihre Aporien," *in* Hendrik Birus (ed.): *Hermeneutische Positionen,* pp. 59–88. Göttingen: Vandenhoeck & Ruprecht.

Apel, Karl-Otto (1979) *Towards a Transformation of Philosophy.* London and New York: Routledge.

Apel, Karl-Otto (1984) *Understanding and Explanation: A Transcendental-Pragmatic Perspective.* Cambridge, MA: MIT Press.

Apel, Karl-Otto, Juha Manninen, and Raimo Tuomela (eds.) (1978) *Neue Versuche über Erklären und Verstehen.* Frankfurt am Main: Suhrkamp.

Armstrong, D. M. (1983) *What Is a Law of Nature?* Cambridge: Cambridge University Press.

Arrow, Kenneth (1994) "Methodological Individualism and Social Knowledge," *American Economic Review (Papers and Proceedings)* 84: 1–9.

Ast, Friedrich D. (1808) *Grundlinien der Grammatik, Hermeneutik und Kritik.* Landshut: at Jos. Thomann, Buchdrucker und Buchhändler.

Barnes, Eric (1992) "Explanatory Unification and Scientific Understanding," *Proceedings of the Biennial Meeting of the Philosophy of Science Association* 1: 3–12.

Baron, Jonathan (1994) *Thinking and Deciding,* 2nd ed. Cambridge: Cambridge University Press.

Baron-Cohen, Simon (1995) *Mindblindness. An Essay on Autism and Theory of Mind.* Cambridge, MA, and London: MIT Press.

Becker, Gary (1976) *The Economic Approach to Human Behavior.* Chicago and London: University of Chicago Press.

Becker, Gary (1996) *Accounting for Tastes.* Cambridge, MA: Harvard University Press.

Blaug, Mark (1992) *The Methodology of Economics,* 2nd ed. Cambridge: Cambridge University Press.

Bodammer, Theodor (1987) *Philosophie der Geisteswissenschaften.* Freiburg and München: Alber.

Böhm, Jan M. (2002) "Kritischer Rationalismus und Hermeneutik," *in* Jan M. Böhm, Heiko Holweg, and Claudia Hoock (eds.): *Karl Poppers kritischer Rationalismus heute,* pp. 203–27. Tübingen: J. C. B. Mohr (Paul Siebeck).

Bohnen, Alfred (1975) *Individualismus und Gesellschaftstheorie.* Tübingen: J. C. B. Mohr (Paul Siebeck).

Bohnen, Alfred (2000) *Handlungsprinzipien oder Systemgesetze.* Tübingen: J. C. B. Mohr (Paul Siebeck).

Bosman, Ronald, Heike Hennig-Schmidt, and Franz van Winden (2002) "Exploring Group Behavior in a Power-to-Take Video Experiment." Bonn: Graduate School of Economics, Discussion Paper 7/2002.

Bougas, Tassos (1991) "Das Ende der Philosophie bei Marx und Heidegger," in Dietrich Papenfuss and Otto Pöggeler (eds.): *Zur philosophischen Aktualität Heideggers,* vol. 1: Philosophie und Politik, pp. 101–17. Frankfurt am Main: Vittorio Klostermann.

Buchanan, James M. (1979) *What Should Economists Do?* Indianapolis: Liberty Fund.

Bühler, Axel (1987) "Die Einheit der wissenschaftlichen Methode und Maximen des Verstehens," *Zeitschrift für philosophische Forschung* 41: 633–44.

Bühler, Axel (1993a) "Der Hermeneutische Intentionalismus als Konzeption von den Zielen der Interpretation," *Ethik und Sozialwissenschaften* 4: 511–18.

Bühler, Axel (1993b) "Replik:, Jetzt verstehe ich meine Absichten besser," *Ethik und Sozialwissenschaften* 4: 574–85.

Bühler, Axel (ed.) (1994) *Unzeitgemäße Hermeneutik. Verstehen und Interpretation im Denken der Aufklärung.* Frankfurt am Main: Vittorio Klostermann.

Bühler, Axel (1995a) "Verstehen: Vernunft und Erfahrung," *Philosophia Naturalis* 32: 271–94.

Bühler, Axel (1995b) "Hermeneutischer Intentionalismus und die Interpretation philosophischer Texte," *Logos* N.F. 2: 1–18.

Bühler, Axel (1998) "Vier Vorurteile über Hermeneutik – Eine Polemik," *in* Bernulf Kanitscheider and Franz Josef Wetz (eds.): *Hermeneutik und Naturalismus*, pp. 83–97. Tübingen: J. C. B. Mohr (Paul Siebeck).

Bühler, Axel (1999a) "Die Vielfalt des Interpretierens," *Analyse und Kritik* 21: 117–37.

Bühler, Axel (1999b) "Autorabsicht und fiktionale Rede," *in* Jannidis Fotis, Gerhard Lauer, Matias Martinez, and Simone Winko (eds.): *Rückkehr des Autors. Zur Erneuerung eines umstrittenen Begriffs*, pp. 61–75. Tübingen: Max Niemeyer Verlag.

Bühler, Axel (2002) "Nutzen und methodische Eigenheiten rationaler Rekonstruktionen im Rahmen ideengeschichtlicher Untersuchungen," *Internationale Zeitschrift für Philosophie* 11, no. 1: 117–26.

Bühler, Axel (2003a) "Grundprobleme der Hermeneutik," *in* Axel Bühler (ed.): *Hermeneutik. Basistexte zur Einführung in die wissenschaftstheoretischen Grundlagen von Verstehen und Interpretation*, pp. 3–19. Heidelberg: Synchron.

Bühler, Axel (2003b) Einführung in die Philosophie der Geistes- und Sozialwissenschaften. Unpublished manuscript.

Bühler, Karl (1934/1999) *Sprachtheorie*, 3rd ed. Stuttgart: Lucius & Lucius.

Carnap, Rudolf (1931) "Überwindung der Metaphysik durch logische Analyse der Sprache," *Erkenntnis* 2: 219–41.

Carnap, Rudolf (1932) "Die physikalische Sprache als Universalsprache der Wissenschaften," *Erkenntnis* 2: 432–65.

Chomsky, Noam (2000) *New Horizons in the Study of Language and Mind.* Cambridge: Cambridge University Press.

Churchland, Paul (1979) *Scientific Realism and the Plasticity of Mind.* Cambridge: Cambridge University Press.

Churchland, Paul (1989) *The Neurocomputational Perspective.* Cambridge, MA, and London: MIT Press.

Cohen, Neal J., and Larry R. Squire (1980) "Preserved Learning and Retention of Pattern-Analyzing Skill in Amnesia: Dissociation of Knowing How and Knowing That," *Science* 210: 207–10.

Conlisk, John (1996) "Why Bounded Rationality?," *Journal of Economic Literature* 34: 669–700.

Coseriu, Engenio (1994) *Textlinguistik*, 3rd rev. edition, Jörg Albrecht (ed.). Tübingen and Basel: Francke Verlag.

Damasio, Antonio (1994) *Descartes' Error: Emotion, Reason, and the Human Brain.* New York: Avon Books.

Damasio, Antonio (1999) *The Feeling of What Happens.* New York, San Diego, and London: Harcourt, Brace.

Danks, Joseph H., Lisa Bohn, and Ramona Fears (1983) "Comprehension Processes in Oral Reading," *in* Giovanni B. Flores d'Arcais and Robert J. Jarvella (eds.): *The Process of Language Understanding*, pp. 193–223. Chichester and New York: Wiley.

Danneberg, Lutz, and Hans-Harald Müller (1983) "Der >intentionale Fehlschluß< – ein Dogma?", I and II, *Zeitschrift für allgemeine Wissenschaftstheorie* 14: 103–137, 376–411.

Davidson, Donald (1963/2001) "Actions, Reasons and Causes," *in* Donald Davidson: *Essays on Actions and Events*, 2nd ed., pp. 3–19. Oxford: Clarendon Press.

Davidson, Donald (1973/2001) "The Material Mind," *in* Donald Davidson: *Essays on Actions and Events*, 2nd ed., pp. 245–60. Oxford: Clarendon Press.

Davidson, Donald (1976/2001) "Hempel on Explaining Action," *in* Donald Davidson: *Essays on Actions and Events*, 2nd ed., pp. 261–76. Oxford: Clarendon Press.

Davidson, Donald (1984) *Inquiries into Truth and Interpretation.* Oxford: Clarendon Press.

Decéty, J., J. Grèzes, N. Costes, D. Perani, M. Jeannerod, E. Procyk, F. Grassi, and F. Fazio (1997) "Brain Activity During Observation of Actions: Influence of Action Context and Subject's Strategy," *Brain* 120: 1763–77.

Dehaene, Stanislas, and Jean-Pierre Changeux (1997) "A Hierarchical Neuronal Network for Planning Behavior," *Proceedings of the National Academy of Sciences USA* 94: 13293–8.

Dennett, Daniel C. (1987) *The Intentional Stance.* Cambridge, MA: MIT Press.

Dilthey, Wilhelm (GS I) (1883/1990) *Gesammelte Schriften, I. Band: Einleitung in die Geisteswissenschaften*, 9th ed. Stuttgart: B. G. Teubner Verlagsgesellschaft and Göttingen: Vandenhoeck & Ruprecht.

Dilthey, Wilhelm (GS V) (1924/1990) *Gesammelte Schriften V. Band: Die geistige Welt. Einleitung in die Philosophie des Lebens. Erste Hälfte: Abhandlungen zur Grundlegung der Geisteswissenschaften*, 8th ed. Stuttgart: B. G. Teubner Verlagsgesellschaft and Göttingen: Vandenhoeck & Ruprecht.

Dilthey, Wilhelm (GS VII) (1927/1992) *Gesammelte Schriften VII. Band: Der Aufbau der geschichtlichen Welt in den Geisteswissenschaften*, 8th unchanged ed. Stuttgart: B. G. Teubner Verlagsgesellschaft and Göttingen: Vandenhoeck & Ruprecht.

Dilthey, Wilhelm (SW I) (1989) *Selected Works, Volume I: Introduction to the Human Sciences*, ed. Rudolf A. Makkreel and Frithjof Rodi. Princeton, NJ: Princeton University Press.

Dilthey, Wilhelm (SW III) (2002) *Selected Works, Volume III: The Formation of the Historical World in the Human Sciences*, ed. Rudolf A. Makkreel and Frithjof Rodi. Princeton, NJ: Princeton University Press.

Dilthey, Wilhelm (SW IV) (1996) *Selected Works, Volume IV: Hermeneutics and the Study of History*, ed. Rudolf A. Makkreel and Frithjof Rodi. Princeton, NJ: Princeton University Press.

Donald, Merlin (1991) *Origins of the Modern Mind: Three Stages in the Evolution of Culture and Cognition.* Cambridge, MA: Harvard University Press.

Donald, Merlin (1998a) "Hominid Enculturation and Cognitive Evolution," *in* Colin Renfrew and Chris Scarre (eds.): *Cognition and Material Culture: The Archaeology of Symbolic Storage*, pp. 7–17. Cambridge: McDonald Institute Monographs.

Donald, Merlin (1998b) "Material Culture and Cognition: Concluding Thoughts," *in* Colin Renfrew and Chris Scarre (eds.): *Cognition and Material Culture: The Archaeology of Symbolic Storage*, pp. 181–7. Cambridge: McDonald Institute Monographs.

Dray, William (1957) *Laws and Explanation in History.* Oxford: Clarendon Press.

Droysen, Johann Gustav (1943) *Historik. Vorlesungen über Enzyklopädie und Methodologie der Geschichte*, 2nd ed. München and Berlin: Verlag von R. Oldenbourg.

Dummet, Michael (1986) "A Nice Derangement of Epitaphs: Some Comments on Davidson and Hacking," *in* Ernest Lepore (ed.): *Truth and Interpretation*, pp. 459–76. Oxford: Blackwell.

Elster, Jon (1986) "Introduction," *in* Jon Elster (ed.): *Rational Choice*, pp. 1–33. Cambridge: Cambridge University Press.

Essler, Wilhelm (1975) "Zur Topologie von Verstehen und Erklären," *Grazer Philosophische Studien* 1: 127–45.

Farah, Martha (2000) "The Neural Bases of Mental Imagery," *in* Michael S. Gazzaniga (ed.): *The New Cognitive Neurosciences*, 2nd ed., pp. 965–74. Cambridge, MA: MIT Press.

Fauconnier, Gilles, and Mark Turner (2002) *The Way We Think: Conceptual Blending and the Mind's Hidden Complexities.* New York: Basic Books.

Fehér, István M. (2000) "Zum Sprachverständnis der Hermeneutik Gadamers," in Günter Figal, Jean Grondin, Dennis J. Schmidt, and Friedericke Rese (eds.): *Hermeneutische Wege: Hans-Georg Gadamer zum Hundertsten*, pp. 191–205. Tübingen: J. C. B. Mohr (Paul Siebeck).

Feick, Hildegard and Susanne Ziegler (1991) *Index zu Heideggers "Sein und Zeit*," 4th rev. ed. Tübingen: Max Niemeyer Verlag.

Figal, Günter (1999) *Martin Heidegger zur Einführung*, 3rd ed. Hamburg: Junius.

Figal, Günter (2000) "Philosophische Hermeneutik, hermeneutische Philosophie. Ein Problemaufriß," *in* Günter Figal, Jean Grondin, Dennis J. Schmidt, and Friedericke Rese (eds.): *Hermeneutische Wege: Hans-Georg Gadamer zum Hundertsten*, pp. 335–44. Tübingen: J. C. B. Mohr (Paul Siebeck).

Fish, Stanley (1980) *Is There a Text in This Class? The Authority of Interpretive Communities.* Cambridge, MA: Harvard University Press.

Flyvjberg, Bent (2001) *Making Social Science Matter*. Cambridge: Cambridge University Press.

Føllesdal, Dagfinn (1979) "Hermeneutics and the Hypothetico-Deductive Method," *Dialectica* 33: 319–36.

Føllesdal, Dagfinn (1980) "Explanation of Action," in Risto Hilpinen (ed.): *Rationality in Science*, pp. 231–46. Dordrecht, Boston, and London: Reidel.

Føllesdal, Dagfinn (1982) "The Status of Rationality Assumptions in Interpretation and in the Explanation of Action," *Dialectica* 36: 301–16.

Føllesdal, Dagfinn (2001) "Hermeneutics," *International Journal of Psychoanalysis* 82: 1–5.

Føllesdal, Dagfinn, Lars Walløe, and Jon Elster (1988) *Rationale Argumentation: Ein Grundkurs in Argumentations- und Wissenschaftstheorie*. Berlin and New York: Walter de Gruyter.

Frankfurt, Harry G. (1978) "The Problem of Action," *American Philosophical Quarterly* 15: 157–62.

Friedman, Jeffrey (1996) *The Rational Choice Controversy*. New Haven, CT, and London: Yale University Press.

Friedman, Michael (1974/1988) "Explanation and Scientific Understanding," *The Journal of Philosophy* 71: 5–19 and reprinted in Joseph C. Pitt (ed.): *Theories of Explanation*, pp. 188–98. New York and Oxford: Oxford University Press.

Gadamer, Hans-Georg (GW 1) (1960/1990) *Gesammelte Werke, vol. 1, Hermeneutik I: Wahrheit und Methode*, 6th ed. Tübingen: J. C. B. Mohr (Paul Siebeck).

Gadamer, Hans-Georg (GW 2) (1986/1993) *Gesammelte Werke, vol. 2, Hermeneutik II: Wahrheit und Methode, Ergänzungen, Register*, 2nd ed. Tübingen, J. C. B. Mohr (Paul Siebeck).

Gadamer, Hans-Georg (GW 10) (1995) *Gesammelte Werke, vol. 10, Hermeneutik im Rückblick*. Tübingen, J. C. B. Mohr (Paul Siebeck).

Gadamer, Hans-Georg (2000) *Hermeneutische Entwürfe*. Tübingen: J. C. B. Mohr (Paul Siebeck).

Gadamer, Hans-Georg (1966) "Notes on Planning for the Future," *Daedalus* 95: 572–89.

Gadamer, Hans-Georg (1976) "The Universality of the Hermeneutical Problem," *in* David E. Linge (trans. and ed.): *Philosophical Papers*, pp. 3–17. Berkeley, Los Angeles, and London: University of California Press.

Gadamer, Hans-Georg (1981) *Reason in the Age of Science*, trans. by Frederick G. Lawrence. Cambridge, MA, and London: MIT Press.

Gadamer, Hans-Georg (1986) "Text and Interpretation," *in* Bruce R. Wachterhauser (ed.): *Hermeneutics and Modern Philosophy*, pp. 377–96. Albany: State University of New York Press.

Gadamer, Hans-Georg (1988) "On the Circle of Understanding," *in* John M. Connolly and Thomas Keutner (trans., eds., and intro.): *Hermeneutics versus Science? Three German Views*, pp. 68–78. Notre Dame, IN: University of Notre Dame Press.

Gadamer, Hans-Georg (1994a) "Truth in the Human Sciences," *in* Brice R. Wachterhauser (trans. and ed.): *Hermeneutics and Truth*, pp. 25–32. Evaston, IL: Northwestern University Press.

Gadamer, Hans-Georg (1994b) "What Is Truth?", in Brice R. Wachterhauser (trans. and ed.): *Hermeneutics and Truth*, pp. 33–46. Evaston, IL: Northwestern University Press.

Gadamer, Hans-Georg (1997) "Rhetoric, Hermeneutics, and Ideology-Critique," trans. by G. B. Hess and R. E. Palmer, *in* Walter Jost and Michael J. Hyde (eds.): *Rhetoric and Hermeneutics in Our Time: A Reader*, pp. 313–34. New Haven, CT, and London: Yale University Press.

Gadamer, Hans-Georg (2003) *Truth and Method*, trans. by Joel Weinsheimer and Donald G. Marshall, 2nd rev. ed. New York: Continuum.

Gazzaniga, Michael S., Richard B. Ivry, and George R. Mangun (2002) *Cognitive Neuroscience: The Biology of the Mind*, 2nd ed. New York: Norton.

Geertz, Clifford (1973) *The Interpretation of Cultures*. New York: Basic Books.

Geldsetzer, Lutz (1994) "Hermeneutik," *in* Helmut Seiffert and Gerard Radnitzky (eds.): *Handlexikon zur Wissenschaftstheorie*, 2nd ed., pp. 127–39. München: Deutscher Taschenbuch Verlag.

Gellner, Ernest (1968) "The New Idealism – Cause and Meaning in the Social Sciences," *in* Imre Lakatos and Alan Musgrave (eds.): *Problems in the Philosophy of Science*, pp. 377–406. Amsterdam: North-Holland.

Gemtos, Petros (2004) *Methodologia ton koinonikon epistimon (Methodology of the Social Sciences)*, vol. 1, 4th enlarged ed. Athens: Papazisis.

Gemtos, Petros (1987) *Methodologia ton koinonikon epsitimon (Methodology of the Social Sciences)*, vol. 2, Athens: Papazisis.

Giddens, Anthony (1993) *New Rules of Sociological Method: A Positive Critique of Interpretative Sociologies*, 2nd ed. California: Stanford University Press.

Gigerenzer, Gerd (2000) *Adaptive Thinking: Rationality in the Real World*. Oxford and New York: Oxford University Press.

Gigerenzer, Gerd, and Reinhard Selten (eds.) (2001) *Bounded Rationality: The Adaptive Toolbox*. Cambridge, MA, and London: MIT Press.

Gigerenzer, Gerd, Peter Todd, and the ABC Research Group (1999) *Simple Heuristics That Make Us Smart*. Oxford and New York: Oxford University Press.

Goldberg, Elkhonon (2001) *The Executive Brain: Frontal Lobes and the Civilized Mind*. Oxford and New York: Oxford University Press.

Goldman, Alvin (1990) *Liaisons: Philosophy Meets the Cognitive and Social Sciences*. Cambridge, MA, and London: MIT Press.

Gomperz, Heinrich (1939) *Interpretation. Logical Analysis of a Method of Historical Research*. Chicago: University of Chicago Press.

Gopnik, Alison, Andrew N. Meltzoff, and Patricia K. Kuhl (1999) *The Scientist in the Crib: Minds, Brains, and How Children Learn*. New York: William Morrow.

Göttner Heide (1973) *Logik der Interpretation*. München: Wilhem Fink Verlag.

Graeser, Andreas (2001) "Philosophische Hermeneutik – ein Plädoyer der Unverbindlichkeit?," *Internationale Zeitschrift für Philosophie* no. 5: 86–92.

Grandy, Richard (1973) "Reference, Meaning and Belief," *Journal of Philosophy* 70: 439–52.

Green, Donald P., and Ian Shapiro (1994) *Pathologies of Rational Choice Theory*. New Haven, CT, and London: Yale University Press.

Greve, Werner (1997) "Erklären verstehen. Grenzen und Probleme nomolo-
gischer Handlungserklärungen," *Psychologische Beiträge* 39: 482–502.

Grice, Paul (1989) *Studies in the Way of Words.* Cambridge, MA, and London:
Harvard University Press.

Grondin, Jean (2000) *Einführung zu Gadamer.* Tübingen: J. C. B. Mohr (Paul
Siebeck).

Grondin, Jean (2001a) *Einführung in die philosophische Hermeneutik,* 2nd rev.
ed. Darmstadt: Wissenschaftliche Buchgesellschaft.

Grondin, Jean (2001b) *Von Heidegger zu Gadamer: Unterwegs zur Hermeneutik.*
Darmstadt: Wissenschaftliche Buchgesellschaft.

Grünbaum, Adolf (1953) "Causality and the Science of Human Behavior," *in*
Herbert Feigl and May Brodbeck (eds): *Readings in the Philosophy of Science,*
pp. 766–78. New York: Appleton-Century-Crofts.

Güth, Werner, and Hartmut Kliemt (2003) "Perfect or Bounded Rationality?"
Unpublished manuscript.

Habermas, Jürgen (1970/1982) "Der Universalitätsanspruch der Hermeneutik," *in* Rüdiger Bubner, Konrad Cramer, and Reiner Wiehl (eds.): *Hermeneutik und Dialektik,* vol. I, pp. 73–103. Tübingen: J. C. B. Mohr (Paul Siebeck),
and reprinted in *Zur Logik der Sozialwissenschaften,* 5th enlarged ed., pp. 331–
66. Frankfurt am Main: Suhrkamp.

Habermas, Jürgen: (1981/1987) *Theorie des kommunikativen Handelns,* vol. 1,
4th ed. Frankfurt am Main: Suhrkamp.

Hahn, Frank (1982) "Reflections on the Invisible Hand," *Lloyds Bank Review*
144: 1–21.

Hayek, Friedrich August von (1948) *Individualism and Economic Order.* Chicago:
University of Chicago Press.

Hayek, Friedrich August von (1960) *The Constitution of Liberty.* London: Routledge.

Hayek, Friedrich August von (1973) *Rules and Order: Law, Legislation and Liberty,*
vol. 1. London: Routledge.

Hayek, Friedrich August von (1979) *The Political Order of a Free People: Law,
Legislation and Liberty,* vol. 3. London: Routledge.

Hayek, Friedrich August von (1988) *The Fatal Conceit.* London: Routledge.

Heap, Shaun Hargreaves, Martin Hollis, Bruce Lyons, Robert Sugden, and
Albert Weale (1992) *The Theory of Choice: A Critical Guide.* Oxford and
Cambridge, MA: Blackwell.

Heidegger, Martin (1927/1993) *Sein und Zeit,* 17th ed. Tübingen: Niemeyer.

Heidegger, Martin (1943/1998) *Was ist Metaphysik?,* 15th ed. Frankfurt am
Main: Vittorio Klostermann.

Heidegger, Martin (1947/2000b) *Über den Humanismus,* 10th ed. Frankfurt
am Main: Vittorio Klostermann.

Heidegger, Martin (1956/1992) *Was ist das – die Philosophie?,* 10th ed.
Pfullingen: Neske.

Heidegger, Martin (GA 63) (1995) *Gesamtausgabe, Band 63: Ontologie
(Hermeneutik der Faktizität),* 2nd ed. Frankfurt am Main: Vittorio
Klostermann.

Heidegger, Martin (GA 24) (1997) *Gesamtausgabe, Band 24: Die Grundprobleme der Phänomenologie,* Friedrich-Wilhelm von Hermann (ed.), 3rd ed. Frankfurt am Main: Vittorio Klostermann.

Heidegger, Martin (GA 56/57) (1999) *Gesamtausgabe, Band 56/57: Zur Bestimmung der Philosophie,* Bernd Heimbüchel (ed.), 2nd ed. Frankfurt am Main: Vittorio Klostermann.

Heidegger, Martin (1958) *What Is Philosophy?,* William Kluback and Jean T. Wilde (trans.). Twayne.

Heidegger, Martin (1962): *Being and Time,* John Macquarrie and Edward Robinson (trans.). New York: Harper & Row.

Heidegger, Martin (1993) *Basic Writings,* David Farrell Krell (ed.), rev. and expanded ed. New York: HarperCollins.

Heidegger, Martin (1999) *Ontology – The Hermeneutics of Facticity,* John van Buren (trans.). Bloomington and Indianapolis: Indiana University Press.

Heidegger, Martin (2000a) *Towards the Definition of Philosophy,* Ted Sadler (trans.). London and New Brunswick, NJ: Athlone.

Heidelberger, Michael (1997) "Ist der Kausalbegriff abhängig vom Handlungsbegriff? Zur interventionistischen Konzeption der Kausalität," *in* Renate Breuninger (ed.): *Philosophie der Subjektivität und das Subjekt der Philosophie. Festschrift für Klaus Giel zum 70. Geburtstag,* pp. 106–16. Würzburg: Königshausen und Neumann.

Hempel, Carl G. (1942) "The Function of General Laws in History," *The Journal of Philosophy* 39: 35–48 and reprinted in Hempel (1965), pp. 231–43.

Hempel, Carl G. (1952) *Fundamentals of Concept Formation in Empirical Science.* Chicago and London: University of Chicago Press.

Hempel, Carl G. (1965) *Aspects of Scientific Explanation and Other Essays in the Philosophy of Science.* New York: Free Press.

Hermerén, Göran (1975) "Intention and Interpretation in Literary Criticism," *New Literary History* 8: 57–82.

Hesse, Günter (1990) "Evolutorische Ökonomik oder Kreativität in der Theorie," *in* Ulrich Witt (ed.): *Studien zur evolutorischen Ökonomik I,* pp. 49–73. Berlin: Duncker & Humblot.

Hintikka, Jaakko (1995) "The Phenomenological Dimension," *in* Barry Smith and David Woodruff Smith (eds.): *The Cambridge Companion to Husserl,* pp. 78–105. Cambridge: Cambridge University Press.

Hirsch, Eric D., Jr. (1967) *Validity in Interpretation.* New Haven, CT, and London: Yale University Press.

Höffe, Otfried (1971/1996) *Praktische Philosophie – Das Modell des Aristoteles,* 2nd ed. Berlin: Akademie Verlag.

Höffe, Otfried (1979/1992) *Ethik und Politik,* 4th ed. Frankfurt am Main: Suhrkamp.

Hogan, Patrick Colin (1996) *On Interpretation. Meaning and Inference in Law, Psychoanalysis, and Literature.* Athens and London: University of Georgia Press.

Holland, John H., Keith J. Holyoak, Richard Nisbett, and Paul Thagard (1986) *Induction: Processes of Inference, Learning, and Discovery.* Cambridge, MA: MIT Press.

Hughes, Claire, and Robert Plomin (2000) "Individual Differences in Early Understanding of Mind: Genes, Non-shared Environment and Modularity," *in* Peter Carruthers and Andrew Chamberlain (eds.): *Evolution and the Human Mind*, pp. 47–61. Cambridge: Cambridge University Press.

Humboldt, Wilhelm von (1836/1998) *Über die Verschiedenheit des menschlichen Sprachbaues und ihren Einfluß auf die geistige Entwicklung des Menschengeschlechts*, Donatella Di Cesare (ed.). Berlin and Paderborn: Ferdinand Schöningh.

Hume, David (1748/1975) *An Enquiry Concerning Human Understanding.* Oxford: Oxford University Press.

Husserl, Edmund (Ideen I) (1913/1980) *Ideen zu einer reinen Phänomenologie und phänomenologischen Forschung*, 4th ed. Tübingen: Max Niemeyer Verlag.

Husserl, Edmund (Ideas I) (1983) *Ideas Pertaining to a Pure Phenomenology and to a Phenomenological Philosophy, First Book*, F. Kersten (trans.). Dordrecht, Boston, and London: Kluwer Academic.

Jaspers, Karl (1978) *Notizen zu Martin Heidegger*, Hans Sauer (ed.). München and Zürich: Piper Verlag.

Jung, Matthias (1996) *Dilthey zur Einführung.* Hamburg: Junius.

Just, Marcel Adam, and Patricia A. Carpenter (1980) "A Theory of Reading: From Eye Fixations to Comprehension," *Psychological Review* 87: 329–54.

Kagel, John H., and Alvin. E. Roth (1995) *Handbook of Experimental Economics.* Princeton, NJ: Princeton University Press.

Kahneman, Daniel, Jack Knetsch, and Richard Thaler (1990) "Experimental Tests of the Endowment Effect and the Coase Theorem," *Journal of Political Economy* 98: 1325–480.

Kahneman, Daniel, and Amos Tversky (eds.) (2000) *Choices, Values and Frames.* Cambridge: Cambridge University Press.

Kalleri, Ekaterini (1993) "Verstehen als grundlegendes Prinzip der Geisteswissenschaften bei Wilhelm Dilthey," *in* Hans Lenk: *Philosophie und Interpretation*, pp. 64–76. Frankfurt: Suhrkamp.

Kempski, Jürgen von (1992) *Brechungen: Kritische Versuche zur Philosophie der Gegenwart, Schriften I*, Achim Eschbach (ed.). Frankfurt am Main: Suhrkamp.

Keuth, Herbert (1989) *Wissenschaft und Werturteil: Zu Werturteilsdiskussion und Positivismusstreit.* Tübingen: J. C. B. Mohr (Paul Siebeck).

Keuth, Herbert (1990) "Über begriffliche Voraussetzungen der Erkenntnis," *in* Dietmar Koch and Klaus Bort (eds.): *Kategorie und Kategorialität: Festschrift für Klaus Hartmann zum 65. Geburtstag*, pp. 345–57. Würzburg: Königshausen & Neumann.

Keuth, Herbert (1998) "Zur Kritik am Anspruch einer universellen Hermeneutik," *in* Bernulf Kanitscheider and Franz Josef Wetz (eds.): *Hermeneutik und Naturalismus*, pp. 63–82. Tübingen: J. C. B. Mohr (Paul Siebeck).

Keuth, Herbert (2000) *Die Philosophie Karl Poppers.* Tübingen: J. C. B. Mohr (Paul Siebeck).

Kim, Jaegwon (1989/1997) "Mechanism, Purpose and Explanatory Exclusion," *Philosophical Perspectives* 3: 77–108 and reprinted in Alfred Mele (ed.): *The Philosophy of Action*, pp. 256–82. Oxford: Oxford University Press.

Kintsch, Walter (1998) *Comprehension: A Paradigm for Cognition*. Cambridge: Cambridge University Press.

Kintsch, Walter, and Teun A. van Dijk (1978) "Toward a Model of Text Comprehension and Production," *Psychological Review* 85: 363–94.

Kirchgässner, Gebhard (1991) *Homo Oeconomicus*. Tübingen: J. C. B. Mohr (Paul Siebeck).

Kistler, Max (2002) "Erklärung und Kausalität," *Philosophia Naturalis* 39: 89–109.

Kitcher, Philip (1981) "Explanatory Unification," *Philosophy of Science* 48: 507–31.

Koppelberg, Dirk (1999) Article: "Naturalismus/Naturalisierung," *in* Hans Jörg Sandkühler (ed.): *Enzyklopädie Philosophie*, pp. 904–14. Hamburg: Felix Meiner.

Kornblith, Hilary (ed.) (1994) *Naturalizing Epistemology*. Cambridge, MA, and London: MIT Press.

Kosslyn, Stephen, and William Thompson (2000) "Shared Mechanisms in Visual Imagery and Visual Perception: Insights from Cognitive Neuroscience," *in* Michael S. Gazzaniga, (ed.): *The New Cognitive Neurosciences*, 2nd ed., pp. 975–85. Cambridge, MA: MIT Press.

Künne, Wolfgang (1981) "Verstehen und Sinn: Eine sprachanalytische Betrachtung," *Allgemeine Zeitschrift für Philosophie* 6: 1–16.

Lambert, Karel (1980) "Explanation and Understanding: An Open Question?" *in* Hilpinen Risto (ed.): *Rationality in Science*, pp. 29–34. Dordrecht, Boston, and London: D. Reidel.

Lambert, Karel (1990) "Prolegomenon zu einer Theorie des wissenschaftlichen Verstehens," *in* Gerhard Schurz (ed.): *Erklären und Verstehen in der Wissenschaft*, pp. 299–319. München: Oldenbourg.

Latsis, Spiro J. (1972) "Situational Determinism in Economics," *British Journal for the Philosophy of Science* 23: 207–45.

Latsis, Spiro J. (1983) "The Role and Status of the Rationality Principle in the Social Sciences," *in* Robert S. Cohen and Marx W. Wartowsky (eds.): *Epistemology, Methodology, and the Social Sciences* pp. 123–151. Dordrecht, Boston, and London: Reidel.

Lenk, Hans (2000) *Kreative Aufstiege*. Frankfurt: Suhrkamp.

Lewis, David (1973) "Causation," *The Journal of Philosophy* 70: 556–67.

Livingston, Paisley (1988) *Literary Knowledge: Humanistic Inquiry and the Philosophy of Science*. Ithaca and London: Cornell University Press.

Livingston, Paisley (1993) "Why Realism Matters: Literary Knowledge and the Philosophy of Science," *in* George Levine (ed.): *Realism and Representation: Essays on the Problem of Realism in Relation to Science, Literature, and Culture*, pp. 134–54. Madison: University of Wisconsin Press.

Löwith, Karl (1984) *Sämtliche Schriften, vol. 8: Heidegger – Denker in dürftiger Zeit*. Stuttgart: J. B. Metzler.

MacFie, Alec (1971) "The Invisible Hand of Jupiter," *Journal of the History of Ideas* 32(4): 595–599.

Mach, Ernst (1917): *Erkenntnis und Irrtum. Skizzen zur Psychologie der Forschung*, 3rd ed. Leipzig: Johann Ambrosius Barth.

Mantzavinos, C. (2001) *Individuals, Institutions and Markets.* Cambridge: Cambridge University Press.

Martin, Michael (2000) *Verstehen. The Uses of Understanding in Social Science.* New Brunswick and London: Transaction Publishers.

Max Planck Institut for Psycholinguistics (2002) *Annual Report.* Nijmegen, the Netherlands.

McClelland, Jay L., and David Rumelhart (eds.) (1986) *Parallel Distributed Processing: Explorations in the Microstructure of Cognition*, vols. 1 and 2. Cambridge, MA: MIT Press.

Meier, Georg Friedrich (1757/1996) *Versuch einer allgemeinen Auslegungskunst, mit einer Einleitung und Anmerkungen*, Axel Bühler and Luigi Cataldi Madonna (eds.). Hamburg: Felix Meiner Verlag.

Misch, Georg (1933/1994) *Der Aufbau der Logik auf dem Boden der Philosophie des Lebens*, Gudrun Kühne-Bertram and Frithjof Rodi (eds.). Freiburg and München: Verlag Karl Alber.

Moran, Richard (2001) *Authority and Estrangement: An Essay on Self-Knowledge.* Princeton: Princeton University Press.

Mumford, Stephen (1998) *Dispositions.* Oxford and New York: Oxford University Press.

Nelson, Katherine (1995) "From Spontaneous to Scientific Concepts: Continuities and Discontinuities from Childhood to Adulthood," *in* Laura W. Martin, Katherine Nelson, and Ethel Tobach (eds.): *Sociocultural Psychology: Theory and Practice of Doing and Knowing*, pp. 229–49. Cambridge and New York: Cambridge University Press.

Nordenstam, Tore (1998) "Verstehen und Erklären in den Humanwissenschaften," *Synthesis Philosophica* 26: 499–511.

Ott, Alfred E., and Harald Winkel (1985) *Geschichte der Theoretische Volkswirtschaftslehre.* Göttingen: Vandenhoeck & Ruprecht.

Passmore, John (1958) "Law and Explanation in History," *The Australian Journal of Politics and History* 4: 269–76.

Pinker, Steven (1994) *The Language Instinct.* New York: Perennial Classics.

Popper, Karl (1934/1971) *Logik der Forschung*, 4th ed. Tübingen: J. C. B. Mohr (Paul Siebeck).

Popper, Karl (1949/1972) "Naturgesetze und theoretische Systeme," *in* Albert Hans (ed.): *Theorie und Realität*, 2nd changed ed., pp. 43–58. Tübingen: J. C. B. Mohr (Paul Siebeck).

Popper, Karl (1957/1991) *The Poverty of Historicism.* London and New York: Routledge.

Popper, Karl (1959/2003) *The Logic of Scientific Discovery.* London and New York: Routledge.

Popper, Karl (1963/1989) *Conjectures and Refutations*, 5th ed. London: Routledge.

Popper, Karl (1963/1994) "Models, Instruments, and Truth. The Status of the Rationality Principle in the Social Sciences," *in* Mark A. Notturno (ed.), *The Myth of the Framework*, pp. 154–84. London and New York: Routledge

Popper, Karl (1969/1993) "Die Logik der Sozialwissenschaften," *in* Theodor W. Adorno, Hans Albert, Ralf Dahrendorf, Jürgen Habermas, Harald Pilot, and Karl R. Popper (eds.): *Der Positivismusstreit in der deutschen Soziologie*, pp. 103–23. München: Deutscher Taschenbuch Verlag.

Psillos, Stathis (2002) *Causation and Explanation*. Chesham: Acumen.

Quine, Willard van Ormen (1960) *Word and Object*. Cambridge, MA: MIT Press.

Quine, Willard van Ormen (1969) *Ontological Relativity and Other Essays*. New York: Columbia Univeristy Press.

Reale, Giovanni (2000) "Gadamer, ein großer Platoniker des 20. Jahrhunderts," *in* Günter Figal (ed.): *Begegnungen mit Hans-Georg Gadamer*, pp. 92–104. Stuttgart: Reclam.

Rescher, Nicholas (1997) *Objectivity. The Obligations of Impersonal Reason*. Notre Dame, IN, and London: University of Notre Dame Press.

Richardson, Alan, and Francis F. Steen (2003) "Reframing the Adjustment: A Response to Adler and Gross," *Poetics Today* 24(2): 151–9.

Rickert, Heinrich (1899/1926) *Kulturwissenschaft und Naturwissenschaft*, 6th ed. Tübingen: J. C. B. Mohr (Paul Siebeck).

Rickert, Heinrich (1902/1929) *Die Grenzen der naturwissenschaftlichen Begriffsbildung*, 6th ed. Tübingen: J. C. B. Mohr (Paul Siebeck).

Riker, William H. (1990) "Political Science and Rational Choice," in James E. Alt and Kenneth A. Shepsle (eds.): *Perspectives on Positive Political Economy*, pp. 163–81. Cambridge and New York: Cambridge University Press.

Rodi, Frithjof (1995) "Gegen die methodische Verstümmelung der Wirklichkeit. Kritische Anmerkungen zum Programm einer 'naturalistischen' Hermeneutik," *Philosophia Naturalis* 32: 193–209.

Rorty, Richard (1992) "The Pragmatist's Progress," *in* Umberto Eco (ed.): *Interpretation and Overinterpretation*, pp. 89–108. Cambridge: Cambridge University Press.

Rothschild, Emma (1994) "Adam Smith and the Invisible Hand," *American Economic Review (Papers and Proceedings)* 84: 319–22.

Rothschild, Emma (2002) *Economic Sentiments*. Cambridge/MA: Harvard University Press.

Ryle, Gilbert (1949) *The Concept of Mind*. London: Penguin Books.

Salmon, Wesley (1984) *Scientific Explanation and the Causal Structure of the World*, Princeton, NJ: Princeton University Press.

Salmon, Wesley (1997) *Causality and Explanation*. Oxford and New York: Oxford University Press.

Schleiermacher, Friedrich Daniel Ernst (1999) *Hermeneutik und Kritik. Mit einem Anhang sprachphilosophischer Texte Schleiermachers*, Manfred Frank (ed. and intro.), 7th ed. Frankfurt am Main: Suhrkamp.

Scholtz, Gunter (1998) Artikel "Rekonstruktion," *in* Joachim Ritter (ed.): *Historisches Wörterbuch der Philosophie*, pp. 570–8.

Scholz, Oliver (1999) "Wie versteht man eine Person? Zur Streit über die Form der Alltagspsychologie," *Analyse und Kritik* 21: 75–96.

Scholz, Oliver (2001) *Verstehen und Rationalität*, 2nd ed. Frankfurt am Main: Vittorio Klostermann.

Schulz, Walter (1953/1954): "Über den philosophiegeschichtlichen Ort Martin Heideggers," *Philosophische Rundschau* 1: 65–93, 211–32.

Schumpeter, Joseph (1908) *Das Wesen und der Hauptinhalt der theoretischen Nationalökonomie*. Berlin: Duncker & Humblot.

Schurz, Gerhard (1990) "Was ist wissenschaftliches Verstehen? Eine Theorie verstehensbewirkender Erklärungsepisoden," *in* Gerhard Schurz (ed.): *Erklären und Verstehen in der Wissenschaft*, pp. 235–98. München: Oldenbourg.

Schurz, Gerhard, and Karel Lambert (1994) "Outline of a Theory of Scientific Understanding," *Synthese* 101: 65–120.

Schwarz Wentzer, Thomas (2000) "Das Diskrimen der Frage," *in* Günter Figal, Jean Grondin, Dennis J. Schmidt, and Fiedericke Rese (eds.): *Hermeneutische Wege. Hans-Georg Gadamer zum Hundertsten*, pp. 219–40. Tübingen: J. C. B. Mohr (Paul Siebeck).

Searle, John R. (1983) *Intentionality*. Cambridge: Cambridge University Press.

Searle, John R. (2001) *Rationality in Action*. Cambridge, MA: MIT Press.

Shackle, G. L. S. (1972/1992) *Epistemics and Economics*. New Brunswick, NJ, and London: Transaction.

Shackle, G. L. S. (1979) *Imagination and the Nature of Choice*. Edinburgh: Edinburgh University Press.

Simon, Herbert A. (1979) *Models of Thought*. New Haven, CT, and London: Yale University Press.

Simon, Herbert A. (1983) *Reason in Human Affairs*. Stanford, CA: Stanford University Press.

Singer, Wolf (2002) *Der Beobachter im Gehirn*. Frankfurt am Main: Suhrkamp Verlag.

Sinclair, Robert (2002) "What Is Radical Interpretation? Davidson, Fodor, and the Naturalization of Philosophy," *Inquiry* 45: 161–84.

Smith, Adam (1776/1976) *An Inquiry Into the Nature and Causes of the Wealth of Nations*, Edwin Cannan (ed.). Chicago: University of Chicago Press.

Smith, Adam (1759/1976) *The Theory of Moral Sentiments*. Oxford: Oxford University Press.

Smith, Adam (1795/1980) *Essays on Philosophical Subjects*. Oxford: Oxford University Press.

Sniderman, Paul (2000) "Taking Sides: A Fixed Choice Theory of Political Reasoning," *in* Arthur Lupia, Matthew D. McCubbins, and Samuel Popkin (eds.): *Elements of Reason. Cognition, Choice and the Bounds of Rationality*, pp. 67–84. Cambridge: Cambridge University Press.

Snow, P. C. (1993) *The Two Cultures*. Cambridge: Cambridge University Press.

Sperber, Dan, and Lawrence Hirschfeld (1999) "Culture, Cognition and Evolution," *in* *The MIT Encyclopedia of the Cognitive Sciences*, pp. cxi–cxxxii. Cambridge, MA: MIT Press.

Starbatty, Joachim (1985) *Die Englischen Klassiker der Nationalökonomie.* Darmstadt: Wissenschaftliche Buchgesellschaft.

Stegmüller, Wolfgang (1983) *Probleme und Resultate der Wissenschaftstheorie und Analytischen Philosophie, vol. I: Erklärung, Begründung und Kausalität,* 2nd improved and enlarged ed. Berlin, Heidelberg, and New York: Springer-Verlag.

Stegmüller, Wolfgang (1986a) *Rationale Rekonstruktion von Wissenschaft und ihrem Wandel.* Stuttgart: Reclam.

Stegmüller, Wolfgang (1986b) "Walther von der Vogelweides Lied von der Traumliebe und Quasar 3 C 273. Betrachtungen zum sogenannten Zirkel des Verstehens und zur sogenannten Theorienbeladenheit der Beobachtungen," *in* Stegmüller: (1986a), pp. 27–86.

Stegmüller, Wolfgang (1988) "Walther von der Vogelweide's Lyric of Dream-Love and Quasar 3C 273," *in* John M. Connolly and Thomas Keutner (trans., eds., and intro.): *Hermeneutics versus Science? Three German Views,* pp. 102–52. Notre Dame, IN: University of Notre Dame Press.

Stegmüller, Wolfgang (1989) *Hauptströmungen der Gegenwartphilosophie,* vol. I, 7th ed. Stuttgart: Alfred Kröner Verlag.

Sternberg, Robert J. (ed.) (1999) *Handbook of Creativity.* Cambridge: Cambridge University Press.

Stigler, George (1981) "Economics and Ethics," *in* Sterling McMurrin (ed.): *The Tanner Lectures on Human Values,* vol. II, pp. 145–91. Cambridge: Cambridge University Press.

Stigler, George, and Gary Becker (1977) "De Gustibus Non Est Disputandum," *Amercan Economic Review* 67: 76–90.

Stroop, H. Ridley (1935) "Studies of Interference in Serial Verbal Reactions," *Journal of Experimental Psychology* 18: 643–62.

Strube, Werner (1985) "Analyse des Verstehensbegriffs," *Zeitschrift für allgemeine Wissenschaftstheorie* 16: 315–33.

Suchanek, Andreas (1994) *Ökonomischer Ansatz und theoretische Integration.* Tübingen: J. C. B. Mohr (Paul Siebeck).

Tallis, Raymond (1999) "Evidence-Based and Evidence-Free Generalizations: A Tale of Two Cultures," *in* Fuller David and Patricia Waugh (eds.): *The Arts and Sciences of Criticism,* pp. 71–93, Oxford and New York: Oxford University Press

Taylor, Charles (1985) *Philosophy and the Human Sciences,* Philosophical Papers, vol. 2. Cambridge: Cambridge University Press.

Thaler, Richard (1980) "Toward a Positive Theory of Consumer Choice," *Journal of Economic Behavior and Organization* 1: 39–60.

Tietzel, Manfred (1988) "Zur Theorie der Präferenzen," *Jahrbuch für Neue Politische Ökonomie* 7: 38–71.

Tomasello, Michael, and Joseph Call (1997) *Primate Cognition.* Oxford and New York: Oxford University Press.

Topitsch, Ernst (1990) *Heil und Zeit.* Tübingen: J. C. B. Mohr (Paul Siebeck).

Tugendhat, Ernst (1984) "Heideggers Idee von Wahrheit," *in* Otto Pöggeler (ed.): *Heidegger: Perspektiven zur Deutung seines Werkes,* pp. 286–97. Königstein/TS: Athenäum.

Tugendhat, Ernst (1992) *Philosophische Aufsätze.* Frankfurt am Main: Suhrkamp.

Tugendhat, Ernst (2001): *Aufsätze 1992–2000.* Frankfurt am Main: Suhrkamp.

Tuomela, Raimo (1984) *A Theory of Social Action.* Dordrecht, Boston, and London: D. Reidel.

Turner, Mark (2001) *The Cognitive Dimensions of Social Science.* Oxford: Oxford University Press.

Tversky, Amos, and Daniel Kahnemann (1991) "Loss Aversion in Riskless Choice: A Reference-Dependent Model," *Quarterly Journal of Economics* 106: 1039–61.

Tversky, Amos, and Richard Thaler (1990) "Anomalies: Preference Reversals," *Journal of Economic Perspectives* 4: 201–11.

Vanberg, Viktor (1975) *Die zwei Soziologien.* Tübingen: J. C. B. Mohr (Paul Siebeck).

Vollmer, Gerhard (1999) "Kritischer Rationalismus und Evolutionäre Erkenntnistheorie," *in* Ingo Pies and Martin Leschke (eds.): *Karl Poppers kritischer Rationalismus,* pp. 115–34. Tübingen: J. C. B. Mohr (Paul Siebeck).

von Wright, Georg Henrik (1971) *Explanation and Understanding.* Ithaca, NY: Cornell University Press.

Vossenkuhl, Wilhelm (1998) ">Verstehen< verstehen – über Analysen und Hermeneutik," *in* Bernulf Kanitscheider and Franz Josef Wetz (eds.): *Hermeneutik und Naturalismus,* pp. 168–93. Tübingen: J. C. B. Mohr (Paul Siebeck).

Watkins, John W. N. (1953) "Ideal Types and Historical Explanation," *in* Herbert Feigl and May Brodbeck (eds.): *Readings in the Philosophy of Science,* pp. 723–43. New York: Appleton-Century-Crofts, Educational Division, Meredith Corporation.

Weber, Erik (1996) "Explaining, Understanding and Scientific Theories," *Erkenntnis* 44: 1–23.

Weber, Max (1922/1985) *Gesammelte Aufsätze zur Wissenschaftslehre,* Johannes Winckelmann (ed.), 6th rev. ed. Tübingen: J. C. B. Mohr (Paul Siebeck).

Weber, Max (1978) *Economy and Society,* Guenther Roth and Claus Wittich (eds.). Berkeley, Los Angeles, and London: University of California Press.

Wessling, Ewald (1991) *Individuum und Information.* Tübingen: J. C. B. Mohr (Paul Siebeck).

Wimsatt, William, Jr., and Monroe C. Beardsley (1946) "The Intentional Fallacy," *Sewanee Review* 54: 468–88.

Winch, Peter (1958) *The Idea of a Social Science and Its Relation to Philosophy.* London: Routledge & Kegan Paul.

Windelband, Wilhelm (1894/1907) "Geschichte und Naturwissenschaft," *in* *Präludien,* 3rd ed., pp. 355–79. Tübingen: J. C. B. Mohr (Paul Siebeck).

Author Index

Subject Index

action calculi, 105
aim, 101
anosognosia, 16
anthropomorphism, 74
antinaturalism, xi, 80, 81, 84–5
argument of the internal
  perspective, 12, 15–18
autonomy of the human sciences, x,
  9, 11ff., 17, 19, 36, 113

backstage cognition, 152
being (*seiend*), 23–4, 28, 30, 34, 49
  being-in-the-world, 27, 39, 75
  being-with (*Mitsein*), 27
  question of being, 22
Being, 23–6, 28–31, 40, 49, 56, 61
  Being-in-the-world, 28, 40
beliefs, 87, 89–90, 98, 102–3, 124,
  133, 142
brain imaging techniques, 17
brain research, 17

care, 27
category mistake, 44
causal explanation, xi
causal nexus, 61, 73–6, 83, 88, 92,
  94, 97, 112–13, 119, 125–6, 130,
  148, 155
choice calculi, 105

circle of understanding, 36
circular reasoning, 24
cognitive problem solving, 14
coming (*Kunft*), 29
conceptual apparatus, 96–7, 110,
  128
conceptual blending, 153
constraints, 103–5
context of discovery, 18
context of justification, 18
convictions, 91
critical rationality, 14

Dasein, 23–31, 34–6, 40, 48–9, 56–7
Dasein-with (*Mit-dasein*), 27
decision, 90, 120
declarative knowledge, 43, 69
deconstruction, 147, 148n27
deduction, x, 13, 41, 81, 143
deductive argument, 95
deductive rationality, 126
descriptive psychology, 7
descriptive system, 17, 147
desires, 89, 91, 98, 100, 102–3, 120,
  133
dilemma of confirmation, 41
disclosedness, 27–8
dispositional explanation, 111
dispositions, 111